SIERRA LEONE

T0322524

DAVID HARRIS

Sierra Leone

A Political History

HURST & COMPANY, LONDON

First published in the United Kingdom in 2013 by
C. Hurst & Co. (Publishers) Ltd.,
41 Great Russell Street, London, WC1B 3PL
This revised and updated edition first published in 2020
© David Harris, 2020
All rights reserved.

Printed in India

The right of David Harris to be identified as the author of
this publication is asserted by him in accordance with the
Copyright, Designs and Patents Act, 1988.

A Cataloguing-in-Publication data record for this book is
available from the British Library.

ISBN: 9781787384125

This book is printed using paper from registered sustainable
and managed sources.

www.hurstpublishers.com

CONTENTS

ACKNOWLEDGEMENTS

For various reasons, both in the past and in more recent times, I would like to thank the following people for their direct and indirect help in writing this book: my wife, Lynda Waterhouse, my brother, Andy Harris, Tom Young, Simona Vittorini, Julia Gallagher, Shaun Milton, Felix Marco Conteh, John Birchall, Ibrahim Madina Bah, Michael Wundah, Charly Cox, PC Thomas Koroma, the late Olu Gordon, Malcolm Jones, Daniel Eyre and Carole Greene. Thank you also to my reviewers, Will Reno, Stephen Ellis, Patrick Chabal and Almami Cyllah. There are many who agreed to be interviewed, often anonymously, who cannot be named here but to whom I am also grateful. Thank you to all.

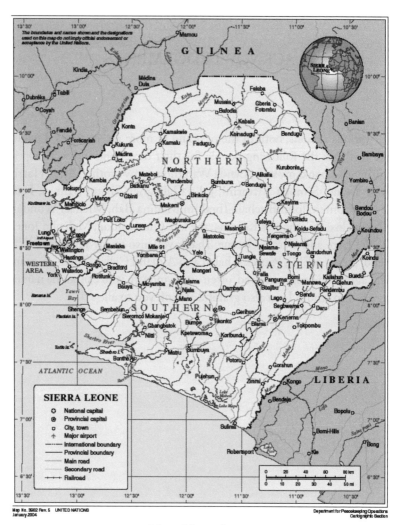

Map of Sierra Leone

FOREWORD

It is absolutely remarkable that the first edition of this book went out of date so soon after its publication in November 2013. In that edition, I referred to predictions that were based on the idea that the iron ore boom would deliver stratospheric growth. At the time, these forecasts were treated by most as unrealistic, but no-one was expecting that in 2014, the bottom would fall out of the iron ore market leading to the closure of the iron ore mines. However, this development has been dwarfed by the outbreak of Ebola in Guinea in December 2013, led to the first known death in Sierra Leone in May 2014 and an epidemic of shocking proportions. Finally, and although the first edition briefly noted the 2012 elections, a more thorough examination is made of these polls in the present edition; but it is the 2018 elections, with a second momentous turnover at the ballot box in just over a decade, that provide the headlines. The first edition could not cover the iron ore price collapse, the national catastrophe that was the Ebola crisis, or the electoral turnover, but this new edition does exactly that.

Hence, considerable space in a new Chapter 10 has been given over to the exploration of the precipitous iron ore price fluctuations, in particular the effect that both the increase and the decrease has had on the economy, government and international relations of Sierra Leone. Research undertaken in 2010 and 2011 for the first edition is supplemented by further, new research that was carried out in 2016, particularly concerning the consequent perturbations in government and its relations with Western donors.

A sizeable proportion of the new chapter is dedicated to the Ebola crisis, its genesis, the domestic and international response that it inspired, and also how it has affected Sierra Leonean politics. In this chapter, I consider the severe criticism of international bodies and the government that emerged during the early stages of the epidemic, which in the later stages remarkably transformed into something close to applause. Since the Ebola outbreak and iron ore boom coincided, I examine their effects on the economy, government and international relations in conjunction. Indeed, the aforementioned research that was carried out in 2016 is also situated within a post-Ebola context. In this chapter, I also look at the centralised model for the Post-Ebola Recovery, which was based on the later stages of the Ebola response.

Finally, my study of the 2012 elections, which was only a brief feature in the short Appendix of the first edition, has undergone a notable expansion in this new edition. The All People's Congress and President Koroma re-emerged as victors in 2012, but the most stunning electoral event was the national polls of 2018, in which Sierra Leone experienced its third opposition victory at the ballot box and the second in just over a decade. The Sierra Leone People's Party regained the power that it had lost in the previous turnover in 2007. Using research undertaken in 2018, in this edition I consider how this new electoral manifestation occurred.

Analysis of the three key developments outlined here—plus responses to critiques from book reviews, evidence and arguments from 20 new books and articles, as well as 30 newspaper and website articles that have materialised since 2013—have also led to a recalibration of the original narrative and conclusions that shaped the first edition. However, this book still rests on its five areas of contention—'traditional' authorities and values, the urban-rural divide, democratisation, the role of outsiders, and continuity and change—but each is reconsidered given the profusion of events that occurred across the 2012–2018 period. The iron ore price fluctuations, the Ebola crisis and the 2018 elections have all thrown new light on these five areas of contention. While this new edition is a considerably updated version of first edition, it is also, crucially, a further testament to the tribulations and fortitude of the Sierra Leonean people.

1

INTRODUCTION

Sierra Leone is a small country, around the size of Ireland or Panama, on the Atlantic coast of West Africa. Along with its two neighbours, Liberia and Guinea, Sierra Leone is situated in the Mano River sub-region, named after the watercourse that separates it from Liberia. The country of between five and six million people is now approaching sixty years of independence from British colonial rule. Despite being rich in diamonds, iron ore and agriculture, Sierra Leone is one of the poorest countries in the world, with very little in the way of development or international influence to show for its primary commodities and sources of wealth. The country would indeed have been a poor and forgotten corner of the world if it wasn't for the cataclysmic civil war in the 1990s and early 2000s—which was beamed onto televisions around the globe and later depicted in a blockbuster Hollywood film—as well as the equally catastrophic and extensively reported Ebola crisis in 2014–16. However, this rather fleeting interest hides more than it reveals and is only a part of the story. There are instead three key reasons why the history of Sierra Leonean politics is of crucial importance.

The first concerns Sierra Leoneans themselves (of whom I am not one), who provide a key imperative for this book. Sierra Leoneans are remarkable people who have given me friendship, humour, debate and the desire to write what is indeed an outsider's perspective on their national story, including the civil war and the Ebola epidemic that has affected so many. It is, however, a perspective which I believe is well-informed and well-researched in a theoretical, empirical and comparative manner, and one which endeavours to ground theory and history in the tangible by providing sketches of political figures, contextual anecdotes and landmarks on the map that signposts many of the important events and personalities. I have spent twenty years visiting, researching and living in Sierra Leone, acting as an election observer in three sets of elections, writing my PhD thesis, which became a book on this country and neighbouring Liberia, engaging in more recent fieldwork to uncover the thoughts of donor workers, government officials and advisers—Sierra Leoneans and others—on the successes of and obstacles to state reconstruction, and approaching Sierra Leone from both an academic and a personal angle. Thus, I hope it is also a view which will provide at least a point of further debate for those who know Sierra Leone and think about its past and its future, and I also hope that this book serves as a solid point of entry for those who wish to know the country.

Second, Sierra Leone is somewhat typical of post-colonial African states in its multi-ethnic and multi-religious configuration, and its faltering efforts to build a cohesive nation and a functioning state from a pre-colonial and colonial legacy. It is also atypical in that it has its own specific national story with quirks of history, people and geography and indigenous and foreign agents who have tried to rule and/or change the country. Through this book, I endeavour to document and analyse what are effectively, in the *longue durée*, the birth pangs of a country. In many ways, looking at Sierra Leone either as a failing and violent entity or indeed as a work in progress on the way to a Western-style nation-state obscures much of the intricate process of politics. Certainly, this is not the path seen in Europe where states and nations were forged in lengthy, organic upheavals; the African people had little say in the initial making of their territories and states. The implications on state-making of a wholly imported idea of the state, the continued dual system of 'traditional' and 'modern' authority and law, and divided loyalties along ethnic and other lines cannot be over-emphasised. However, one might see the ongoing creation of a Sierra Leonean nation, if not yet a state, which has echoes in other African countries and elsewhere but is also peculiarly Sierra Leonean. There are now myths and narratives, such as the national catastrophes of the war and the Ebola epidemic, which come together to create a distinctive Sierra Leoneness, even as it still competes with strong sub-national identities. This is an unfinished, highly unpredictable and very difficult and painful process, but the idea that a

INTRODUCTION

Sierra Leone is being made, for good and ill, with its own societal processes, its own notions of modernity and, to some extent, its own agency
despite the considerable influence and lure of the outside world, is more
than plausible.

Finally, there is the position of Sierra Leone in global affairs and discourse. It might indeed be seen by some as a poor backwater even on
the African stage, but it clearly is not. The precious gems in the title of
the Hollywood film *Blood Diamond* and the Ebola epidemic which took
on global proportions are a part of the story, but there is much more.
After colonisation by Britain, Sierra Leone has never really become dis-
connected: Sierra Leonean and British people continue to travel back
and forth. The part of London near where I live has been referred to as
'Little Freetown' and my wife, Lynda, has taught many children from
Sierra Leonean-origin families. However, it is in recent times that the
connections have become wider and thicker. During and after the conflict, British military and governmental involvement in Sierra Leone
increased significantly, with the former Prime Minister Tony Blair leading the way, and was re-invigorated in the Ebola and post-Ebola periods. International interest does not end there: each with their own
particular reasons, Libya, Liberia, Nigeria and various Western states
have felt the urge to impose their presence. The reasons behind involvement, particularly the protracted stay of the UK and other European
states, can be seen through the lens of shifts in global discourse over
international intervention, liberal peace, state-building, post-conflict
justice and international public health emergencies. Sierra Leone is then
of global significance, in that it has been at the centre of the manifestation of this considerable discursive shift which led to much larger
interventions as in Afghanistan and Iraq and is in many ways one of
the guinea pigs for such new ideologies. This book is, then, equally
designed to be an investigation of the effectiveness of the liberal intervention and the responses of Sierra Leoneans, and to be a contribution
to current thinking on these issues of global importance.

Surprisingly, there have been few attempts to write the political history
of Sierra Leone in its totality. In 1979, there was Christopher Fyfe's sem-
inal *A Short History of Sierra Leone*, in 1981 C. Magbaily Fyle's concise *The
History of Sierra Leone*, and in 1990 Joe A.D. Alie's school-oriented *A New
History of Sierra Leone*. Another work, *Sierra Leone at the End of the Twentieth Century: History, Politics and Society*, was compiled in 1999 by Earl

Conteh-Morgan and Mac Dixon-Fyle. Conversely, much has been written on certain aspects of Sierra Leone during and since the war. For instance, the nature of colonial and post-colonial authority is debated in the ground-breaking *Corruption and State Politics in Sierra Leone* (1995) by Will Reno, which introduced the notion of the 'shadow state' as a way of thinking about the degradation of the Sierra Leonean state.

Many have considered the war. The first major effort, Paul Richards' *Fighting for the Rainforest: War, Youth and Resources* (1996), took the RUF project seriously and was subsequently taken to task by Ibrahim Abdullah and others in an academic journal which subsequently became *Between Democracy and Terror: The Sierra Leone Civil War* (2004), and by Lansana Gberie in his *A Dirty War in West Africa: The RUF and the Destruction of Sierra Leone* (2005). Marianne Ferme's ethnographic approach based on the Mendes emerged as *The Underneath of Things: Violence, History and the Everyday in Sierra Leone* (2001), and David Keen's *Conflict and Collusion in Sierra Leone* (2005) and Kieran Mitton's *Rebels in a Rotten State* (2015) brought psychological factors to the fore to explain the extremity of the violence. Danny Hoffman's *The War Machines: Young Men and Violence in Sierra Leone and Liberia* and Krijn Peters' *War and the Crisis of Youth in Sierra Leone* (both 2011) revealed analyses based on youth within the factions, and Natalie Wlodarczyk considered the role of magic in *Magic and Warfare: Appearance and Reality in Contemporary African Conflict and Beyond* (2009).

Key works have also been written by scholars on the post-war environment. Tim Kelsall explores the problems of international justice in *Culture under Cross-Examination: International Justice and the Special Court for Sierra Leone* (2009), and Rosalind Shaw also critiques transitional justice in several publications. On elections, this author wrote *Civil War and Democracy in West Africa: Conflict Resolution, Elections and Justice in Sierra Leone and Liberia* (2011), and article-length electoral analyses by Jimmy Kandeh and this author link with those on post-war violence by Mats Utas. Post-conflict liberal reconstruction and its limits have been analysed in a series of articles and reports by Richard Fanthorpe, Bruce Baker, Felix Marco Conteh and others, and the texture of post-war political life is explored in several pieces by authors such as Yusuf Bangura, Christopher Clapham, Felix Marco Conteh and Luisa Enria.

In this book, I endeavour to use the wealth of recent and past literature alongside my own knowledge and research in Sierra Leone to provide a wide-ranging discussion of Sierra Leonean history, politics and society and many of the surrounding debates. Further, this book is intended to provide a theoretical thread that runs through the narrative. A central concept within the book is a complex state-society relationship which has evolved and yet has maintained many of its key features and is also somewhat similar to and somewhat different from other parts of Africa. The notions of change and continuity constantly reappear in the book and are considered with respect to state-society relations, in terms of the structural conditions and the agency of individual actors who endeavour (or not) to alter these relationships, and to the international environment. The book is thus organised as a narrative but one which is intertwined with key theoretical arguments about African politics and history, such as the arguments over colonial legacies, dependency, extraversion, neo-patrimonialism, political culture and reciprocity, and various notions of conflict, democracy, justice and liberal state-building.

Specifically, there are five areas of contention which appear and reappear under different guises and at different times in the narrative. The first is the critical position of 'traditional' authorities and values. From the colonial era right through to contemporary times, the relationship between primarily the chiefs—whether Paramount, section or village—and the 'modern' state has been thoroughly intertwined yet simultaneously fraught. Chiefs have been, and to a large degree remain, central to the way in which the colonial and post-colonial state has exerted some control over its people. At the same time, they have also emerged, somewhat counter-intuitively, as key players in the various attempts at democratising the countryside and decentralising the state which have occurred under various regimes. Even further, 'traditional' authorities have played a contested role in the sporadic outbreaks of violence aimed against either the state or chieftaincy or both—as in the 1890s, 1950s and 1980s—and in the civil war, and more recently in the Ebola crisis. This is all the more understandable when it is considered that value-systems, which include 'traditional' norms and practices such as communalism, reciprocity, deference, ethnic solidarity, 'secret societies' and African religious beliefs, remain extremely important, if far from static, and bound up in the roles of 'traditional' authorities who may or may not perform their functions satisfactorily for all concerned.

The next two areas follow on directly from these problematic relationships. There is the very visible urban-rural divide. This is about wealth and opportunities, but it is also about the legal bifurcation of the state where rural areas come very much under local 'customary' jurisdiction while urban areas, to a much greater degree, fall within the sphere of the state. These issues run through Sierra Leonean history but came to a head in the build-up to the war. Then, there are the attempts at democratisation which began throughout Sierra Leone in the colonial 1950s, were stymied in the 1970s and re-emerged in the 1990s. The notion of what exactly constitutes democracy is brought into sharp relief when one considers that since the 1950s the rather fragile Sierra Leonean variety has been underpinned, even if cut through by other imperatives, by ethno-regional bloc voting, patronage and the role of chieftaincy, and yet has delivered three, albeit contested, opposition electoral victories in 1967, 2007 and 2018.

Fourth, at a tangent, what one will then find repeatedly appearing is the role of outsiders. It is not, though, solely colonial outsiders who have shaped Sierra Leonean history. Many have come since independence with varying motives and not inconsiderable influence, and we can include such recent narratives as the response to the Ebola crisis, the role of the Chinese and the effects of the volatile iron ore industry. However, in what has been labelled 'extraversion', Sierra Leone's leaders have been equally adept at using outside actors, whatever their particular motives. Whether it is President Siaka Stevens playing off both sides in the Cold War and indeed the international diamond industry, or President Ahmad Tejan Kabbah relying on international forces, particularly the Nigerians and the British, to keep him in power (or not) during the war, or the current aid machine which keeps the Sierra Leonean government afloat, the international is always conspicuous. It is rare not to have an outside interest endeavouring to influence or being used at key moments in Sierra Leonean history.

Finally, and directly related to the idea of continuity and change and notions of tradition, the urban-rural divide, democratisation and extraversion, there must be consideration, whether the political and social changes that occur are structural or merely procedural. This deliberation has enormous consequences for the likely success of contemporary reform efforts in Sierra Leone or indeed in many other African states. Attempts at state reform and democratisation have been tried on several occasions before with limited success, but it is in the aftermath of the war and Ebola that the latest and most lengthy exertions have been made. Progress so far in post-conflict and then post-viral conditions, including large-scale liberal intervention, has been slow, but whether the combination of conditions and intervention is a potent coupling for structural change remains open to question.

There are many facets of countries in the rest of Africa which bear comparison with Sierra Leone, particularly those with British colonial history and those that have endured conflict. The *longue durée* of the state of Sierra Leone, through foreign settlement in the eighteenth century, through colonialism in the nineteenth and twentieth centuries, and independence since 1961, has encompassed both quieter passages and severe turbulence, but at each juncture sits in an African and global context worthy of investigation. For instance, the geography of Sierra Leone, a small country with few internal barriers, would seemingly make it a less likely candidate for strife than say Angola, Sudan or the Democratic Republic of Congo (DRC). Equally, the conservative nature of successive Sierra Leonean governments makes a striking comparison with what happened just across the border in Sekou Touré's Guinea. Recent liberal state rebuilding is analogous, for instance, to similar processes nearby in Liberia and further afield in a much larger state, the DRC. It is the intention here to make these comparisons to illuminate the Sierra Leonean case and to situate Sierra Leone in an African and global context.

The starting point for the book is the arrival of the first black settlers in 1787, but the key analysis starts with the onset of British colonial rule over the entirety of Sierra Leone in 1896. From 1787 onwards, the embryonic state builds on an early relationship between black settlers, who over time merge into a Creole or Krio identity, and British overseers. Confined to a small coastal area, the state was forced to expand both geographically and institutionally after the Berlin Conference of 1884–85 and the British-Krio duality enlarged to a three-way British-Krio-indigenous pattern. Such a pattern served as a model for post-independence relationships, with the British replaced by the independent state and with a diminishing role for the Krio. More often than not, however, the pattern proved a hindrance to the consolidation of this same state. Drawing on an idea of the amalgamation of British indirect colonialism and Krio and indigenous political cultures, the first two substantive chapters build a picture of state-society relations, including the genesis of the various disconnects and divisions, in the colonial period. Emphasis is placed on the decade before independence when key players and political parties emerged and relationships solidified.

The second pair of chapters takes the narrative into the post-independence era and constitutes an investigation into the severe challenges to state and nation building faced first by the Sierra Leone People's Party (SLPP) and the Margai half-brothers, Milton and Albert, and later by the All People's Congress (APC) under Siaka Stevens and Joseph Momoh. The responses, particularly from the Margais and from Stevens, offer an insight into the strengths and weaknesses of these two governments and the personalities and motivations of the key figures. Given such an environment, and the first turnover of power at the ballot box in 1967 and the military coups that began at the same time, the book asks how much of the ultimately ruinous political methods of the one-party state era and the ensuing conflict is the responsibility of the long-time leader Stevens, how much is due to Sierra Leone's exceptional state-society relations, and indeed, how much is related to outside factors.

The conflict in Sierra Leone was particularly nasty and, partly because of this, generated considerable academic heat. The book gives over two chapters to the conflict: essentially the beginning and first five years of the war and the many reasons that have been offered for its outbreak, followed by the last five years, the war's conclusion and the various factors influencing its culmination. Whether blame for the war is placed on Stevens and his dismantling of the formal state or on diamonds, Liberian interference and the Revolutionary United Front (RUF), seen by some purely as bandits, and whether we see the combatants as forced, opportunistic or with genuine grievances and as emerging from an urban or a rural milieu, informs to a large extent the way solutions to the instability and its legacies were and are envisaged. The later entry of armed forces from other states, including Nigeria and the UK, and from international organisations in the post-Cold War environment, was a precursor of further post-conflict international involvement in Sierra Leone and elsewhere and had a considerable impact on the trajectory of the civil war.

The final three substantive chapters bring us up to date. State-society relations stubbornly persist into the current day and continue to confound state-builders, now of the post-Washington Consensus liberal persuasion. Analysis focuses on continuities but also on change brought about either by the war, by the considerable and largely imported liberal reform measures, or by organic shifts in society. Key processes must include the 2002 electoral landslide of Kabbah and the SLPP, decentralisation, state reform, the Anti-Corruption Commission (ACC), the Sierra

Leone Special Court (SLSC), the Ebola crisis and its aftermath, huge iron ore price swings, the Chinese presence, the second and third over-turns of power at the ballot box in 2007 and 2018, and the return of the APC under Ernest Koroma and the SLPP under Julius Maada Bio. Tak-ing all into consideration, this question needs to be asked: how profound are the changes within these processes and indeed those afoot in soci-ety? Liberal reforms continue at a painfully slow pace and most prob-lems as outlined above have not gone away, but there is reason to believe that Sierra Leone is not exactly the same as it was before the conflict. In the latter part of the 2000s and 2010s, global politics has also altered, with the introduction of China and India as key players in Africa and the accompanying threat to Western influence, and Sierra Leone is far from immune to these shifts. Change, in the form of either the momen-tous second and third democratic turnovers or the mutating nodes of power in the Sierra Leonean body politic and in the outside world, should challenge us to constantly re-examine our analysis.

2

THE RISE AND WANE OF KRIO DOMINANCE, 1787–1951

It is almost a given that the history of the Sierra Leonean state begins in 1787 with the momentous and unprecedented arrival of black settlers in Africa from Europe and the Americas and the formation of the first settlement which became known as Freetown. There is little to argue against here as, prior to 1787, the notion of Freetown or Sierra Leone did not exist or rested solely in the minds of Portuguese sailors who may have thought that from a certain angle the mountains of the Freetown peninsula somewhat resembled a lion. Equally, the notion of forming society and government along lines more akin to those in the West, rather than the forms that existed in indigenous political hierarchies, was largely novel. Thus the beginnings of a Western-style state, based on demarcated territorial lines and, however incompletely, on ideals of individualism, meritocracy, liberal democracy and the public-private divide, were only introduced in the late eighteenth century.

However, that assumption would be to set aside important people and processes which have greatly informed how the Sierra Leonean state has been moulded and shaped and how it looks today. For over a hundred years, the nascent state was limited to what was referred to as the Col-ony, which consisted of the Freetown peninsula and assorted islands off the coast south of the peninsula. With a predominantly settler or Krio population under the administration of the Colony in towns such as Hastings, Waterloo, York and Sussex, the links to the interior were largely concerned with trade. Most important, though, all of this changed after the Berlin Conference of 1884–85 and subsequent treaties when Africa was sliced up amongst the European powers. The rest of Sierra Leone, named the Protectorate, was claimed by Britain in 1896, shifting the course of history. However, the need to engage with the vastly more numerous population of the Protectorate also changed the rules of the game. Suddenly the Krio were less important and the interior chiefs took on a vital role in the creation of order and stability for the expanded colonial state. Thus, the following two chapters explore the premise that the important state-society relations emerged after 1896, and the analytical emphasis of the colonial period will as a consequence fall on the period 1896–1961.

A short history of the Krio-British state in the first century is, though, important in establishing the social and political foundations of the more extensive post-1896 colonisation. Freetown owed its existence to British organisations and activists dedicated to the abolition of slavery who turned to the idea of 'repatriating' emancipated slaves and 'free persons of colour' from Britain and the Americas to Africa. The initial settlement of predominantly black Londoners on the Freetown peninsula in 1787 failed owing to the settlers' arrival in the rainy season, disease, lack of preparedness for tropical agriculture, and disputes with indigenous chiefs. The first settlement was named Granville Town after the British abolitionist Granville Sharp. Ironically, it is the local Temne sub-chiefs who have key parts of Freetown named after them to this day: King Jimmy, who burned down Granville Town in 1789; his predecessor, King Tom, with whom the original deal for land was brokered; and Pa Demba. King Jimmy's Market leads down to the shoreline from the centre; the King Tom peninsula west of the city centre houses the King Tom Power Station; and Pademba Road is a main artery heading west which in turn gives its name to the notorious Pademba Road Prison. Naimbana, the chief above King Tom who did not accept the 1787 treaty and renegotiated in 1788, has his head on the 100 leone coin.

Subsequent settlers, however, succeeded in putting down firmer roots. They arrived in three waves. First came the Nova Scotians—former soldiers who had fought for the British in the American War of Independence with the promise of freedom and land. Once Britain had lost the war, it was decided that the land in question would be in the British colony of Nova Scotia in Canada, which proved to be less than satisfactory. Some 1,200 left Nova Scotia in 1792 for West Africa. Despite the French incursion and burning of Freetown in 1794, the settlement survived. The current central Freetown layout dates from this rebuilding with the huge Cotton Tree, then as now, at its heart. The second wave also came from Nova Scotia in 1800 but they were originally Maroons from Jamaica who had revolted against slavery and escaped to the mountains, and were then recaptured and shipped to Canada. Their arrival was timely for the British as the rebellion of Nova Scotians, driven by the charging of land rent and the desire to self-govern, was underway. Maroons and British soldiers put down the rebellion. Built in 1820, St John's Maroon Church still notifies everyone of its original congregation on Siaka Stevens Street. All settlers, however, were threatened by King Jimmy's successor, another King Tom, who attacked Freetown in 1801. With the help of a Loko chief, Ngombu Smart, the Temnes were beaten back and by the time of the 1807 treaty were driven from most of the Freetown peninsula.

The number of settlers was then swollen through the first half of the 19th century by the third wave, the 'recaptives'. These were Africans, particularly Yoruba and Igbo people from what is now Nigeria, who had been liberated from Portuguese and Spanish slave ships by the British navy and taken to Freetown. By 1815, over six thousand had landed and in the 1820s and 1830s thousands more arrived each year until the final shipload disembarked in 1863. Some came from as far afield as the Congo and settled and left their mark in Congo Town in the west of Freetown.[1] Emmanuel Cline was a successful Hausa recaptive from Nigeria who traded goods and land in what was to become Cline Town in the east of the capital. Other recaptives were sent into the hills and further eastwards along the coast to the new settlements of Regent, Leicester and Kissy. Up-country people also became assimilated through residence in Freetown or within Krio families.

From this motley collection of people emerged over the following century a relatively cohesive Krio identity. Most important were its Western influences of church, Western-style education, small family size, professional trades, dress sense and names such as Thorpe and Bright. Krios would often refer to the UK as 'home'. However, it also had African influences from recaptives and from up-country, such as 'secret societies' like the Yoruba-origin Oje and Hunters' societies, and its own language derived from English but incorporating words from Yoruba (*kushe* or hello; *awoko* or gossip), Portuguese (*poto* or white man; *pickin* or child), French (*boku* or a lot) and up-country languages (*yaba* or onion,

from Temne). By the end of the 19th century, differences between settlers, recaptives and some of the local Africans who had either moved to
the Colony, been raised as wards of Krio families or integrated through
marriage or as 'outside wives' had become blurred and all were considered Krio, although this was not a uniform identity.[2] Despite the decline
in importance of Maroon or Nova Scotian descent or ancestors among
one of the 'Seventeen Nations' of the recaptives, there were still class divisions and sub-groups such as the Akus or Muslim Krios. Akus, formerly
Yoruba-speaking liberated Africans, are sometimes regarded as an entirely
separate group from Krios because of their differentiated culture and religion. Indeed, some suggest that Krios did not become politically or
socially unified until the 1960s.[3] Others, meanwhile, assert that Krios
had largely integrated with indigenous Sierra Leoneans by the same time,
which has elements of truth in that they remained part and parcel of
Sierra Leonean society and government after independence.[4] However,
considerable important and longstanding distinctions are observed by
most even today.

It could be summarised that Krios are a reasonably cohesive social
group which is acknowledged as African, but is striking in its cultural
and linguistic difference from the mass of the population, and in mores
that are partially derived from the colonial metropole. However, Krios
can be seen as substantially, although not completely, different from white
settlers in southern Africa. Divisions in society, which included in addition racial divisions in the case of South Africa and Rhodesia/Zimba-
bwe, have never hardened to anything like the same degree in Sierra
Leone. Equally, the Krio have never held the same political power as
whites in southern Africa. One might also make the comparison across
the border in Liberia. Black Americo-Liberian settlers arrived in Liberia from the USA over an approximately forty-year period from 1822
onwards. Similarities to the Krios can be found in the problems of settlement, the addition of recaptives freed in this case by US ships, the
amalgamation into a roughly cohesive culture, and the dominance of
social attitudes and mores from outside Africa. Differences, though, lie
in the lack of interest in colonialism in the USA at this point in time and
the concomitant ability of the Americo-Liberians to assert power and
declare an independent republic in 1847. In addition, there are the Angolan Creoles who are often of both Portuguese and African ancestry, but
who were aligned for many years with Portugal and Brazil and performed

similar colonial tasks to their West African counterparts. Indeed, for several centuries up to the early 1900s, a cosmopolitan and powerful Creole aristocracy ran the administrations of Luanda, Benguela and other coastal towns and, until the 1830s, the Atlantic slave trade from Angola. In an experience similar to that of the Krios, their societal dominance was usurped by Portuguese immigrants during the twentieth century, while their place in the small *assimilado* class, about 1 per cent of Angolans in 1960, assured them continued benefits.[5] Creoles then effectively seized power after independence through their predominance in the Movimento Popular de Libertação de Angola (MPLA). Importantly, Krios have been influential in Sierra Leone but never hegemonic like the other settlers or Creoles in South Africa, Rhodesia/Zimbabwe, Liberia and Angola.

Perhaps most interesting about all of these groups is their relationship with hinterland peoples. There are elements of the '*mission civilisatrice*' or 'civilising mission' of French and British colonialism which can be seen in Creole attitudes. Until the 1970s, the Liberian Constitution referred to the 'enlightenment of the benighted continent'. Although not formally enshrined as such, the Krio stance was similar. As 'interpreters of Western culture to other Africans', they saw themselves as socially superior to indigenous Sierra Leoneans and in a paternal sense responsible for educating them in the benefits of more appropriate ways of living.[6] An eminent Krio, Sir Samuel Lewis, was an early advocate of British expansion into the hinterland, partly for economic reasons but partly also 'to spread the ameliorating influence of European civilisation' of which he was of course very much a part.[7] In Angola, the disdain for the *matumbo*, the 'ignorant native', was common among *assimilados* under Portuguese colonialism.[8] Krios were also seen and saw themselves as 'the intellectual leaders, the vanguard of political and social advance in West Africa'.[9] In 1853, Colony inhabitants were given British citizenship, which officially put them on a different footing to the bulk of other Sierra Leoneans when the colonial enterprise was later expanded.

During the nineteenth century, Krios quickly put aside farming and were able to benefit from the economic opportunities, particularly the import-export trade, exchanging produce such as groundnuts, palm oil and timber for European goods. They could also be found not just in Sierra Leone but all along the British West African coast and even in the Congo Free State, working as government officials, doctors, magis-

trates, teachers and missionaries. J.F. Easmon became a doctor of medicine, rose to be head of the medical department in the Gold Coast (later
Ghana) colonial government, and isolated blackwater fever as a separate
disease. James Africanus Horton, a son of recaptives, qualified as a doctor and from 1859 served for over twenty years in the British Army. John
Thorpe, a descendent of Maroons, became the first Sierra Leonean, as
early as 1850, to be called to the English Bar. Lewis was called to the bar
in 1871 and returned to Freetown the next year as Acting Queen's Advocate, in effect Attorney-General. A vociferous yet loyal critic of the government, he built his practice, became the first mayor of the reconstituted
Freetown Municipality in 1895 and was the first Black African to be
knighted by a British monarch.[10] His statue still stands in Murray Town
in the west of the capital. Some like Bishop Samuel Ajayi Crowther, the
first pupil of the Christian Institution after it moved to Fourah Bay in
1827, went abroad to proselytise, in Crowther's case returning to Yorub-
aland. Schools, such as the Annie Walsh Memorial School which emerged
from the Christian Female Institution in 1877, flourished in the Colony.
Fourah Bay College, now seated high on one of the hills overlooking the
capital but created from the Christian Institution in Fourah Bay in 1848,
was affiliated to the University of Durham in the UK in 1876.

The political power of the settlers within the Western-style administration, while never great, did wax and wane over the first century. The
first Governor of Granville Town, Richard Weaver, was a settler, but
under the rule of the Sierra Leone Company, from 1791 to 1807, Freetown was not self-governing and was directed from London. The failed
Nova Scotian rebellion of 1800 was partly based on the desire for self-
rule. New rules were temporarily issued by the rebels but the defeat ultimately allowed the Company to ban the election of settler representatives.
In 1807, having lost money, the Company passed the Freetown peninsula over to the British Crown and it became a Crown Colony. Direct
rule from London continued, however, and petitioning and the increasingly active press became the sole methods of influencing the Governor,
particularly after any pretence of local self-government in the first Freetown Municipality was abandoned in 1821. Given the education and
professional and commercial success of the Krios, many increasingly
believed some form of self-government to be preferable. However, in
1863, despite a new constitution and the establishment of an Executive
and Legislative Council, just two appointed seats on the latter council

were reserved for the community. Three more were added later, so progress was made, but representation in the first century of the settlement continued to be circumscribed. Perhaps most important, though, a means of governing utterly alien to those outside the Colony was being created with some Krio participation or at least acceptance, either inside or outside the government. Krio desires, often articulated in a plethora of newspapers and magazines, were to change the membership or policies rather than to radically reform or re-create the institution on the basis of something more African.

The ramifications of the Berlin Conference of 1884–85 and the Scramble for Africa changed everything for the British, the Krios and the hinterland population. Africa was the last great landmass left to colonise but European powers had thus far been reluctant to go much further than their coastal enclaves. Expense, disease, some unwelcoming Africans, the largely unknown material attractions of the interior and the comfortable levels of existing trade led to an entrenched status quo. However, the invention of better weapons and medicines coincided with increasing need for raw materials and markets in European economies, the ratcheting up of political tensions in Europe and the belligerence of certain African polities such as the Asante in the Gold Coast (later Ghana). Britain, France, Germany, Portugal, Italy, Spain and the King of Belgium, but certainly not Africans, became the main negotiators. Britain, for its part, was required to reverse its policy of non-expansion and demonstrate, in the terms of the Conference, 'effective occupation' of the hinterland of coastal claims. In Sierra Leone these were the Freetown peninsula and southwards down to Sherbro Island, the latter nominally and rather reluctantly annexed in 1861 in the face of French expansionism. The proximity of the French in the north also hurried this process along. Territorially, the result was the declaration of the Protectorate in 1896 and the tenfold geographic expansion of Sierra Leone from the peninsular Colony to its current borders with Guinea to the north and east and Liberia to the south. Societally, the effects were just as momentous.

First, although never in huge numbers, many more British administrators began to arrive in Freetown. The effects were felt strongly by Krios in that they were sidelined from state jobs that had previously been their domain, causing some to seek work elsewhere in the empire. The 18 of about 40 senior government posts held by Krios in the Colony in 1892 were reduced to 15 of 92 by 1912 and five of these 15 posts were subsequently abolished when their incumbents retired.[11] Bo School, established by the government in 1906 to educate sons and nominees of chiefs, expressly disqualified Krio teachers, and Krios were almost entirely excluded from administrative positions in the Protectorate. Equally, the limits of Freetown were extended further into the hills to allow British officials in the 'white man's graveyard' to live in a slightly cooler European Reserve, named Hill Station. The shift was received as a slight on Krios, accompanied by a loss of the rental income on their property portfolios in the city centre. Second, the Lebanese, who were collectively known for a while as Syrians and began to arrive in the 1890s, had by the end of the first quarter of the nineteenth century supplanted the Krio trading mandarins, often aided by the British authorities and firms.[12] The influx greatly exercised Krio opinion, and hostility culminated in the 1919 anti-Syrian riots.

Third, there was a fairly clear change of heart from the British colonisers, switching preference to a rather romanticised view of indigenous Sierra Leoneans away from the 'savvy niggers' or 'trousered' Africans, by which the Krio and other 'detribalised' Africans elsewhere had derogatively become known.[13] Reasons given for Krio exclusion from Bo School included the need to retain the students' 'pristine purity free from modernising tendencies' and to 'strengthen tribal patriotism'.[14] There were limits to these views as some saw far less noble qualities and even those who were sympathetic emphasised 'superficial emotional qualities' over 'intellect'.[15] The Krios still maintained their privileged status vis-à-vis other Sierra Leoneans. Indeed, up to independence and beyond, jobs in the professions, academia, the civil service and the judiciary were still taken mostly by Krios, when not filled by Europeans. In 1950, Krios comprised 67 of the 70 qualified Sierra Leonean medical doctors. However, the vocal allegiance to Britain, exemplified by H. C. Bankole-Bright who was seen as a troublemaker by the British but still spoke of his 'organic connection with the British Crown', and J. C. O. Crowther, who insisted that 'everyone of us should be proud of our British connection', meant that the Krio response to the new British attitude was one of immense disappointment.[16] In many ways, the British policy was a systematic attack on Krios due to the greater presence of British colonials and the notion that white men could do a better job than black men. The relative meritocracy of the 1800s was overruled by considerations of colour in the 1900s. This was an era when 'racial prejudice was reaching new heights of absurdity'.[17] Added to the new racism, the shortcomings of a few Krio notables and the notion that Krios had played a part in fomenting the 1898 Hut Tax War sealed the change in British attitudes. Finally and most crucially, though, there had also been a sea change in political circumstances within colonial expansion.

The debate concerning colonialism across Africa often runs on the lines of how powerful it was and what it was trying to achieve. The first aspect tends to polarise into two ways of thinking. From one angle, particularly focused on the Congo, European imperialism is seen as all-conquering, the *Bula Matari* or crusher of rocks to use the Congolese phrase.[18] From a different angle, predominantly of British colonialism, the whole project is 'hegemony on a shoestring'.[19] The relative significance of either slant depends very much on which colonial territory is being scrutinised. Inevitably, British colonialism in Sierra Leone is a mixture of the two, but as will become evident, it is more of the latter. The second aspect of the debate regards the relative importance of geopolitics, economics and the 'civilising mission' in the colonial project. Geopolitics was clearly important in the timing of the Berlin Conference and subsequent expansion, but whether the prime motivation over time was geopolitical, economic or social will concern us during the rest of this chapter.

As with all other colonial acquisitions in Africa, and despite its deliberately vague terminology, the requirement of 'effective occupation' was a serious challenge. Officially, the colonial methodologies were miles apart. French direct rule treated one small area (the Four Communes of Senegal) as almost a part of France, and allowed some Africans assimilated into French culture to obtain full French citizenship, while the majority of African '*sujets*' were governed directly by French administrators at all levels. By contrast, British indirect rule, based on ideas developed in Northern Nigeria by Lord Lugard, saw rule by proxy through the African political hierarchies, such as the emirs and kings of Nigeria and the chiefs of Sierra Leone. In practice, the differences were not so great. The willingness of the French state to spend money on Africa was almost as circumscribed as that of the British state. Colonial officials came in small numbers to West Africa: in the 1930s, British tropical Africa had just 1,223 administrators and 43 million Africans and French West Africa had 3,660 administrators and 15 million Africans across even larger territories, in stark contrast to the Japanese who in the same period in Korea alone had approximately 45,000 officials.[20] With limited resources and European personnel, both Britain and France used coercion where necessary in subduing scattered people in large territories, but deal-making and incorporation of chiefs into the colonial hierarchy were much more common methods of securing occupation. The French then relied almost as much on their African counterparts as did the British to maintain law and order. Colonialists in Africa have been described as 'neither administrators nor conquerors'.[21] Equally, the idea that Africans would be imbued with the republican notions of *liberté, égalité, fraternité* was undermined by the French reliance on chiefs, who were more inclined to preserve their own cultural mores.[22] The British were not immune to the challenge of a civilising mission but, through a mixture of policy and parsimony, faced the same obstacles as the French.

In effect, in a sea change of considerable proportions, the African political hierarchies of the Protectorate had suddenly become immeasurably more important to the Sierra Leonean colonial project. In the former Protectorate today, ethnic identities include the Mende in the South, who constitute around 30 per cent of the population; the Temne and Limba, who make up around 30 per cent and 8.5 per cent of the population respectively, and occupy the Northern Savanna areas and have greater connections with Islam and the peoples of Guinea; and other smaller but important groups such as the Kono and Kissi in the East and the Koranko in the North. At the same time, no ethnic group is solely Islamic or Christian, with the exception of the smaller largely Muslim Mandingo and Fula communities. It is often estimated that 60 per cent of Sierra Leoneans are Muslim, 20–30 per cent Christian and 5–10 per cent followers of traditional beliefs, but this is very misleading as the figures are not accurate and because many are Christian or Muslim whilst also following traditional beliefs. Temnes are more often Muslims and Mendes often Christians, reflecting the early Islamicisation of the north and the subsequent preference of Christian missionaries for the south. Many, though, share cultural, linguistic and religious connections, in particular chieftaincy, the important Poro (for men) and Bondo and Sande (for women) 'secret societies' and the need for chiefs to consult over important actions. The 'traditional' institutions provide to this day much of the policing, judicial, citizenship and spiritual requirements of the rural population.

Identities and authority, however, were much more fluid in pre-colonial times. In a pattern repeated over much of sub-Saharan Africa, languages mutated over space and time and people often held greater loyalty to a local hierarchy than to an ethnic group. There were kingdoms and chieftaincies which governed groups of people through kings, chiefs, elders and 'secret societies'. These differed from European and Krio notions of governance, under construction to some extent in the Colony, in two crucial ways. First, the emphasis of pre-colonial control lay with people not territory. In a setting where there was a vast amount of land and few, dispersed people, territory was rarely demarcated. Instead, people owed allegiance or gave tribute to a king or chief, often influenced by necessities of the time, most often security. The relationship between chief and subject was thus unequal but one firmly based on reciprocity, where reneging on the arrangement from either side might annul the relationship. Second, the method of governing was not based on written rules and policies, but on the combination of reciprocal imperatives, decisions of a hereditary hierarchy, and religious and cultural mores.

In many ways it was the colonial period that did most to codify rules, territorially define chiefdoms and solidify and politicise ethnic identities. British notions of scientific classification and the need to parcel people into groups for administrative purposes meant the gradual reifying of ethnicity and chieftaincy. Equally, the response of African local leaders was often an attempt to use this new environment to their own benefit, which led to the same need for grouping and consequent reification and politicisation of identity. It has been argued that 'tradition' was invented during colonialism, but it has also been noted that, whilst holding some truth, the idea of inventing 'tradition' wholesale is unlikely as the colonial authorities required something legitimate and recognisable on which to build.[23] Perceiving identity as somehow primordial and unchanging is of course fanciful, but it is also important to see the limits of both constructivism and the notion that identity has little other substance than its instrumental use to gain advantage or resources. Change and continuity are both seen in these critical processes.

The history of the Sierra Leonean hinterland and the internal and external interactions should then be understood in its pre-colonial yet evolving state. Internally, political flux was evident in pre-colonial times, as might be expected. Conflicts would break out and die down for a variety of reasons. Notable wars include the 18th-century Islamic takeover of the Futa Jallon in contemporary Guinea by the Fulas, which drove Susus and Yalunkas southwards into Temne, Limba, Koranko and Loko areas, creating greater diversity all the way up to the level of chief. Tension between Loko and Temne chiefs around the Colony erupted sporadically in the first half of the nineteenth century. In the south, the inland Mendes began to threaten the wealthier coastal chiefdoms and, although not a unified people, earned themselves a tough reputation as warriors. Nearby chiefdoms and the British Army employed Mende soldiers. Trade wars broke out in the 1880s, often pitting Mende against Mende and Temne against Temne, enlisting British assistance wherever possible.

Externally, the mouth of the Sierra Leone River, ruled to the north by a Loko chiefdom and to the south by Temnes, was an important docking area for traders and slavers as well as the British Empire right up to the Second World War. Portuguese traders were followed by their British counterparts and in time the slavers. Renting small islands, such as Bunce Island in the Sierra Leone River estuary where ruins remain today, or land at the mouths of other rivers, European slavers would barter for up-country people captured by coastal or up-country chiefs in battle. Both sides benefited from this arrangement, although the export of people was not of benefit to either those involved or the larger economy. Sierra Leone was not a main centre of trans-Atlantic slaving, but still some 3,000 left every year and the trading of slaves to the outside world was not eradicated until 1850 when the Rogers family of Gallinas country (later partly in Liberia) signed the last of such treaties with the British.[24] Indeed, a new form of chief emerged when European traders intermarried with local dignitaries, creating such dynasties as the Rogers and the Tuckers and Caulkers (originally Corkers) of Sherbro country.

In establishing the Protectorate, Governor Sir Frederick Cardew (1894–1900) was instrumental. He was the first European to tour the entire territory, and formulated the plans for how the Protectorate would be run. It was he who proposed the idea of the Protectorate and a form of indirect rule which preceded Lugard's more famous introduction of the policy in Nigeria. Chiefs would continue ruling, assisted and restricted by European District Commissioners.[25] Some, such as Lewis, argued for a comprehensive British takeover, but admitted that rapid wholesale introduction of 'English laws and customs' would probably be destabilising.[26] Another Krio, J.C.E. Parkes, a leading expert of the time on interior people who became head of the Aborigines Department and later the Department of Native Affairs, was also in favour of full legal control but, crucially, foresaw trouble if this was attempted.[27] Indirect rule thus became the solution. Railway lines would indeed be built and the territory would be kept in order by the recently-created Frontier Police, but this was of course still a very cheap option, being reliant mostly on Africans. It would cost money, though, and the British government insisted on it being financed internally. Thus Cardew brought in the five shillings Hut Tax, in the firm belief that his experience in Zululand, his personal attempts at explanation and the ability of many Protectorate householders to pay would make resistance unlikely.[28]

British colonial authorities were, however, given early warnings about the legitimacy and coherency of local power and the limits of coercive actions. If Samori Touré's exhausted Sofa warriors were relatively easily defeated in the Kono area, the Hut Tax War of 1898 led by the Temne chief Bai Bureh was a different matter. Known for his professional military prowess, Bai Bureh was made Chief of Kasseh and had a long history of fluctuating relations with the British. Given the imposition of the house tax and the belligerent stance taken by Cardew against chiefs who did not accept his efforts of explanation, Bai Bureh resisted.[29] A similar extensive uprising ensued in Mendeland. Grievances concerning the tax, Krio traders, unpopular chiefs, the Frontier Police and British expansion in general came together in full scale insurrections. This was guerrilla warfare with scorched-earth tactics on both sides. Many lost their lives, including Chief Thomas Neale Caulker, one of those who paid the taxes, hundreds of Krios and seven American missionaries. Nine months later, the revolt was finally put down by the overwhelming coercive power of the Frontier Police. Bai Bureh and others such as the Mende leader Nyagua were deported to the Gold Coast.[30] Bai Bureh returned in 1905, was reinstated as chief until his death around 1909 and now appears as a hero on 1,000 leone notes and in the name of a main highway in the east of the capital. Cardew's name does live on in a small street in the East End of Freetown, but he does not have a main artery in the capital named after him like his successors, Sir Charles King-Harman (1900–4) and the historian of Malaya, Sir Richard Wilkinson (1916–22).

Notwithstanding military victories, British colonial fingers had been burned. Indeed, the British Secretary of State for the Colonies, Joseph Chamberlain, and the Special Commissioner sent to investigate were both against the continuance of the tax and it was only due to Cardew's insistence that it remained.[31] But despite these coercive actions, the establishment of the Protectorate was still mostly achieved by negotiation and incorporation: the limits of British power were already becoming clear. British solutions might be summarised as stick and carrot. After the Hut Tax War, many larger kingdoms or chieftaincies were broken up and in some cases pliant chiefs installed, although this was rarely a smooth process.[32] Bizarrely, the Reverend D.F. Wilberforce was made Paramount Chief of Imperi.[33] There is evidence that the British administration deliberately fostered divisions between ethnic groups and between Colony and Protectorate.[34] Strengthening 'tribal patriotism' was indeed an aim and some in the Colony were dismayed to see attempts to portray the Krio as 'degenerate' and 'an interloper' in the Protectorate.[35] On the other hand, in some cases, such as that of the Kissi people whose political entities were small and localised, chiefs of greater areas were created or allowed to emerge.

At the same time, there were many others alongside Caulker who entered into the colonial bargain, including the raising of taxes, and benefited. Before the Berlin Conference, Britain had been extremely reluctant to expand beyond the Colony but also needed to trade. The solution was to make treaties with local rulers and pay them stipends, and allow Krios to act as middlemen on the same basis as the slavers but in greater numbers. Later, leaders like the female Mende chief, Mammy Yoko, whose name adorns a hotel in the Aberdeen area of Freetown, Momo Kai Kai in Pujehun and Kai Londo in Kailahun welcomed British rule and were often able to consolidate and extend their own authority and benefit from connections with the colonial state. Remarkably, Kai Londo managed to persuade the British to have the Liberian and Guinean borders redrawn so that the whole of his newly-expanded chiefdom fell within Sierra Leone, although this was divided into two after his death.[36] His face appears on the 500 leone coin.

All in all, chiefs lost some powers and gained others within a 'traditional' system which was now even more questionably 'traditional', was codified and territorialised, and allowed greater scope for local level abuses as long as British relations were kept in order. The important notion of reciprocity and the balancing of chiefly power through consultation remained, but were distorted by the presence of the new state and by the potential for chiefs to renege on some of their reciprocal responsibilities to their people if they had the backing of the central power. One observer has gone as far as labelling these new era chiefs in British colonies and post-colonies as 'decentralised despots'.[37] At the same time, the Sierra Leonean institution of chieftaincy had survived and retained a good proportion of its legitimacy during the transition. The effect was to co-opt the chiefs into the colonial system, where obedience was rewarded and resistance punished by removal from office. The patron-client system with the state as the ultimate patron, the chiefs as middlemen and the people as clients was thus born. Krios were significantly relegated in importance. Crucially, because it was 'hegemony on a shoestring', the system was one of incomplete colonial domination or what might be described as a negotiated political arena or the 'politics of collaboration'.[38] This particular stick and carrot system was not lost on post-independence leaders who went on to adopt similar methods to counter similar problems.

Moving on to the reasons behind the colonial project, it is often assumed that, after the initial geopolitical push, extraction was the predominant colonial priority. Trade with the hinterland had indeed been vital to the Colony. Thus the first railway in British West Africa, connecting Freetown and the interior, was begun in 1895 and reached its eastern terminus at Pendembu, passing through Bo and Kenema, in 1908, and its northerly branch line terminus at Makeni in 1914. Its main function was to transport agricultural goods bound for Europe: exports rose fourfold from 1900 to 1918.[39] Passenger travel was clearly not the aim given the dearth of lines, the high fares and the extremely slow trains, but if the process created local capitalists, then so much the better. Another railway designed for passengers was built in Freetown but this service existed purely to give British colonial commuters a route from their attractive and airy homes in Hill Station, some of which still stand, to their jobs in the centre.

However, it was not until the 1930s that the mining of two extremely important minerals began. In 1931, the Sierra Leone Development Company (DELCO) was formed to exploit the Marampa iron ore mines in Port Loko District, for which a 52-mile railway was built to take the ore to ships at Pepel. More importantly, diamonds were discovered in 1930 in Kono District and soon graduated to become the mainstay of the economy, simultaneously proving immensely difficult to control. This discovery and its implications were to reverberate through subsequent Sierra Leonean history. The colonial government quickly signed long-term, country-wide deals with a De Beers subsidiary, Sierra Leone Selection Trust (SLST), in 1932–33. Both SLST and the colonial government

feared the onset of illicit mining. They were right to be wary as the diamonds were mostly alluvial and simple to dig up and the chiefs effectively controlled both the land and people. Kono and Kenema Districts
attracted many migrant miners who worked on a tributor basis where
earnings depended entirely on finding the stones.[40] No amount of legislation was able to deter illicit mining overseen by the chiefs, traders from
Freetown and the Lebanese community. In an unsuccessful attempt to
bring chiefs in, their official incomes were increased substantially. In
Kono, chiefs' incomes grew from around £500 per annum before mining
activities began to nearly £10,000 in the late 1940s, a process which did
not reduce illicit mining but did serve to further increase chiefly power.[41]
Importantly, and despite these problems, the colony moved quickly in
the 1930s from deficit to surplus.

On the other hand, while the British did not subscribe to French and
Portuguese notions of assimilation and the 'civilising mission', Britain
certainly had its own version. This was the era of ideas of sociocultural
evolution and stages of social development in which the British considered themselves leaders. At the highest level, there was the extension of
the Colony state to the Protectorate. Some features of the modern liberal state were decidedly lacking, such as the juridical equality of the cit-
izenry, a separation of state powers and, until the latter stages, democratic
institutions. Extended into the interior, however, were a precisely demarcated territory and centralised structures including a capital, a permanent coercive force, a permanent bureaucracy, national taxation, codified
law—although in both 'state' and 'customary' forms—and a partially reg-
ulated market. One could suggest that most of this was required for economic exploitation and one might baulk at the notion of a state that had
only partial hegemony over its population and such limited resources to
effect its extension, but the idea of a country, a state and a public realm
were deliberately and somewhat successfully introduced.

At societal level, as one author succinctly notes, there were 'aspects of
traditional government that were distasteful to the British, such as ritual murder'.[42] More commonplace, slavery and female circumcision were
seen in a similar way by the colonial state while polygamy, 'witchcraft'
and 'traditional' religious beliefs were opposed by missionaries. All were
subject to colonial or missionary efforts to bring about change. As early
as 1863, a Colonial Office civil servant in London questioned the British presence on Bonthe Island if it could not 'exercise power and do

good'.[43] The first Bo School Prospectus, a document of conflicting ideas, is indicative at least of the thinking of Governor Sir Leslie Probyn (1904– 10). Training in morals including assumed British traits of the time— truthfulness, work and self control—and a particular directive on increasing respect for women by teaching the lives of Florence Nightingale and Queen Victoria sat alongside the non-interference in and prohibition of speaking against 'Native Customs and Institutions.... excepting of course any custom that is repugnant to humanity'.[44] Ironies abound and the exact manner in which these two sets of cultural mores could be accommodated is not at all clear.

However, to further underline the drive for some forms of social change and the concurrent limits of imperial power, the actions against slavery— a policy which the British and the Krios would seemingly hold dear— are instructive. Prior to 1896, governors and Krios were often keen to extend British rule, despite reluctance in London, so as to eliminate the slave trade, and it was indeed abolished throughout Sierra Leone in 1896.[45] However, it took until 1928 for actual slavery to be outlawed. Slaves were so important to chiefly economics that the British administration adopted a very cautious approach. Indeed, the trade in goods, which was deemed legitimate and had been avidly promoted for some time as an alternative to slave trading, was itself reliant on the capital that many societies had in abundance: slaves.[46] It is important to differentiate here as there were many categories of slave. Many in Sierra Leone were dependent by choice or inheritance, often being part of the household and given land to cultivate, as well as those who were bought or captured.[47] Much derives from the greater importance of people than land in an under-populated milieu. Britain, however, was embarrassed by discussions at the League of Nations after the First World War. Sierra Leone was the last colony in British West Africa to abolish slavery, but even at this point the practice of non-voluntary unpaid community work, administered by the chiefs, continued. Forced labour, one of a chief's 'customary rights', was officially recognised in 1902 and restated in the Forced Labour Ordinance of 1932. Chiefs could use this labour as they felt fit, even extending to work on a chief's commercial farm.

Female circumcision has weathered the efforts of colonialism and indeed the more recent global onslaught at eradication, and still affects some 90 per cent of the female population across all ethnic groups except the Christian Krios.[48] Syncretism, the simultaneous belief in Christianity or Islam and the power of traditional spirituality, remains common today. The Poro and Bondo societies still thrive and 'witchcraft', especially when it is alleged to be in the service of prominent people, is a frequent story in the newspapers. The spirit world of the forests is seen by many to deeply affect events in the physical world and the secret societies continue to police the border areas between the two worlds, supervise the important coming of age and circumcision rituals, and provide the spiritual glue which holds rural and often urban society together. Thus, the extent to which the British were able to shift Protectorate society into Western ways of thinking and doing, which might fit with Western techniques of governance and economy, was rather limited. Change had indeed come about through the colonial presence, and some changes in the economic, political and social organisation of the Protectorate were of substance, but much was maintained or, perhaps more accurately, the changes of substance were often partial and not at all as intended. This has implications that resonate even today, of which more later in the book.

The difference in administration and laws between Protectorate and Colony further exposes colonial prerogatives and deficiencies. Although it was far from a parliamentary democracy, the administration in the Colony had nothing to do with chieftaincies. On the other hand, administration in the Protectorate was left to a great extent in the hands of Africans. The Protectorate was divided into five districts with both District Commissioners and the newly created Paramount Chiefs, a pattern which survives with only a few differences today. The Legislative Council could make laws for the Protectorate, but in a display of expediency, chiefs could also use their own laws. Chiefdom courts were officially recognised in 1902. More Paramount Chiefs, eventually exceeding two hundred, were created. A confusing twin track legal system with many regional perturbations was thus created, which again survives to a large degree into the contemporary age. For instance, it is unclear how long the North can continue to forbid women chiefs while in the South they have long been allowed and the central state maintains laws of non-discrimination. Many Colony laws, particularly those pertaining to land tenure and ownership, were not extended to the Protectorate. It was declared that Protectorate land belonged to the people and could not be bought and sold. These legal divisions have proved remarkably resilient.

At the same time, education and state infrastructure in the Protectorate lagged far behind the Colony. Despite the creation of new educational facilities and state infrastructure in the twentieth century, the Protectorate remained grossly underdeveloped by comparison with the Colony. In 1921, for example, there were 103 schools in the Colony but still only 70 in the Protectorate, in spite of its significantly greater population.[49] Indeed, Bo School did not offer a European-style education until the 1930s. Most children still attended 'secret society' or Koranic schools. A few went to missionary schools, predominantly in the south, which were taken over by the government in 1929, and a primary teacher training college was established at Njala which was later to become part of the University of Sierra Leone. Pre-Second World War Western-style education, and similarly health provision, in the Protectorate did improve, but they were little more than drops in the ocean. Crucially, alongside social, political, economic and legal differences, the urban-rural gap was thus created and solidified.

In sum, the reluctant British colonists of the late nineteenth century were stung into action in Sierra Leone by global concerns. They also clearly had one eye on profits from agriculture and subsequently minerals. The importance of trade had been clear for a long time and remained so, and the news of the discoveries of diamonds and iron ore was no doubt gratefully received, even though their existence was unknown at the start of the colonial project. It would, in addition, be remiss to ignore the other colonial eye fixed on changing society, however unsuccessfully in the long term. British colonialism—however faltering, misguided and circumscribed—established the modern state, introduced Western-style schooling, suppressed slavery, endeavoured to 'civilise' the ways of Sierra Leoneans towards British thinking and in the latter stages instituted formal democracy. This all suggests that colonial imperatives changed over time but also that colonialism was driven as much by socio-political concerns as by the usual suspects of geopolitics and economics. One might reduce colonial imperatives to those of control and change, where the former always took priority in the frequent clashes of interest.[50] Control was required, on the cheap through indirect rule, in order to govern and exploit the resources of the colony, while the imperative to 'civilise' Sierra Leoneans or to bring Sierra Leone in line with the 'modern' world was always serious but liable to cause trouble and so subordinated to the more pressing needs of control. Again, these concerns still resonate today within the priorities of Sierra Leonean government and indeed international bodies.

The decision to integrate the Colony and Protectorate initiated a fraught and piecemeal process that lasted from 1922 to 1951 and further changed the political balance, thus undermining the Krios in the important 1950s pre-independence decade. The Freetown City Council had been re-established in 1893 and consisted of a mayor and twelve elected and three nominated councillors. This arrangement was amended in 1927 to a president, four nominated and four elected members. In 1926, following an inquiry into the performance of the City Council, E.S. Beoku-Betts became the last elected leader until after the Second World War and control of the Council was turned over to the colonial government. The rural areas of the Colony were divided into four—Wilberforce, Kissy, York and Waterloo, the former two now considered as part of Greater Freetown—and run by a Rural Commissioner and a Rural Area Council. In other words, the rollercoaster ride of Krio representation in the Colony continued. At the same time, the Executive Council remained an all-white affair until 1943 when two Africans were appointed, but the Legislative Council was reformed in 1924 in the first attempt to amalgamate Colony and Protectorate. In a rather half-hearted attempt riddled with ambiguities, the new Legislative Council included three members elected by literate property-owning Colony voters, two more selected by the Governor and three Paramount Chiefs. Beoku-Betts and H. C. Bankole-Bright were elected in the Colony and were prominent in the politics of the period up to the Second World War. This was, of course, not an amalgamation and contained varying notions of criteria for selection, but it showed that the Protectorate was beginning to be included in central government.

The period immediately before and after the Second World War saw, on the one hand, mostly Krio proto-nationalist agitation for African rights, and on the other hand, much more movement in the process of amalgamation of Colony and Protectorate. While the Sierra Leonean branch of the National Congress of British West Africa (NCBWA), led by Bankole-Bright and other Krios, had been active since 1920, its raison d'être was not nationalist as such but to articulate grievances to the colonial government. Similar anti-colonialist but not nationalist agitation can be seen elsewhere in Africa.[51] I.T.A. Wallace-Johnson was a brief but fiery challenge to the NCBWA. Widely travelled as a journalist and trades unionist, Wallace-Johnson was a founder member of the West African Youth League (WAYL) and, on his return to

Sierra Leone in 1938, became leader of the Sierra Leonean branch (SLYL). He simultaneously frightened the Krio establishment and the colonial government with his pro-worker rhetoric which appealed to both Colony and Protectorate. The SLYL swept the Freetown City Council elections and the unions became more demonstrative. In a time of international tensions Wallace-Johnson was eventually detained from 1940 until the end of the war. His time of greatest influence was brief, but he is recognised by a statue and a street name in central Freetown for his efforts in the first stirrings of nationalism. Many, however, are circumspect about his success in uniting the Colony and Protectorate people as the SLYL was Krio-dominated, and further note that he drove a wedge into Krio politics.[52]

Much speculation and notions of balancing of the Colony and Pro-tectorate gave way in 1947 to the Stevenson Constitution propagated by Governor Sir Hubert Stevenson (1941–47). In recognition of the shift in global politics towards the new superpowers and self-determination of nations, and the shift in British thinking after the Second World War leading to acceptance that independence was now much more imminent, Africans were now to be in the majority in the Governor's Executive Council and the Legislative Council. Just as important, in the final guise of the latter body, fourteen members would represent the Protectorate and seven the Colony. In a *volte face* of some proportions, Wallace-Johnson, alongside Bankole-Bright and the National Council of Sierra Leone (NCSL) formed in 1950, led the vociferous Krio protestations at their loss of political status. They saw the Krios at the forefront of polit-ical agitation and at all costs did not want to be pushed aside. In 1951, two Protectorate organisations and one Colony party, led by Reverend E.N. Jones who changed his name to Lamina Sankoh and committed himself to Protectorate-Colony solidarity, came together to form the Sierra Leone People's Party (SLPP). In the same year, accompanied by counter-arguments from the SLPP led by the future first prime minis-ter of independent Sierra Leone, Dr Milton Margai, the new constitu-tion came to life. Indeed, with a population ratio of about two million to sixty thousand, the Colony was seemingly getting a good deal but, if historical, educational and prior political considerations are taken into account, this was not so clear.

The distinction between Protectorate and Colony was not really removed by the time of the 1951 elections as the imbalances remained and Protectorate voting was indirect with the chiefs still playing an overbearing role in the selection of Protectorate members of the Legislative Council. The Protectorate Assembly, established in 1945–46, included 26 seats for Paramount Chiefs and just two for educated Protectorate Africans. In this situation the Assembly and the District Councils would then have elected an overwhelmingly chiefly body of men as members of the Legislative Council. The Sierra Leone Organisation Society (SOS), established in 1946 and headed by John Karefa-Smart, who would subsequently gain considerable prominence, fought this chiefly influence. A schism between the two Protectorate groups was bridged by the diplomacy of Milton Margai and recognition of the need for some balance by the colonial administration.[53] Reforms to the Protectorate Assembly in 1950, where the educated Protectorate elite could take up six seats, allowed two other future prime ministers, Albert Margai and Siaka Stevens, to be elected to the Legislative Council, but chiefly influence remained very great.

The 1951 elections returned three NCSL, two SLPP and two independent candidates, including Wallace-Johnson, in the Colony. Of the fourteen emerging from the Protectorate, four were card carrying SLPP members including Stevens and the Margais, but all, including the Paramount Chiefs, subsequently declared for the SLPP. Despite Bankole-Bright's assumption that the NCSL would somehow assume power, this was a clear victory for the Protectorate and the SLPP.[54] As a consequence, the Governor subsequently chose only SLPP members for his African nominations to the Executive Council. Albert Margai became Minister of Local Government, Education and Welfare, Stevens took on the post of Minister for Land, Mines and Labour, and Milton Margai became Minister of Health, Agriculture and Forests and, one year later, Chief Minister.[55] Meanwhile, the Freetown City Council was reconstituted in 1948. It included nine elected councillors and three elected aldermen, but voting rights were also extended to non-Krio Freetonians, a right not held by Krios living in the Protectorate. In many ways, despite further Krio efforts to turn back the clock examined in Chapter 3, the political shift was almost complete.

Pertinently, it has been noted that the state inherited from the colonial power was dominated by Krios, while politics was dominated by people and interests from the former Protectorate.[56] Indeed, the rather lightweight Western-style state manned by Krios and Europeans had already been thoroughly compromised in its reliance on 'traditional' authorities to pacify the hinterland. By 1951, the Protectorate, underpinned by the non-Western institutions of chieftaincy and 'secret societies' and imbued with notions of ethnicity, communalism and traditional spiritual beliefs, was penetrating deep into its vulnerable machinery. The constitutional changes allowed for the beginnings of rule by the majority, but opened the doors for chiefly patronage politics to supplant narrow elitist Krio politics which nonetheless had had some sense of citizenship, liberal democracy and the rule of law associated with the Western-style state now implanted at the centre. The disconnections and divides in the body politic were considerable. Current reformers concerned with democratisation and decentralisation still face an environment not unlike that of the constitutionalists of the colonial era.

This state of affairs one can attribute to the failure of British 'hegemony on a shoestring' or the resilience of African society. In addition, the legacy of British governing and commercial structures, of the separation of Colony and Protectorate and of the influence of the Freetown-based Krios is still visible, and a source of contention, even today. This was to some extent a rural-urban bifurcation of the state.[57] The heavy political involvement of the chiefs might suggest that the bifurcation lies in a broader elite versus non-elite sense, but it is more pronounced than even most other social and economic gaps in British colonial and post-colonial systems, although now involving an expanded African elite. By the 1950s, the Krios may have given way in politics to their hinterland compatriots, but the system had been fashioned for those that followed. Peculiarly, given the Krios' mission to bring the benefits of Western civilisation to Africa, and the wealth of education and the assimilationist structure of Krio society, their unintended legacy was a distended social, political and economic gap between the elite and the rest of the Sierra Leonean population. Paradoxically, the gap was connected by a continually reinforced patron-client political structure, but this was not even a remotely fair connection and it was one imbued with assumed superiority from above and the associated deference from below.

A developmentally unbalanced state thus began to emerge, now presided over by a politically and economically over-centralised, institutionally weak, somewhat patronising and numerically restricted regime. Indeed, one might tentatively conclude that Krio elitism and chiefly elitism combined and reinforced one another to produce this more extreme social and political environment. Until the political battles of the 1950s, the non-Krio elite was incorporated into Krio society, even 'Creolised'.[58] One keen observer noted in 1989 that the Krios''status as a social reference group to be emulated belongs to the past', but in so saying acknowledged their influence and how at crucial times they were indeed emulated.[59] One reading of Liberian history suggests exactly this sort of convergence, although Liberian Creole dominance was always much greater than that in Sierra Leone.[60] Another reading of African history suggests the reassertion of modified pre-colonial patterns of rule or 're-traditionalisation' of the imported state.[61] It is not outlandish to suggest that the history of Sierra Leone incorporates to some extent both of these processes. We will return to these notions in the next and later chapters.

3

KEY PLAYERS IN A DECEPTIVELY QUIET DECOLONISATION, 1951–1961

The process of integrating the Protectorate and Colony, politically at least, was finalised in 1951 and led to nationwide political party contestation, in particular the two pre-independence elections of 1951 and 1957, and the first Sierra Leonean Legislative Council with an African majority. The decade also witnessed increased agitation across Africa for independence. Sierra Leone had its own proponents of independence, who also saw the fragility of European rule after the Second World War, the independence of countries like India and Pakistan, and the notion of self-determination enshrined in the new United Nations, and acted accordingly. At the same time, Britain acknowledged these new realities, ushering in self-rule and significantly increasing investment in Sierra Leone. The decolonisation process was almost entirely peaceful, even more so than the relatively calm decolonisation processes of other West African colonies, at least up to the point of independence, and much more so than in Cameroon or Kenya. It had, though, one unusual twist, in that Krios began a rather convoluted political trail towards independence and hinterland people took over the reins of power; and one more familiar twist, in that it began to expose some of the forthcoming ruptures within the political elite. Finally, while independence was historic, peaceful and ostensibly a fundamental break with the colonial period, it actually amounted to a rather conservative version of change.

The 1951 elections, described in Chapter 2, were only a foretaste of democracy given the restrictions on suffrage. In contrast, the 1957 elections allowed Sierra Leoneans in both the Colony and the Protectorate a much greater taste of democratic processes. The two sets of elections recorded victories for the SLPP, which was to become one of the two dominant post-independence parties and hold power for long stretches, over the Krio parties. Clearly, the 1950s was the decade in which Krio influence declined further and the Sierra Leonean national political elite fundamentally changed. These elections were not identical, but did hold within them some of the keys to understanding the decolonisation process and post-independence politics.

Paradoxically, but in line with other British, French and Portuguese colonies and even the Republic of Liberia next door, the decade before Sierra Leonean independence witnessed accelerating economic and infra-structural development. Men flocked to the diamond mines in Kono and Kenema Districts in the East to dredge for alluvial stones. There was lit-tle the colonial government or the SLST could do to prevent such ille-gal activities in a sector that provided 65 per cent of state revenue in 1951 in spite of the illicit mining.[1] By 1956, after another diamond rush, an estimated 50–70,000 people were mining and fortunes were there to be made.[2] The SLST official monopoly was not viewed well in the diamond fields and illicit miners attacked SLST security and a police station in 1955, attacks which the colonial authorities were ill-equipped to coun-ter. In response, the government paid SLST compensation in the same year to give up its nationwide deal and concentrate on the particularly rich areas near Yengema and Tongo. All other diamondiferous ground was opened to small-scale licensing under the Alluvial Diamond Min-ing Scheme (ADMS), provided that the local chief and the existing land-holder agreed. Unsurprisingly, although this was a serious attempt to legalise widespread alluvial mining, illicit operations did not cease and the stranglehold of the chiefs and predominantly Lebanese traders on the industry was not mitigated by this policy shift. In 1959, the govern-ment Gold and Diamond Office (GDO) was established in order to buy all non-SLST diamonds for export. Some trade did shift to the legal sphere up to the mid-1960s, but the prices paid were not good and state control over the diamonds remained unconvincing.[3]

Iron ore became the second export product in 1940 and in the 1950s the Marampa Mines supplied 40 per cent of Britain's iron. During this period, there was also mining of gold in Tonkolili District, chrome in Kenema District and platinum on the Freetown peninsula. The result of this activity meant, first, that by 1961 minerals contributed a massive 87 per cent of total exports and, second, that labour migrated from the agricultural sector to the mines, in particular the diamond mines. The Sierra Leone Produce Marketing Board (SLPMB) was established in 1949 and made attempts to incentivise farmers with guaranteed prices and to add value to agricultural products through such initiatives as palm oil mills and cigarette manufacturing. At the same time, by 1956, just six European companies controlled between 82 and 95 per cent of the produce trade.[4] Labour, however, bled out of the farms and the price of rice soared to the point that government was forced to import. Economic hardships, in particular the price of food, sparked a strike for pay rises to compensate in February 1955, which turned into four days of rioting in Freetown and the stoning of the houses of Sierra Leonean ministers. On the other hand, import businesses thrived with the money that was being made from diamonds.

The revenues from mining were, to some extent, ploughed back into Sierra Leone. Roads and bridges were built in the interior which replaced porterage and boat transport and eventually began to sideline the railways. A deep water quay was finished in the east of the capital and air connections began briefly at an airport near Waterloo until its proximity to the hills forced the beginning of construction in 1947 at the current site across the river in Lungi. Public electricity supply, restricted to Freetown before the Second World War, reached Bo in 1949 and Kenema in 1953. Education expanded from its paltry levels before the war. Numbers of students in primary and secondary schools and teacher training colleges increased almost fourfold between 1945 and 1961. By independence, 86,000 were attending primary school and 7,500 were in secondary. In the same time period, students in technical and vocational schools increased from none to nearly 1,200 and those in higher education increased six-fold to 300. Fourah Bay College began relocation to its current site on Mount Aureol in 1948 and, in 1960, became the University College of Sierra Leone with Dr Davidson Nicol as the first Sierra Leonean principal. By 1957, four new hospitals and health centres in many of the larger towns had been built.[5]

Oppositional politics established itself in the Legislative Council. The NCSL opposed many SLPP measures, almost all of which subsequently went through, and proposed their own which were mostly defeated. Debates were rancorous and often revolved around Krio and hinterland identities rather than policy.[6] Bankole-Bright described the Krios and the hinterland people as 'two mountains that can never meet' and, as early as 1950, associated the birth of the Protectorate with 'the massacre of some of our fathers and grandfathers....in Mendeland because they were described as "Black Englishmen"'. Milton Margai replied that the Krios were a handful of foreigners to whom their forefathers had given shelter, who imagined themselves to be superior because they aped Western modes of living but who had never breathed the true spirit of independence.[7] Interesting to note that in these exchanges both sides saw each other as foreigners; from the Krio angle the fact that they were British citizens while all others were not. Krio anxiety could be seen in the burgeoning of Freemasonry, with one estimate that the number of lodges doubled between 1947 to 1952.[8] Some agreement was reached over the SLST diamond contract changes and education in the Protectorate, but the NCSL obsession with Colony rights did not abate. The NCSL was joined in this crusade by the Settler Descendants Union (SDU) in 1952, the former agitating for separate independence for the Colony and the latter aiming to prove the legality of the ownership of the Colony by settlers. Many court cases ensued. Further parties joined the ranks including the Sierra Leone Independence Movement (SLIM) under Edward Blyden in 1956, the Kono Progressive Movement (KPM) in 1955 led by Tamba Briwa and, most important, the United Progressive Party (UPP).

Founded in 1954, the UPP represented a possible bridge between Colony and Protectorate. It was not that there were no connections between the two. Two SLPP members of the Executive Council were A.G. Randle, a Krio from Bonthe, and M.S. Mustapha, a Muslim Krio from Freetown. Lamina Sankoh and Constance Cummings-John were in the SLPP. Cummings-John was the first woman to be elected to the Freetown City Council in 1938 and established the women's wing of the SLPP in 1955 with Patience Richards and Etta Harris. Richards and Cummings-John, both Krios, won their seats for the SLPP in 1957 in Freetown, only for the former to be unseated and the latter to resign when presented with electoral petitions.[9] The SLPP motto was then and remains today 'One People, One Country'. In contrast, the UPP had a predominantly Krio leadership but reached out to the Protectorate. The party was founded by Wallace-Johnson and the lawyer C.B. Rogers-Wright who defended many Protectorate clients after the disturbances in the mid-1950s. A populist stance reaped some dividends

at the expense of the NCSL but also amongst some Protectorate voters in the 1957 elections.

Institutionally, the 1950s continued the same trajectory set by the
promulgation of the new constitution in 1951. Recommendations from
an electoral advisory commission established in 1954 brought the Colony and Protectorate voting criteria closer together. The Protectorate
franchise included males who paid the local head tax and females who
paid tax, all of whom had to be over twenty-one, while the Colony franchise was much closer to universal suffrage in that it included anyone
over twenty-one years old who had lived in the Colony for six months.
However, the adopted SLPP proposals for the new House of Representatives which would replace the Legislative Council continued to favour
the Protectorate. The NCSL proposed equivalence in 15 Protectorate
and Colony seats apiece, but the end result was much closer to the SLPP
proposal of a 30–12 split. There would be 57 members including 14 from
the Colony, two from each of the 12 Protectorate Districts, one from Bo
and 12 Paramount Chiefs. Significantly, the year 1961 was first men-
tioned then as a date for independence.

The other key development in this period between elections was the
aforementioned disturbances in 1955–56. Following on from the Freetown strikes and riots in February 1955, violence broke out in November in the Protectorate. As with the Freetown events there was an
economic cause, but in the provinces the issues were tax and its administrators, the chiefs. Taxes were raised in 1955 and imposed on greater
numbers of young men. At the same time, in a marked breakdown in
reciprocity, abuse of the chiefs' considerable local power had grown.[10] The
riots in 1955, which began in Port Loko District and spread throughout
the Protectorate into 1956, were aimed at chiefs who had enriched themselves with houses and cars through local tax corruption, tribute including forced labour, and market protection.[11] Their style of life had now
much in common with that of the urban elite.[12] In many ways, chieftaincy subjects were demonstrating against abuse of power but not against
chieftaincy *per se*. Considerable force was used to quell the disturbances
and many people were killed. A commission decided that local governing bodies were in fact to blame and five chiefs were deposed and five
resigned. Most important to note, however, is the continued importance
of the chiefs in Sierra Leonean politics, and despite the removal of ten
chiefs, the institution of chieftaincy maintained its relevance and hence

its vulnerability to abuse. Further, within a few years, some were demanding the reinstatement of the deposed chiefs.[13] To emphasise the point, the indirect elections in the Protectorate in 1951, coupled with the continuing relative weakness of the intelligentsia there, put chiefs in a strong position to continue protecting their own interests.[14] Even in the 1957 direct elections, 59 per cent of candidates (72 per cent for the SLPP) and an extraordinary 84 per cent of all successful candidates still had chiefly kinship ties.[15] In addition, House of Representative seats were reserved for the twelve elected Paramount Chiefs.

The 1957 election results were catastrophic for the NCSL in that it lost all its seats, but a small yet ultimately pyrrhic victory for the UPP and a grand triumph for the SLPP. The NCSL failed to adapt to mass politics and, in an election dominated by identity, was seen as almost solely a Krio party and lost ground to the UPP. Bankole-Bright continued to campaign in English, not even Krio, and lost his Freetown seat to the SLPP along with his deposit.[16] In all, the SLPP took 23 seats, including nine out of 14 in the Colony, and the UPP five, leaving 11 to independents including the KPM leader Tamba Briwa and none to any other party. Eight of the independents and all of the Paramount Chiefs subsequently sided with the SLPP. Amongst the chiefs was the first female member of the House of Representatives, Ella Koblo Gulama. The UPP had indeed gained considerable ground in taking seats in the districts at the centre of the tax riots, one in Kambia, two in Port Loko and one in Moyamba, but had no real purchase on Protectorate politics as it had little access to the chiefs and none to the influential Poro society. Except in rare cases where the SLPP slipped up in its choice of candidates—as in Bo where a Krio-Mende businessman was selected over the son of a Paramount Chief of Bo who was then able to use his connections and others' obligations to win as an independent—the SLPP held all the Protectorate cards.[17]

It is worth describing at this point the backgrounds of the main players in 1950s Sierra Leonean politics. There were still the longstanding Krio participants such as Beoku-Betts, Bankole-Bright and Wallace-Johnson, who by the mid-to-late 1950s were near the end of their careers and near the end of their lives. Beoku-Betts passed away in 1957, three months after becoming the first Sierra Leonean to be knighted in sixty years. Bankole-Bright followed in 1958, and Wallace-Johnson died in a car accident in Ghana in 1965. Others, such as Randle and Mustafa, were forging their careers within the new politics. It was, however, the new politics, predominantly of the Protectorate, that mattered. Within Protectorate politics it was the chiefs that dominated but, as pointed out before, both Margais, Stevens and Karefa-Smart all emerged from the nascent and still very small Protectorate intelligentsia. All assumed important positions in the run-up to, and aftermath of, independence, and so it is these characters and their relations with the Protectorate that need further examination.

Sierra Leone's first Chief Minister, Milton Margai, became its first Prime Minister in 1958. Born in 1895 in Gbangbatoke in Mende-speaking Moyamba District in the South of what was about to become the Protectorate, he was of an older generation by the time of the run-up to independence and died three years afterwards in 1964. His life was one that saw huge changes but also one that was firmly rooted in the past. On the one hand, in an illustrious career he became the first Protectorate African to graduate from the Krio educational bastion, Fourah Bay College, and after graduating from the Durham College of Medicine in the UK became the first British-trained medical doctor from the Protectorate. On returning to Sierra Leone in 1927, he worked in nearly all districts and was awarded Member of the British Empire (MBE) for services to midwifery in 1947. A knighthood followed in 1959.[18]

On the other hand, and this is extremely important, Milton was the grandson of a Mende Paramount Chief and the son of a chief. His uncle was an influential Mende chief during the time of his political career. After retiring from government service and taking up politics in 1950, he became an unofficial adviser to many chiefs. It was his friendship with chiefs that mended the bridges between the Protectorate intelligentsia organisation, SOS, of which he was Deputy President, and the chiefly Protectorate Assembly, and this allowed the SLPP to rise. Indeed, Milton was partly responsible for the SLPP being far from a mass-based party, instead almost entirely working through 'traditional' authorities. Africa around independence was not overwhelmed with mass-based parties, but anti-colonial movements like Kwame Nkrumah's Convention People's Party (CPP) in the Gold Coast (later Ghana) and the Parti Démocratique de Guinée (PDG) under Sekou Touré at least maintained a rhetorical and to some extent actual distance from the chiefs. Not so the SLPP, where first president Milton adopted the Poro men's society symbol, the palm leaf, as the party's symbol in 1951, a motif which continues into the present day. Whether this was an anti-colonial stance, given the association of the palm leaf with the Poro role in the Hut Tax War, or simply a statement of allegiance to the Poro, it served notice of the close alignment of the SLPP with the 'traditional' order.[19] Chiefs' obligations to the Poro were used by Milton and the SLPP to garner bloc votes. Further, Milton's midwifery work endeavoured to foster modern practices but often within the confines of the Bondo women's initiation society.

Clearly, Milton had some commitment to modernisation, but one would equally call him conservative or (very) gradualist.[20] He believed that a ruler's legitimacy derived from his status.[21] He was reluctant either to speak to the general populace or to build the party at a grassroots level.[22] He was a listener, but one who changed few of his opinions. He noted that 'it would be awkward for a leader to say one thing at one time and then change later'. Highly cautious, it was said that he 'drove with the brakes ready'. Age, maturity and experience were paramount and he was unenthusiastic in promoting younger Sierra Leoneans to positions of authority.[23] At the same time, he was reported not to be corrupt or ostentatious. One might say that Milton's conservative and diplomatic disposition made the transfer of power from the British seamless and non-violent. One might also observe an elitism born of membership of, allegiance to and reliance on, the upper echelons of a very hierarchical society: upper echelons which had maintained their sway but undergone some profound changes, not always for the best, especially in their relations with colonialism.

Similarly, the first Protectorate lawyer was Albert Margai, another founder of the SLPP, a member of the 1951 Executive Council, Finance Minister and Sierra Leone's second Prime Minister. He was Milton's half-brother and was also born in Gbangbatoke but fifteen years later in 1910. He returned to Sierra Leone in 1948 after four years studying law in the UK. He was knighted in 1965. However, he was, like his half-brother, of chiefly stock. He showed at times that he might try to distance himself from the chiefs and was on several occasions impatient enough with Milton's gradualist approach to take matters into his own hands, most importantly when he briefly left the SLPP in 1958. Significantly, though, in the aftermath of the tax riots in 1956 he was moved to 'assure the chiefs that we are very confident that the position of chieftaincy is very necessary and must continue'.[24]

Greater contrast is provided by Stevens. Born in Moyamba District in 1905, he was supposed to be of Limba stock, but his ethnicity was made increasingly uncertain as it later served him well to obfuscate on this issue. His father had worked for the Governor of the time, hence his son's middle name, Probyn. Stevens attended secondary school and worked for the police before moving to the Marampa mines where he engaged in trade union activities. He attended Ruskin College, the trade union college in Oxford. Using his role as co-founder and Secretary of the United Mine Workers Union as a platform, Stevens was able to embark on his rather unusual, at the time, Protectorate political career. Stevens served from 1951 as a minister and was a founder of the SLPP, which he left in 1958 to create a more progressive party; later he became the third Prime Minister and first President of Sierra Leone. His name still lives on in Siaka Stevens Street, one of Freetown's main arteries heading past the Cotton Tree, and the town of Masiaka. Significantly again, but perhaps showing he was a touch more instrumental and modernising in tone, Stevens noted in the aftermath of the tax riots that 'chieftaincy is an office which is very useful and which we will need for a very long time'.[25]

Again born in Moyamba, but this time in Rotifunk in the north of the district and effectively the north of the country, Karefa-Smart made his way into Protectorate elite politics through education at Fourah Bay College and in the USA before becoming a medical doctor and administrator. After briefly resisting chiefly power as head of the SOS, he co-founded the SLPP, and became Minister of Lands, Mines and Labour in 1957 and Minister of External Affairs in 1962 before being dismissed by Albert in 1964. He continued thereafter to play a significant part in post-independence politics. There were, in other words, non-chiefly Protectorate routes to positions of authority but each came through the SLPP system, even if it was to leave at a later date, and all adopted or were forced to adopt SLPP-developed methods of political support.

The immediate phase before independence tested the diplomatic skills of Milton. More constitutional changes in 1958 made him Prime Minister and reduced the power of the British Governor. The Governor maintained control of foreign affairs, defence and security, but in all other areas acted on the advice of the Executive Council whose members he now appointed from the House of Representatives on the recommendation of the Prime Minister. However, Milton encountered much greater challenges from within his own party. Seemingly dismayed by the slow pace of progress and the reliance on the chiefs, some dynamic members sought change. Perhaps as a part of this dismay but possibly also in a case of rivalry between older and younger factions, Albert made a bid for the leadership of the SLPP. He was successful but was persuaded to stand down in favour of his half-brother by grandees of the party.

As a consequence, key people including Albert Margai and Stevens left the SLPP to form the People's National Party (PNP). The new party called for a faster pace of decolonisation, increased social spending and foreign non-alignment, and crucially was more critical of chiefs, but only up to a point. A PNP policy statement of 1959 stated, 'the People's National Party strongly maintains that chieftaincy has and will continue to have a most important place in our national development for a very long time'.[26] Worryingly for the SLPP, the PNP began to expand when in 1959 three more SLPP legislators defected and Wallace-Johnson joined. The party also started to pick up support amongst the young and educated. Meanwhile, the KPM had merged with the SLIM to form the Sierra Leone Progressive Independence Movement (SLPIM) and this amalgamation in turn merged with the PNP to form a significantly broader movement, the PNP-Alliance. In 1959, Krio politics also shifted when several UPP legislators, disgruntled with Rogers-Wright's leadership, split off and formed the Independent Progressive People's Party (IPP).

The turmoil at the top led Milton in 1960 to perform one of his diplomatic juggling acts and persuade many to join a United National Front (UNF) which would arrange independence from Britain. Parties agreed to be led by Milton in exchange for a place at the London Constitutional Conference in April–May 1960 and a post in the SLPP cabinet. Agreement was reached in London and all bar Stevens signed the document which would lead to independence on 27 April 1961. Stevens, as a representative of PNP and in a foretaste of events to come, refused to sign, his purported reason being related to Sierra Leone's defence arrangement with Britain. On returning home, Albert became Minister of Natural Resources and later Minister of Finance and Rogers-Wright of the UPP became Minister of Housing and Country Planning and later Minister of External Affairs. Posts also went to the new IPP but not to Stevens.

Stevens returned to Sierra Leone earlier than the rest after surprising the Constitutional Conference with his refusal to sign, and rather opportunistically formed the Elections Before Independence Movement. He attracted Wallace-Johnson, educated PNP supporters who disliked the alliance with SLPP, and elements of the urban poor looking for a different political outlet. His success allowed him in September 1960 to form the All People's Congress (APC), a new political party which would go on to threaten the SLPP as it had not been threatened before and become the other main party during fifty years of independence. Two months later the APC shocked the establishment by winning the elections to the Freetown City Council. While not exactly promoting socialism akin to that across the border in Guinea, Stevens' rhetoric of greater opportunities for all, a desire for a faster pace of change and a younger, more militant brand of politics struck a chord in the urban setting of Freetown.

Meanwhile, in 1961, the member parties of the UNF, including the PNP, agreed to dissolve their formal structures and merge into the SLPP. The APC unveiled its plans for a general strike and was then accused of aiming to wreck the independence celebrations with violence. Milton panicked, declared a state of emergency and arrested forty-three APC members, including Stevens and Wallace-Johnson, a week before the event. They remained in jail for a month while the celebrations took place. Thus the future Prime Minister and President of Sierra Leone spent 27 April 1961, the most important day in Sierra Leonean history, behind bars.

Despite APC protestations, the independence declaration and celebrations went smoothly. At midnight at the start of 27 April 1961, the green, white and blue flag was unfurled to the crowds in Brookfields Playground in Freetown, and during the ensuing day the Duke of Kent, the Queen's cousin, handed over the constitutional instruments to Sir Milton Margai in the new Parliament building. The Duke stayed at Government House which boasted a brand new wide paved avenue up from the Cotton Tree. The British Queen remained Head of State and the British Governor became the Governor-General, later replaced by a Sierra Leonean, the lawyer Sir Henry Lightfoot-Boston, after whom a central Freetown street is now named. The Queen subsequently visited Sierra Leone to a reception by crowds on the streets during a tour of West Africa later that year.

Notwithstanding the rather draconian state of emergency, the entire process of decolonisation appears at first glance to be largely free of complications. Broad agreement at the London Constitutional Conference attended by all parties and a smooth transition of power from coloniser to colonised was what many hoped for. The anti-colonial disturbances of the Gold Coast (later Ghana) and Guinea, where strikes and boycotts had contributed to ousting the British early in 1957 in the former case and where the French had left taking with them everything portable— even light bulbs, it was reported—after a 'no' vote in the 1958 French Community referendum in the latter, were not a feature in Sierra Leone. The violence of Cameroon or Nyasaland (later Malawi) and the outright war footing in the settler colonies of Kenya and Rhodesia/Zimbabwe and the Portuguese African territories of Angola, Mozambique and Guinea-Bissau were unthinkable in this corner of West Africa. The Sierra Leonean process was more akin to that in Côte d'Ivoire, where the francophile and conservative Félix Houphouët-Boigny had already served as a member of parliament and minister in Paris and resisted complete decolonisation for as long as possible, or in Nigeria, where intra-Nigerian squabbling was of most importance, culminating in a very unsteady coalition to welcome in independence. Some structures of self-rule had been in place in Freetown for a decade and the civil service was staffed by a cadre of educated and experienced Sierra Leoneans, albeit mostly Krios. This was a far cry from the Belgian Congo where elections were very hastily organised to create the first Congolese political institution in 1959, the year before independence. The underpinning of the Sierra Leonean economy in primary products, largely from the mining sector, was a scenario repeated all over Africa and at least afforded a fiscal base to build on. Further, while education levels were still low in Sierra Leone, primary attendance figures were much better than in French colonies like Niger or Upper Volta (later Burkina Faso). Sierra Leone had vocational institutions and also a university college, which was one more than in the whole of French Africa.

However, the relative serenity and levels of development disguised a series of problems. The economy was heavily reliant on the diamond sector over which the government had only a tenuous hold. The chiefs retained considerable influence in this industry, as they did in the political system. Despite the formation of the UNF, elite politics fractured alarmingly, was pasted together and then fractured once more, all in the three years before independence. This was a taste of things to come. Whether through association or increasing need, Milton maintained extremely close relations with the chiefs and other 'traditional' bodies.

The chiefs, meanwhile, had consolidated their place in the system and some took the opportunity to abuse their position, leading in particular to widespread rioting in the mid-1950s by those aggrieved that the reciprocity underpinning chiefly obligations was breaking down.

There was no anti-colonial violence, but there were simmering problems. As the Krios were politically vanquished, the tensions were no longer along Colony-Protectorate lines but were intra-Protectorate. In another auspicious sign, ethnic politicisation was yet to emerge—but its precursor was the battle line drawn between those who relied heavily on chiefly support and those who sought the votes of the people marginalised by the same chiefs. This crucial battle continued through the 1960s until the SLPP method was finally adopted across the board. One might see these lines of mostly non-violent tension as healthy political disputes, but they also raised the spectre of limits to nationalist feeling. Elsewhere in Africa, in Ghana, Guinea, Tanzania, Zambia and Angola, parochial concerns often played havoc with even the most committed nationalists.[27] In Sierra Leone, the push for independence was rather muted and more parochial matters, such as chieftaincy and elite divides which soon led to ethnic politicisation, appeared to be more prominent concerns than Sierra Leonean nationalism and nation-building.

The process of establishment of an independent Sierra Leonean state was a far cry from that experienced in the home countries of those who had come to colonise. In a relatively densely populated Europe, nation-states were often created in adversity. Threatened from outside, there was an urgent need to strengthen the centre, unify the population, collect taxes and demarcate and protect borders.[28] In Sierra Leone and much of Africa, the new states did not come about in the 1960s from outside threats but instead were imposed as an idea from outside. In one reading, these were 'quasi-states' with external recognition in the form of juridical sovereignty but little domestic legitimacy.[29] Despite rhetorical pronouncements, the imperatives to create a functioning central state with real penetrative power and authority, and indeed a cohesive nation, were thus not so immediate, and were subordinated to more disquieting shorter-term priorities of some sort of control and sub-national considerations.[30] These were far from ideal circumstances in which to bring a new nation-state to birth.

In a similar vein, the state-society model with its disconnections and divides described in Chapter 2 had also moved on, but this was to incorporate the key changes in Sierra Leonean leadership and mass elections. Similar to developments in other African colonies at the time and many African countries today, a dual system of 'modern' and 'traditional' had emerged, survived and intertwined. Some saw the development of a 'weak state' and a 'strong society'.[31] The central governments, lacking legitimacy in the face of 'traditional' ties, encountered a decision on whether to modernise or to rely on the 'traditional' for authenticity. The SLPP swung completely to the latter, creating a new indirect rule: a highly hierarchical system reliant on 'traditional' authority on top of the paternalistic model developed under the British and the Krios. Now the key imperative was to foster Protectorate support, but the prior imperatives of control had not gone away. In the process, the tensions in the substance of democratic transition and majoritarian rule were starkly revealed. The contradictions in the idea of a civic national politics versus 'traditional' or chiefly values of privilege and norms of patronage and strong local identities and concerns came rushing to the fore.

In a reciprocal relationship similar to that between chiefs and people, and similar to the methods of the now departing colonial administration, the Sierra Leone parties at the top end of the chain needed to keep the chiefs and 'big men' on board by supplying them with resources and favours. A very hierarchical and societally underpinned patron-client system of central government legitimacy, thoroughly endorsed by the SLPP, was on the way to being firmly established. On the other hand, one might consider whether conservatism did not extend to outside relations, especially when taking into account the deference shown by Krio society to Britain. One should ask, whatever one's final conclusion, whether such deference did not affect many of the national elite, particularly considering the rather modest nationalist movement, the sidelining of alternative visions of how Sierra Leone might be governed, and indeed the welcome given to the return of the British in the 1990s, 2000s and 2010s.[32] At the same time there are indications that national leaders, in particular Stevens, used the negotiations with outsiders quite successfully for domestic political gain. This would not be the last time that Stevens would adopt this strategy. There were those trying, for whatever reasons, to buck the conservative trends, but judging by some of the comments of Stevens and Albert Margai and the incarceration of Stevens, such a political project would be difficult to maintain even rhetorically.

4

IMMEDIATE AND SEVERE CHALLENGES

DEMOCRACY AND COUPS, 1961–1968

The declaration of independence was indeed momentous, but the ensuing years from 1961 to 1968 might easily be seen as the most crucial political period in Sierra Leonean history. Within this short stretch of time, the first leader of the SLPP and of Sierra Leone, Milton Margai, died and Albert Margai took his place. Regular elections were held and, astonishingly, in 1967 the opposition APC emerged victorious, an event almost unprecedented in Africa at the time. Sierra Leone's cleanest, fairest and most straightforward elections occurred in the late 1950s and early to mid 1960s, viewed by some as a 'model of democratic multiparty competition'.[1] Elections during this period were open and competitive. Although mostly within the elite, a wide ideological perspective was seen in political debate, public discussions, democratically organised non-governmental organisations and an active, critical and combative press.[2] The economy held up well and much seemed auspicious. However, problems relating to exactly how political support was generated, including the emergence of the political north-south ethno-regional divide, came to the fore. Equally worrying and certainly more eye-catching was the succession of military coups and subsequent military regimes which began a matter of days after the 1967 elections and just moments after Stevens had been sworn in as prime minister.

The ruling SLPP duly became the largest party in the first post-independence elections to the Parliament, the successor to the House of

Representatives, in 1962. All adult men and women were now allowed to vote. The SLPP was left just short of a majority when it took 28 of the 62 non-chieftaincy seats. But there were other pertinent processes which significantly enhanced the SLPP position. Of the remaining non-chieftaincy seats, a large number, 14, went to independents. As was noted at the time, the idea of voting for an independent so that on winning he or she could side with the ultimate victors was a popular notion.[3] This makes clear sense in a political game predicated on winner-takes-all elections. In line with such thinking, eight of 11 'independents' had sided with the victors in 1957, and once again 12 'independents' subsequently sided with the SLPP in 1962. Further, despite the official non-partisan status of the Paramount Chiefs, it might be assumed that many, particularly in the South and East if not all, would support the ruling party for the same reasons as the independents. Thus the SLPP manufactured a good working majority in Parliament.

The elections, however, signalled a historic rupture in Protectorate politics which would reverberate around Sierra Leonean politics into the current era. On the back of its Freetown City Council victory, the APC, led by Siaka Stevens, became the main opposition in Parliament. In an alliance with the SLPIM, the predominantly Kono party, the APC won twenty seats where it had previously held none. Taking 22.5 per cent of the nationwide vote of 663,674 compared with the SLPP's 35 per cent, the APC-SLPIM alliance had hit the ground running. The UPP was consigned to history, winning just 0.25 per cent of the national vote.

The APC's populist appeal, based on Stevens' anti-elitist rhetoric and his recent history of opposition to the conservative SLPP, significantly helped the party. The APC delivered overt appeals to the 'common man's class interest, regardless of tribe' and, continuing his stance in the latter days of colonialism, Stevens' trades-union credentials contrasted starkly with the SLPP's pro-chief conservatism.[4] There is, however, no escaping the fact that the APC gained most of its seats in the Northern Province and the former Colony, now renamed the Western Area. APC successes came in 12 of the 18 Northern seats, alongside four out of 12 in the Western Area. Concentrated in just four hinterland districts, the APC won all three constituencies in Kambia, three out of four Bombali constituencies, likewise in Tonkolili, and three out of five constituencies in Port Loko. These were districts involved in the tax riots in the mid-1950s and the results suggest anti-chief sentiment might have played an important role in the vote. They are also all Northern.

Indeed, the APC won with large majorities, two in Kambia of over 3,000 and one in Bombali of nearly 3,000. The SLPP victories over the APC in Freetown were not nearly as convincing. The whitewash in Kono in the East, where all four constituencies went to the alliance, was attributable almost entirely to the SLPIM. Majorities here reached nearly 8,000 in Kono North and around 6,000, 4,000 and 3,000 in the other constituencies.[5] The SLPIM, formed out of the KPM which was established in 1955, was easily the most successful deliberately localised movement in the hinterland, gaining support from the contradiction of central neglect and immense diamond wealth. The SPLIM had in the past used such radical terminology as 'imperialist exploitation', almost unknown in Sierra Leone, but it was still essentially a Kono party, in terms of geography and Kono ethnicity.[6] Ethno-regional imperatives were beginning to clarify across the country. Although the SLPP could still claim to be a nationwide party, its power-base was now clearly focused in the South, in particular amongst the Mendes.

The rise of politicised ethno-regionalism is certainly not limited to Sierra Leone or indeed Africa. Outside Africa, the politicisation of identity is clear in far flung places such as Lebanon, India, Belgium and Northern Ireland. However, African ethno-regionalism has specific characteristics and the Sierra Leonean version its own peculiarities. The reification of ethnicity and reliance on chieftaincy for colonial control in Africa were juxtaposed with the arrival of a modern state system. Brought forward into the post-colonial era, the still highly relevant, albeit modified sub-national identities and 'traditional' authorities thus became key constituencies in the struggle for power in the independent state. Underpinning this struggle was the distribution of state resources. The state is simultaneously dominant, in terms of resources as there are no societal or business formations that even come close in institutional terms, and weak in that it is very difficult for it to impose its policies and presence on much of society. The colonial and then post-colonial states were superimposed on the reciprocal structures of pre-colonial polities. Those in posts in the state often owe their positions to others from their community and, in a reciprocal sense or in a sense of common identity, are obligated to use their position for the benefit of their community—whether ethnic, village or family—not the ministry or department in which they work.[7] Resource distribution along ethno-regional lines also becomes an efficient way of building constituencies in a post-independence setting. Nation-building is thus as problematic as state-building and both are intertwined.

The relative sharpness of the north-south divide seen in Sierra Leone is not replicated everywhere in Africa, although similar dominant bipolar divides can be seen in Ghana and Côte d'Ivoire. Here, we may consider it is the demographic environment, in particular the existence of two large ethnic groups, Mende and Temne, which lends itself to a rather rigid bipolar political division.[8] At the same time, Sierra Leone had no leader like Kwame Nkrumah, Sekou Touré or Julius Nyerere who would seek to forcefully build nationalism and eliminate parochial concerns such as ethnicity in the name of modernisation or socialism. It is rather instructive to note that the projects of even these leaders were very limited in their successes, although arguably Nyerere provided a disparate Tanzania with a national political, if not economic, base from which to move forward.

In many ways the growing ethno-regionalism can easily be seen in the bias in the distribution of posts at the top of politics. Some thought of the UNF as a convenient front for Mende dominance.[9] The Margais were of course Mende and other top positions in the UNF had gone to Krios in the SLPP, UPP and IPP. Karefa-Smart was one of the few prominent northerners in the UNF and no ministerial positions were occupied by Konos. In these terms, the APC-SPLIM alliance makes more sense. The recent imbalances at the top built on the perceptions that the South had always been favoured. Note that the two early Protectorate Schools, Bo School and Harford School for Girls, were both situated in Mendeland and that in 1938, 80 per cent of Western-style Protectorate schools were similarly located. Missionaries preferred the less Islamicised South. Bo School took in sons and nominations of chiefs from all over the country but Mende students were in greater numbers. In addition to the educational advantage, the railway lines extended largely to the South and East and perceptions of regional wealth disparities ensued. Prime Minister Milton Margai clearly recognised these disparities and did make efforts to achieve an ethno-regional balance in government.[10] In a typical Milton manoeuvre, at once both co-opting and inclusive in intention, the 1962 post-election cabinet contained seven Mendes, four Temnes, five Krios and one Sherbro.[11]

Elections, and the crucial importance of both numbers and resource distribution therein, bring ethno-regionalism into sharp relief. Cold War era modernising thinkers told us that a level of economic, educational and class development is necessary for substantive democratisation to occur (and it is only with post-Cold War liberal thinking that the cart and the horse have been switched round and it is considered that democracy can deliver development).[12] Prosperity and education thus allow the electorate an element of autonomy in choice and thinking, leading to a democracy based on policies rather than distribution on communal lines and allegiance to 'traditional' values and authorities. A class system, as opposed to an ethno-regional basis for society, indicates solidaristic groups which are fluid and vie for power on ideological grounds. These are highly contested ideas, but they are ideas that suggest a limit to the depth or, perhaps more accurately, the type of democratisation and hence elections that might occur, and to a large extent did ensue, in the Sierra Leonean conditions of the 1960s. Inevitably, these notions return in the re-democratisation period in the 1990s and through to the current day.

Equally noticeably, the conservative nature of the Milton-led SLPP hierarchy showed no signs of changing. Representation of chiefs in District Councils was expanded in 1961 in order to nullify the threat of progressive elements when electing Paramount Chiefs to the Parliament. Indeed, the newly elected Paramount Chief for Port Loko District in 1962 had been heavily criticised in the Commission of Inquiry into the 1955–56 riots, labelled by the Commissioner as displaying conduct 'unworthy of a Paramount Chief'. Chiefdom courts were given powers to control local party political activities and the Chiefdom Police Forces, which continue into the present day, were inaugurated between 1959 and 1961. In the mid-1960s a major obstacle to the SLPP in Kono, Tamba Mbriwa, leader of SLPIM, was tried and convicted in a chiefdom court for conspiring against a Paramount Chief.[13] While ethno-regionalism grew, the role of 'tradition' was systematically maintained.

If state-building can be described as rapid and economic planning as largely state-led in immediate post-colonial Africa, then despite the conservative nature of the SLPP government Sierra Leone was very much part of this drive, in line with contemporaneous global economic discourse. Almost immediately, education and health facilities were expanded and a raft of new acts and state institutions came into being: the National Health Plan; the Development Act; Sierra Leone Investments Limited in 1961; the Bank of Sierra Leone in 1963; Njala Training College as a university in 1964; King Tom Power Station in 1965; the Opportunities

Industrialisation Centre in Bo; and the National Dance Troupe. The state-run Sierra Leone Produce Marketing Board (SLPMB) continued to be the official exporter of agricultural products. Financing the expansion was difficult in all African countries and Sierra Leone was fortunate when bauxite, an aluminium ore, and rutile, from which titanium is obtained, were added to its list of exportable minerals. The former is located in Moyamba District and the latter, one of the largest natural rutile deposits known in the world, in Moyamba and Bonthe Districts. Gross domestic product increased by nearly 5 per cent per annum in the first decade of independence and debts remained relatively small during this period.

On the other hand, it might also be observed that Sierra Leone fell into the category of African states which were conservative and nominally capitalist, like Kenya or Côte d'Ivoire, as opposed to transformative and socialist, like Ghana and neighbouring Guinea, and that state expansion was of a more cautious variety. Nationalisation of foreign assets was never considered and the government made its intentions abundantly clear. The state did not then need to expand as much as elsewhere in order to manage a greater number of state-owned enterprises. Foreign investment was indeed welcomed with tax breaks and mining and farming remained in the private sector. Foreign policy was non-aligned but links to Britain were maintained and Sierra Leone remained firmly within the Commonwealth.

Equally, it was often observed that the Sierra Leonean state had a sizeable educated cadre to draw on and the stabilising presence of experienced, mostly Krio civil servants in testing political circumstances.[14] In 1962, 70 per cent of 1,111 senior civil service positions were held by Krios. In the mid-1960s, 51 of 74 administrative officers were Krios.[15] The Krio class did indeed display some of the universalistic tendencies required of a modern meritocratic state, in that they tended to promote the independence of the judiciary, the neutrality of the civil service, a free press and free political competition. However, one might also observe a particularistic leaning in these defences as the Krios were endeavouring to protect the last bastions of their power in precisely these sectors. When threatened by encroachment, the independence of the judiciary might equally be an attempt to uphold the integrity of the state and to uphold Krio positions in a manner more recognisable in emerging hinterland politics.[16]

The first juncture in independent Sierra Leonean politics arrived in April 1964 when the ailing Milton died in office. There were three long-standing SLPP members who were possibilities for succession: Musta-pha, who had on occasions acted as Prime Minister, the Minister of External Affairs Karefa-Smart, and Milton's half-brother, Albert. It was the latter who ascended to the leadership. The difficulty with the succession was that it was shot through with ethno-regional considerations. Mustapha was a Krio, but more important, Karefa-Smart was the Northern choice and Northerners in the SLPP believed it was their turn. When Albert assumed power, there was considerable criticism from within the party. Four non-Mende ministers, including Mustapha and Karefa-Smart, were sacked, halving the number of Temnes and reducing Northerners in the cabinet by three; six Mendes, four Krios, one Sherbro and just two Temnes remained. The SLPP had shifted far further South overnight and Northern leaders subsequently drifted away to the APC. Other areas of the state were not spared the slide towards ethnic homogenisation. Africanisation of the military became an exercise in promoting Mendes in the army in order to reward supporters but also to shore up control of the security apparatus for Albert. British officers numbering fifteen in 1964 were whittled down to just three by 1967, most being replaced by Mendes.[17] Under Albert, the number of Mendes rose from 26 per cent to 52 per cent of the officer corps.[18] Brigadier David Lansana, another Mende and brother-in-law of Paramount Chief Gulama, was viewed by Milton as an 'ill-educated incompetent', but was selected to replace a British officer as Force Commander.[19] In a pattern noticeable up to the present day, supposedly apolitical civil service posts up to the top echelons were also handed to supporters, thus accelerating erosion of the independence of the civil service.

At first glance, one might be forgiven for thinking that two of the more radical politicians of the late colonialism era, Albert Margai and Stevens, were now facing each other across the political divide and that radical policies might be the order of the day. In a small number of ways this was indeed the case. Albert was not like his half-brother; he was described variously as an innovator, acquisitive, robust and having an imposing personality, all traits that would not immediately be assigned to Milton.[20] Albert had showed in the past his dislike of the SLPP reliance on the chiefs. More state-led and mostly state-owned enterprises such as large plantations, a cement factory, an oil refinery and the Cape

Sierra Hotel in the very west of Freetown were constructed. Diplomatic relations with the Soviet Union and socialist Guinea were strengthened, the latter sharing a mutual assistance agreement against internal subversion which was invoked by Albert after an alleged coup attempt in early 1967. On the other side of the house, the APC hectored the SLPP for being beholden to the elite. In the APC party newspaper, *We Yone*, Ibrahim Taqi insisted that the APC was 'a party of the masses', guided by socialism, and did not command 'the financial resources of the SLPP nor the patronage of the chiefs'.[21]

However, even if the APC could benefit from these pronouncements in opposition, the populist and mildly leftist leanings of Albert were greatly circumscribed by his party and the political environment. Further to the promotion of Southerners in the military and civil service, Albert embarked on a series of actions to shore up his power. Not having the kudos of an independence leader or the stature of Milton, many saw Albert as a step down in leadership quality. He was equally shorn of support in the important areas that the dismissed cabinet members represented. His response was to attempt to legislate and administrate his way out of trouble. Within the SLPP, a top to bottom reorganisation and the establishment of a party headquarters and party press made many grandees fear a centralisation of power. Women were appointed Mammy Queens and charged with rallying support amongst other women for the party. Outside the party, Albert increased the size of the Freetown City Council, an action that subsequently backfired when the APC won eleven seats against the seven won by the SLPP. His confidence in winning such elections was partly derived from his instructions to the Sierra Leone Broadcasting Service (SLBS) not to give the APC airtime and the passing of a bill that made Parliament seats vacant if their holders were absent for thirty days. In 1965, four APC MPs jailed for unlawful assembly were thus unseated. In a particularly conservative move, another bill gave chiefs extraordinary powers of assembly and instructions went out to chiefs to make life more difficult for the APC in the countryside, a far cry from the actions of Albert's friend Sekou Touré, who had by this time, officially at least, abolished chieftaincy in Guinea. At least one chief was successfully removed in Sierra Leone for not aiding an SLPP electoral candidate.

Albert, though, will always be primarily known as the first leader who tried to introduce the one-party state and the first leader to lose at the ballot box. These two events are not unrelated, but neither is considered particularly inspiring in Sierra Leonean history, although it has been suggested that Albert was not a great advocate of the one-party state and was persuaded by others.[22] In 1966, in a move not out of step with other events in Africa and the wider world, he tried but failed to introduce one-party legislation. Various rationales for introducing one-party rule—from the urgent need to strengthen the state and focus political and economic efforts to the equally urgent need for nation-building which was viewed by proponents as unlikely to emerge from divisive democratic politics—became popular around this time.[23] Indeed, Sierra Leone finally became a one-party state in 1977, under the leadership of Stevens, who in 1966 vehemently opposed the notion. He was not, however, the only one in opposition to the proposal, as the rest of the APC and the Krio bastions of the judiciary and academia were also firmly against. Albert had sought to emulate Kwame Nkrumah in Ghana and some contrasted Ghana's apparent one-party success with turmoil in Nigeria, but when Nkrumah was toppled in a military coup and public disapproval in Sierra Leone rose, the idea was dropped.

The 1967 elections, however, were the foremost political disaster for Albert. Although this was a momentous occasion, being the first victory for a West African opposition party through the ballot box, in many ways the events of 1967 set Sierra Leone on an extremely difficult course. Albert's attempt and failure to introduce the one-party state, and indeed at one point a presidential republic, was one part of the defeat, but there were many other components. One might first note economic matters. The largely state-owned plantations and industries were hastily planned and proved to be uneconomical. The SPLMB, with substantial reserves at independence, encountered such financial difficulties that it could no longer pay farmers and produce was smuggled abroad. Sierra Leone, previously a rice exporter, became a rice importer. The loans and contracts for building were on unfavourable terms and the government was forced to ask for a US$7.5million IMF loan at the end of 1966.[24] In the haste and expansion, corruption took hold. One might rightly argue that corruption was part and parcel of the patron-client system of politics, but it was the scale of the diversion of resources under Albert that was particularly noticeable. A symptom of the malaise was the relatively small issue of customs duty waived on the Prime Minister's Cadillac car, which was made into serious electoral point-scoring.[25]

Underhand tactics emerged. A bill was pushed through to increase election candidates' deposits by 150 per cent, clearly benefiting the incumbent, and six SLPP candidates, including the Prime Minister, were to run unopposed as the opposition candidates had been disbarred for rather frivolous reasons, such as misspellings or omitted initials.[26] The alleged coup plot of February 1967 might be seen as a sign of desperation on the part of the military or on the part of Albert. If it was actually plotted, those who were imprisoned, led by the Northern Deputy Force Commander, John Bangura, and including several senior officers of Northern extraction, clearly saw which way the armed forces were heading under Lansana. If it was not plotted, which many alleged, then it was designed as a political weapon to use against the opposition, further stripped the armed forces of Northern and Krio officers, and was thus another sign of a state of anxiety in government. No trials were ever held to test these waters.

Key to all of the above is the paramount importance of the hardening ethno-regional divide. Politically, the sidelining of Karefa-Smart and the skewed appointments to positions in government and the military were further alienating Northerners. The Chief Electoral Commissioner, a Northerner, was replaced by an SLPP sympathiser and an ally, Gershon Collier, became Acting Chief Justice. Given the necessity of having a representative in government or the state to ensure that parochial needs were catered for, Albert can be seen to have pandered to some while alienating others. However, in a society so finely balanced demographically as Sierra Leone, one cannot be seen to shift too far to one region. Equally, given the fine balance, other more minor factors assume a level of importance that one might not first consider crucial. Hence, the attempt at introducing the one-party state and the stories such as those surrounding the coup and the Cadillac took on greater weight.

At the same time the APC was ready for this election in a way that the SLPP was not. The APC had organisation and embarked on 'exhaustive campaign sweeps throughout the country'.[27] It had a leader in Stevens who was charismatic and charming. It also had a solid base of support in the North and to some extent in the West, and an anti-elitist ideology of sorts which maintained some traction. Indeed, the SLPP attempts to control the chiefs, particularly in the North, was far from universally successful. One chief indicated in Krio that he was 'SLPP *na face*, APC *na heart*', a foretaste of 'watermelon politics'—SLPP green on the outside, APC red on the inside—which was to emerge in later decades.[28] Where the SLPP was successful, it forced the APC into emphasising its anti-elitist stance, which played well amongst other voters. Further, though, Albert's rather autocratic style of leadership, particularly in comparison with his predecessor, alienated even those within his own party. By the time of the elections, the SLPP was a divided party. It was also not convincing in its organisation. Despite efforts to secure as many unopposed seats as possible, it achieved just six. In another foretaste of elections to come right through to the present day, extra ballots were made available for incumbent supporters. However, on some occasions not enough were handed out to make a difference, and they were distributed in such an uncontrolled manner that some found their way into APC hands.[29]

In this environment, Albert and the SLPP were launched into the 1967 elections. The results were extremely close. Voting took place on 17 March for the non-chieftaincy seats and four days later for the Paramount Chiefs, a timing which was to have extraordinary consequences for the final outcome. In an expanded Parliament containing 66 non-chieftaincy seats, the APC emerged as the largest party with 32 seats. The SLPP, however, were close behind with 28 seats and the six independents thus held the balance of power. The APC took 44 per cent of the 647,581 valid votes cast against 36 per cent for the SLPP and 20 per cent for independents. The APC won all bar one seat in the North, all bar one uncontested seat in the West and one, Moyamba West, which abuts the Western Area but is in the South. The SLPP won most seats in the South and in Kenema District in the East, all seats in Kailahun District again in the East, and one in Koinadugu District in the North. A state of emergency was declared in Kono District when disturbances erupted over suspected irregularities. Kono was split, the APC finally taking two constituencies and the SLPP three.

Crucially, all the independent victories occurred in the South and East and it was assumed by some that these winners would side with the SLPP, thus creating a majority out of a minority. Quite the reverse occurred, but for several days the results were portrayed as even closer than they actually were by deliberately including some of the independents in the SLPP total. Interim results were broadcast always with SLPP leading until the morning of 21 March, at which point the Sierra Leone Broadcasting Service announced that SLPP had 32 seats, APC had 31 and independents two, with the Moyamba West result inexplicably held back. Superficially, it was a dead heat, but Albert had burned his bridges with at least four of the former SLPP independents. As 21 March wore on, they came out against him, though not necessarily against the SLPP if there was a new leader, and effectively placed their support behind the leading party, the APC, writing to that effect to Governor-General Lightfoot-Boston.[30] One further independent wrote asserting his independence. The SLPP electoral coup had failed. Having already unsuccessfully attempted to persuade the leaders to form a coalition government, Lightfoot-Boston announced on the same day that in the late afternoon he would appoint Stevens as Prime Minister. He did not consider it necessary to wait for the results of the Paramount Chief elections which were also taking place on that day.

It is an indication of the confusion in the dual system of rule—the modern state and the chieftaincies—that it was not clear whether general elections results could legally be announced before the Paramount Chiefs had been elected. Paramount Chiefs are not allowed to campaign under party banners and so, as elders, are expected to be above party competition and support the government elected with the wider mandate. In many ways they do support the government, if only because the government is the fount of many resources for their chieftaincy and because they also do not want to face the possibility of being deposed for opposing central authority, a tool that colonial and post-colonial governments have found to be very useful, although problematic. Paramount Chiefs may well support the ruling party most often, but whether this can be assumed is another matter. Exactly these issues had been discussed prior to the elections between the Secretary General of the APC, the Attorney-General and the Governor-General of Sierra Leone. The decision from the latter two officials was that the Governor-General should, in line with the Constitution and the precedents of 1962 and 1964, determine which person was likely to command the support of the majority of the Parliament, but also that Paramount Chiefs should be taken into account as members who were free to opt for the party of their choice.[31]

It is thus clear that Lightfoot-Boston could and did use his judgement to calculate the likelihood of support for Stevens, but not whether he should have waited for the Paramount Chief elections. It is undoubtedly clearer that Brigadier Lansana's reasons for having Lightfoot-Boston, Stevens and other cabinet members arrested at State House minutes after

Stevens had been sworn in on 21 March were not entirely based on his stated justifications: to protect the constitution and maintain law and order. After seizing power in this strikingly easy fashion, Lansana made much of the 'unconstitutional' manner in which Lightfoot-Boston had appointed Stevens as Prime Minister. He repeated the fanciful notion that the parties were level at 32 seats each and noted that the results of the Paramount Chief elections were still awaited. Just two hours later, these results began to be announced and 10 of the 12 Paramount Chiefs duly declared their allegiance to the SLPP.[32] During the following two days, Lansana went on to also decry political tribalism and its potential effect on stability. However, Lansana's other reason for what can only be described as a drastic and disproportionate course of action—when other courses, for example through Parliament, were available—must then be considered: his desire to return Albert, to whom he owed his own job, to the prime minister's office. As a footnote, the arresting officer was Lieutenant Sam Hinga Norman, who would later play a significant role in the civil war and its aftermath.

Indeed, the main motive given for the second coup less than 48 hours after the first was that Lansana was about to impose Albert as Prime Minister. Major Charles Blake announced on 23 March that Lansana had been deposed. The Dove-Edwin Commission investigation into the elections came to similar conclusions later that year. It is generally understood that elements of the SLPP supported the first coup, especially given the connections between Lansana, Albert and Paramount Chief Gulama, and that SLPP consultations with the armed forces had intensified in the immediate post-election period, including the presence of top-level SLPP members in Lansana's private residence. Indeed, the military build up in Freetown commanded by Mende officers had been visible since the day after election day.[33] However, political tribalism in general and the economy were also put forward by Blake as key concerns, and he further announced that a national government representative of all the country would be established and that as an interim measure a National Reformation Council (NRC) would be formed. Heading the NRC were its Chairman Lieutenant-Colonel Andrew Juxon-Smith, a long-time opponent of Lansana, and its Deputy Chairman, the Commissioner of Police William Leigh. Making up the rest of the Council was a group of army and police officers, including Blake. The constitution was duly suspended, political parties officially dissolved and all political activity prohibited.

Lightfoot-Boston was put under house arrest and then given six months leave. On taking up the chairmanship, Juxon-Smith gave what he described as a 'funeral oration' for tribalism, pointed at the 'demoniac and hydra-headed monster' of bribery, corruption and nepotism, and forcefully outlined the necessity and seriousness of martial law. At the same time, he extolled the virtues of the Paramount Chiefs whose prestige was to be enhanced as the natural rulers of the country.[34] Thus, whether or not we take the justifications of Blake and Juxon-Smith seriously, they were clearly no closer to addressing the complex and often debilitating political relationships within Sierra Leone.

This was not, though, an unusual course of events in Africa at the time. The number of military coups d'état in Africa was rising through the 1960s and some felt that the acute problems of nation- and state-building demanded such interventions. In line with thinking on one-party states, it was articulated in many different circles that democracy was a luxury that African states could ill afford. Equally, the military was seen as organised, educated and holding the well-being of the country as its core principle. Its allegiance was to the state, not to the particularistic constituencies of political parties. Reasons for intervening were often given as the need to redeem, reconcile and unify the country and in the process eliminate corruption and resurrect the economy. Clearly, some such as Lansana were not as serious in their stated aims and were driven more by particularistic motives, but others were more serious. Some, for instance Flight-Lieutenant Jerry Rawlings in Ghana, had a degree of success in accomplishing their aims, while others such as General Ignatius Acheampong, one of Rawlings' predecessors, significantly worsened the situation. Difficulties within the armed forces, in particular ethnic division or deliberate homogenisation, often played a part in the build-up to coups also, which can be seen in the Sierra Leonean case. In many ways, the armed forces intervened because they could; African states were and are concentrated primarily in the capital and thus relatively easy targets for those with the guns and the will. Much of the above, however, points less towards military capabilities or solutions and much more to the contradictions and structural problems of the state. The state is indeed weak and prone, but coups are also rooted in state-society relations which restrict the state from functioning in the way it is envisioned; hence the often declared need for redemption, reconciliation, unity and anti-corruption drives.[35] Most important, it quickly became clear that the adverse repercussions of the coups in Sierra Leone were easily going to outweigh any advantages.

Initially, however, the NRC set about its tasks with gusto. Ministers and their deputies were ordered to return government cars and vacate state housing. Juxon-Smith reduced the fourteen government ministries to nine departments and took over the Finance Department himself. The Forster Commission investigation into assets declared that SLPP ministers and civil servants must pay back thousands of ill-gotten leones. The conclusions of the Beoku-Betts Commission of Inquiry into the Sierra Leone Produce Marketing Board were to reappear in the 1996 elections in the form of an unflattering account of Ahmad Tejan Kabbah's civil service record. The Dove-Edwin Commission inquired into the conduct of the 1967 elections. The Commission was tainted to some extent when it became known that Justice Dove-Edwin had been one of those persuading Lightfoot-Boston to appoint Stevens quickly, but its conclusions pointed to irregular SLPP electoral practices, the legitimacy of the APC victory and the validity of Stevens' appointment. Unpopular austerity measures were brought in, including a reduced budget, the cessation of uneconomic state projects, retrenchment of workers and higher taxes on income and diamond dealers.

While the austerity measures made the NRC resented at home, it was also increasingly nervous of the plans filtering across the border from Guinea where the APC languished in exile. Stevens and the former Force Deputy Commander Colonel Bangura were resident there with Sekou Touré's knowledge and the training of guerrillas to reinstate them in Freetown had commenced. In the meantime, a third coup rocked the country. One further reason for coups in Africa internal to armed forces has involved disgruntlement over pay and conditions. The 'Sergeants' Revolt' of 17 April 1968 encompassed such complaints as part of its justification, although the conspirators were mostly Northern. Demonstrating further the fragility of power at that time and the severe schisms within the armed forces, a faction led by Warrant Officer Patrick Conteh and Private Morlai Kamara overthrew the NRC, imprisoned the officers and formed the Anti-Corruption Revolutionary Movement. A National Interim Council was formed to oversee a return to civilian rule. Colonel Bangura returned from exile to head the junta and Lightfoot-Boston was recalled from leave. When he did not take up the offer, Justice Banja Tejan-Sie was made (initially Acting) Governor-General.

Events moved fast and Tejan-Sie invited the electoral victors for con-sultation on 26 April 1968. Stevens was re-appointed Prime Minister with the new SLPP leader Salia Jusu-Sheriff as Deputy. A national coali-tion was proposed with cabinet posts shared between the APC, the SLPP, independents and Paramount Chiefs, but typically Stevens had other ideas and swiftly took control of the levers of power. It was, though, the longer process of taking real control which proved to be the making of Prime Minister and later President Stevens. He was appointed Prime Minister in extraordinarily difficult circumstances: Stevens was faced with the same problems of weak and barely legitimate administration, troublesome elections, the urban-rural/'traditional'-'modern' divide and assertive sub-national identities with which the Margais had grappled, but crucially with a significantly less certain power base.

First, the election was won by only a slim majority, particularly if the uncertain allegiances of the Southern-based independents who removed their support from the SLPP in 1967 are taken into account. Second, Stevens' support was heavily concentrated in the North and West with very little to show in the South and not much more in the East. Third, his party's ideological stance against chiefly influence, although now watered down, meant there was a key problem in ensuring compliance and support in the countryside, particularly of course in the South and East. Fourth, Stevens could not trust the armed forces. There was a Mende bias in the officer corps and the armed forces had shown they were riven with often ethno-regional divisions. Most important, soldiers and offi-cers of all ranks had shown that power could be taken, and taken rela-tively easily. While most African states are indeed concentrated in the capital, Freetown's Wilberforce Barracks is almost in the backyard of the SLBS and the leaders' residences. His legitimacy as Prime Minister was clearly threatened from many angles. Thus, it was Stevens' responses to these multiple and seemingly intractable problems that enabled him to remain in office for far longer than might be expected and mapped out the course of Sierra Leone up to the current day. These responses were at the same time not utterly untypical of the times and yet also some-what idiosyncratic to Stevens.

5

THE CHOICES OF SIAKA STEVENS

VIOLENCE, PATRONAGE AND THE ONE-PARTY STATE, 1968–1991

The APC and Siaka Stevens finally emerged front stage on 26 April 1968. They were immediately faced with a raft of potentially terminal problems including, in no particular order, the inherited weak state, the economy with its over-reliance on diamonds, debt, corruption, politicised armed forces with a taste for power, a marginal electoral mandate inordinately skewed towards the North, a much more divided nation along the north-south axis, and an ambivalent relationship with the power in the countryside, the chiefs. They did, however, hold a few advantages: they had some electoral legitimacy, they would most likely have a honeymoon period as a new party in power, and they had a convincing party machine and a popular, charismatic leader. The APC used these advantages but would be far more wide-ranging in its strategies to hold on to power, particularly as less expected and somewhat self-inflicted problems emerged. Indeed, Stevens' particular blend of personality, patronage and persecution was to leave a vast and long lasting legacy.

The most immediate threats, however, were presented by the armed forces. Evidence emerging from across Africa, particularly in the nearby West African states of Ghana, Nigeria and Dahomey (later Benin), and indeed in Sierra Leone itself, indicated that coups were likely and that one coup often led to others. Alongside party political, parochial and sometimes internal military reasons, elements within African militaries often saw themselves, and to some extent still do if one considers the publicised justifications of recent coups in Guinea and Mali, as defenders of the nation. Stevens could easily be a repeat victim of any of these rationales, most of which had emerged during the 1967–68 coups and attempted coups, and so took urgent and immediate remedial action. At the top, Colonel Bangura was made Force Commander in May 1969. He had been arrested by Albert Margai's government on suspicion of a coup plot in early 1967, had spent time in exile in Guinea with Stevens assembling a guerrilla unit, and was one of just two officers out of prison and still in the army after the April 1968 coup. His appointment, however, did not stop several coup plot rumours and attempted coups against the APC regime emerging from various quarters. Indeed, the 1971 military coup, led by Bangura himself, came close to seizing control.

Whilst many imprisoned officers were released during the first year, a select few were put on trial. The former coup-plotters and junta officials Lansana, Blake, Leigh, Hinga Norman and Juxon-Smith were in the latter group of which an example would be made. A new officer corps was constructed by pensioning off Mende officers. Within eighteen months, there remained just one Mende among the ten most senior army officers and Mendes were reduced to just 32 per cent of the total number of officers, a huge turnaround from the SLPP years.[1] At the same time, Stevens extended a carrot to the armed forces in the form of a substantial increase in military spending. The army, rather than the police, was then put to work to quell disturbances during two declarations of a state of emergency. The first was declared following clashes during by-elections in the south and east. The second was altogether more troublesome for Stevens.

The emergence of a new and potent political party in October 1970 presented a clear threat to Stevens. Most important, the United Democratic Party (UDP) was headed by former APC ministers and Northerners, particularly Temnes. In the week before its official formation, there had been clashes between APC partisans and supporters of the new group, following which the second state of emergency was declared. The UDP lasted eighteen days before it was banned and its leaders arrested. The further problem for Stevens, however, lay in his use of the army to make the arrests, which opened the military to division on APC-UDP lines. Stevens began the dismissals of some suspected UDP supporters in the armed forces and refused to lift the ban on the party. On

23 March 1971, Bangura launched his coup. Gun fights around Stevens' home and office, from which he escaped, were followed by Bangura's announcement on state radio that he had taken control. His 'tenure', however, lasted a mere few hours. Fortunately for Stevens, the coup was put down by loyalists in the army led by Lieutenant-Colonel Sam King. Stevens' swift responses in the aftermath were first to sign a new defence pact with the Guinean President Sekou Touré whereby Guinean troops arrived in the capital just six days after the coup attempt—they remained until 1973—and second, in a show of intent, to have Bangura and three of his co-conspirators swiftly executed. This coup was the first significant appearance of the future RUF leader, Foday Sankoh, who was imprisoned for failing to inform the authorities of the coup attempt. Finally, he appointed the future president, a Limba, Colonel Joseph Saidu Momoh, as Force Commander.

Over the ensuing decades of APC rule, the armed forces were further Northernised, the top brass kept firmly within the patron-client network and the army emasculated. The army and police were kept comfortable by quotas of low-priced rice and access to the spoils of elaborate pre-financed contracts. The heads of the forces were appointed to Parliament and the cabinet after the attempted coups. Although some officers remained committed to their duty, recruitment was often made by the 'card system' which allowed politicians to guarantee a person's entry to the military.[2] The army became widely known as 'One Bullet' owing to its lack of equipment. Serious domestic security problems were dealt with from 1979 by the armed Special Security Division (SSD, or 'Siaka Stevens' Dogs' in common parlance), which began life as the Internal Security Unit (ISU, or again alternatively, 'I Shoot U') in 1971–72. The ISU was part Cuban- and part Israeli- and British-trained and both ISU and SSD effectively acted as an APC militia.[3] Its absorption into the police force did not mean that it was not answerable at all times directly to Stevens.[4]

If Stevens' troubles with the army were not enough, then the political issue of the UDP compounded his problems in the early years. The UDP comprised several former APC big guns including Karefa-Smart, newly returned to the country from a post at the UN, the former Minister of Finance Mohamed Sorie Forna, the former Minister of Information Ibrahim Taqi and the former Minister of Development Mohamed Bash-Taqi. In his letter of resignation, Forna accused Stevens of 'megalomaniac syndrome' and of seeking to impose an executive presidency on Sierra Leone, and Taqi was dismissed for criticism of corruption within the party.[5] Importantly, most UDP leaders, including the four above, were Temne, from the ethnic backbone of the APC. After the arrests, some UDP leaders were released in February 1971, but Karefa-Smart fled to Geneva in March and the UDP was no more. Forna and Taqi, however, were still perceived as a threat and detained until July 1973. Then, in a largely stage-managed trial and despite evidence to the contrary, both were implicated, alongside Juxon-Smith, Lansana and several others, in an alleged attempted coup in July 1974. Indeed, there had been an explosion of some derivation at the house of the Minister of Finance, later Vice President, Christian Kamara-Taylor, on the night in question. All, in any case, were convicted of treason and hanged in July 1975.[6]

Another key area of concern for Stevens was the other older opposition party, the SLPP. As noted above, by-elections were called in 1968 after SLPP MPs were unseated by successful election petitions. Violence had not been entirely absent in earlier elections, what was new was the scale and frequency of the new inter-party violence which commenced in 1968 and returned to haunt each Sierra Leonean electoral campaign right up to the current day. It is perhaps a measure of Stevens' uncertainty over his power that he resorted to violence so quickly. It is also key that the by-elections were in SLPP territory and that any APC victory would shore up the precarious numbers in Parliament. Equally, though, the SLPP seemed quite willing to counter violence with violence. However, more by-elections were held in 1972, in which the SLPP was prevented from even nominating candidates in what were its strongholds.

Multi-party nationwide polls were held in 1973. Following on from the 1972 by-elections, these polls were a far cry from the open national processes of the 1960s. At the close of nominations, 46 APC candidates for a Parliament further expanded to 85 seats stood unopposed, thus guaranteeing a majority.[7] Then, after harassment and beating of party candidates and the attempted assassination of its leader, Salia Jusu-Sheriff, the SLPP withdrew altogether, allowing the APC to sweep the board. A few independents gained seats but the APC took almost complete control of the government at the expense of the legitimacy of the elections. The cabinet announced after the elections demonstrated from where the APC took its strength: ten Temnes and two Limbas constituted half of the cabinet, the numbers being made up by five Krios, four from smaller ethnic groups, and just three Mendes.[8]

Four years later, after violent confrontations between demonstrating students, first at Fourah Bay College and later in schools, and APC militants, early national elections were announced and the SLPP felt more able to compete. Despite widespread violence and intimidation and 12 out of 21 Southern seats being declared unopposed for the APC, the SLPP re-emerged as a semi-viable opposition party, with 15 seats. The incumbents took four of the Southern seats and 11 of the contested elections, but the SLPP showed it was still a force in its strongholds, taking nine seats in the Eastern Province, five in the Southern Province and one in the Western Area; 29 of the 32 Northern seats were declared unopposed for the APC, and the final three were won in contested elections.[9] The ethno-regional division line clearly remained but the contest was far from fair.

Probably concerned by the SLPP's electoral performance in 1977 and a number of outstanding electoral petitions against leading APC members, including the two Vice Presidents, Stevens called for a referendum on the establishment of a one-party state. Official reasons given were similar to those put forward in 1966 by Albert Margai and various other contemporaneous African leaders, namely unity and efficiency, but a further reason—as a panacea for the escalating political violence—was also, rather scurrilously, proffered. Stevens argued that the Mende tradition of 'hanging heads' was a Sierra Leonean version of African consensual politics and a solution to violence and so justified the one-party state.[10] The result of the referendum was duly reported as a very suspect 95 per cent vote in favour. Stevens announced his responsiveness to 'public demands' and, having already turned Sierra Leone into a republic and made himself President and Sorie Ibrahim Koroma Prime Minister and Vice President in 1971, he created a one-party state in 1978. The SLPP was not to return to national political life until the 1990s, although some SLPP politicians felt the need to join the APC in order to remain in their profession. The Parliament was thus finally emasculated and any pretence that it held the legislative power and influence it had in the 1960s vis-à-vis the executive was removed. Parliament sat on just 29 days in 1982.[11]

The introduction of the one-party state did not diminish electoral violence, intimidation and irregularities, which in some areas actually became worse. Ethnic violence in Koinadugu District, stirred by political interference at a national level, was a disturbing development in the one-party elections held in 1982. Competition shifted from the national to the chiefdom level, thereby continuing or even exacerbating the violence.[12] Many standing MPs did their level best to limit opposition within the party, for instance passing legislation making it difficult for civil servants, teachers and lecturers to stand. There was, however, considerable competition between candidates. Despite the absence of political parties, it has been recognised that the more effective one-party states, such as Tanzania and Côte d'Ivoire, administered competitive elections in the sense that the government or the electorate could use these occasions to shuffle those in the top seats at central and/or local level. This could be argued to some extent for Sierra Leone, as one-party elections held some consequences for candidates and government. In 1982, 52 per cent of MPs and 17 per cent of ministers (a total of four out of 24, of which 14 were returned unopposed) were ousted from Parliament.[13] If the man at the top could not be displaced, then many of his supporters could. These shuffles of the pack, however, could not be described as oppositional politics, and made little difference to the general trend of government actions.

In 1985, the Force Commander Major-General Momoh became a surprise choice by the octogenarian Stevens to replace him as leader, bypassing the two Vice Presidents, Koroma and Kamara-Taylor. Seemingly, Stevens did not trust either of his deputies to secure his retirement, or perhaps did not see either as a strong leader.[14] Koroma had also suffered debilitating injuries in a car crash. Once selected by the party, Momoh stood in a presidential election in which there was only one candidate, but before which he embarked on a tour of the country meeting people, listening to complaints and making promises. A much-improved parliamentary poll in 1986, a year early, marked the first one-party elections under Momoh, who appeared eager to quieten the violence and remove some of the previous inequities. A cabinet minister and two ministers of state were disqualified for use of violence. Boundaries were redrawn in order to avoid ethnic conflict, particularly in Koinadugu District. In the elections, 90 per cent of seats were contested and the number of allowed candidates for a seat was increased from three to five. Indeed, 30 per cent of MPs and 33 per cent of ministers (a total of five out of 15 of which five were returned unopposed) lost their seats; only 49 of 105 MPs in the new parliament were incumbents.[15] It would seem that Momoh had reversed some of the electoral trends under Stevens and had at least partly succeeded in his task of creating credible one-party elections, but the 1986 polls were to be the last for ten years.

Outside the armed forces and official party politics, Stevens and Momoh also faced significant societal pressure, in particular from two very dissimilar sources: students and chiefs. As a general first line of attack, Stevens endeavoured to co-opt or replace those who would stand in his way. Opposition was often substantially weakened by the co-optation or exclusion of various heads of, for instance, unions, professional organisations, agricultural associations and university departments and colleges. The head of the Sierra Leone Labour Congress and the teachers' union president were both appointed to Parliament, in these cases after threatening strikes during the 1970s. On the other hand, the Secretary General of the Labour Congress, James Kabia, was arrested after a successful nationwide strike in 1981 and replaced by Stevens' brother-in-law, Ibrahim Langley, who was simultaneously appointed to Parliament.[16] In the same year the offices of the independent newspaper, *The Tablet*, were destroyed in an explosion.[17] Stevens also adopted a strategy of attacking rivals by commissions of inquiry. Cases of embezzlement from state institutions were 'discovered', for instance in the Kilowatt Scandal of the mid-1970s in the Sierra Leone Electricity Company, in the Vouchergate and Squandergate affairs in the early 1980s and, under Momoh, in the Milliongate inquiry in the latter part of the same decade. These were used to remove often high profile rivals from office or to ensure loyalty by arranging a verdict of innocence at the inquiry. The hiring and firing made Stevens, like Mobutu in Congo/Zaïre, a master of the job shuffle, keeping officials on their toes and in the process making short term gains an even greater imperative for these same officials.

However, in 1977 the Stevens regime faced considerable civilian pressure on the streets and reacted not with attempts to co-opt or replace, but with force. Initially, it was the students of Fourah Bay College in Freetown who stood up to the APC militias and Stevens' politically oriented ISU and its hired thugs. After considerable violence against students, unrest spread outside Freetown, forcing Stevens into early elections. An explanation of the focus of resistance in the student body has been put forward as the combination of radical leftist and pan-African ideas and the position of students in urban culture. Alienated youths of the Freetown shanties, known as '*rarray* boys', who met, drank and took drugs in their own urban spaces or *potes*, were often harnessed by the APC through its militias. However, the linkages between this disaffected urban milieu and students grew in the 1970s, culminating in the anti-APC demonstrations and subsequent violence of 1977. The foundations of the RUF have been placed by some scholars in this urban cultural conjunction and the brutalisation of these youths in both APC militias and the anti-APC disturbances.[18] As youth went on to become a key element of the war, it is most likely that a significant number, although far from all, of the youth involved in the war emerged from and were conditioned by these events. Again in 1985, unrest broke out in Fourah Bay College following a purge of those suspected of militancy inspired by Qaddafi's *Green Book*, and retaliatory violence and arrests ensued. Then, two years later, students from Njala College burned down the Provincial Secretariat in Bo in an anti-government demonstration.

On the other hand, APC animosity towards chiefs rapidly abated. District Councils, a node of local power competing with the chieftaincies, were abolished in 1972 and were, significantly, not to return until renewed efforts at decentralisation in 2004. Chiefs remained hugely influential at a local level, still retaining considerable legitimacy, judicial authority and the power to distinguish 'natives' of a chiefdom who would have accompanying land rights, and at a national level as power brokers.[19] At the same time, Stevens felt the need to rein in the chiefs, stating that 'no chief can keep his job without the support of the government'.[20] The five-year period from 1968 to 1973 saw a considerable increase in violence in some chieftaincies where local lineage cleavages were used by members of the regime to oust those who had not switched allegiance to the APC. Importantly, casualties were low probably because the aims centred on changes of rulers rather than—and this is of course significant—a dismantling of the chieftaincy system.[21] However, attempts by the regime to impose compliant chiefs, much as the colonial administration had done, sometimes met with considerable opposition. Occasionally, the protests were successful, as in Kenema and Kono Districts, both in the East of the country. Indicative of local Southern sentiments was the Ndorbgowusui (Mende 'bush devil') defiance campaign in the district of Pujehun in 1983. Similar to the resistance against chiefly imposition, the campaign was provoked by an attempt by the APC's future Vice President under Momoh, Francis Minah, to impose a parliamentary representative in 1982. One opponent was killed, with further rumours of ritual murders. The rebellion, centred on the rival candidate and SLPP veteran Manna Kpaka, was put down in brutal fashion, leading to the displacement and exile in Liberia of many rural people, some of whom went on to join the RUF eight years later.[22]

Underpinning Stevens' pragmatism in co-opting, eliminating and harassing opposition, whether in the military, party politics or society, was his strategy of placing himself at the pinnacle of a patron-client system which had as its foundation the diamond trade and which increasingly starved the formal state of resources. In theoretical discussions, neo-patrimonialism, a hybrid system of power which amalgamates pre-colonial patrimonial hierarchies with the trappings of the modern state, is often seen as having considerable explanatory capacity in African politics. Within this system, reciprocity, sometimes attributed to pre-colonial African political culture and sometimes linked more to everyday necessities of politicians and people alike, plays a key part.[23] To underscore the direct reciprocal relationship of political power and the distribution of resources, one African author put it thus: 'a true, great African leader gives gifts, ceaselessly, every day'.[24] 'Politics of the belly' incorporates the common idea in Africa of 'eating', which can be quite literal but simultaneously refer to the acquisition of goods and power and the notion of being able to grow fatter on the proceeds.[25] A ubiquitous Krio proverb says '*Usai u go tie cow, e go for eat*', meaning that wherever you place a cow, or person, he or she will 'eat'. Reciprocity and the urgent needs of ordinary people mean that the public—as well as those in the state—plays a considerable role in the system, but as it is coupled with an inbuilt gross unfairness and lack of transparency, the public has at the same time a rather ambivalent attitude towards it.[26]

Thus, following on from colonial patterns of control, patrons in the state disburse state resources to clients in a cascading vertical chain in exchange for vital political support in an uncertain political arena, whether authoritarian or democratic. The networks often flow along lines of ethnicity or even more localised identities or family linkages. However, once the doors have thus been opened to illegal resource distribution for political and communal benefits, what can be seen as a blurring of the public-private divide that underpins state integrity, the way is then open to many other forms of self-enriching corruption. As might be expected, these latter forms are then seen by the public as less legitimate than the reciprocal forms. Equally, while such a system (if well-managed) provides a semblance of stability in some African countries, it is grossly inefficient in an economic sense as it prioritises distribution which is politically rational and largely consumptive over that which is economically productive.

At the extreme end of this thinking, the patrimonial networks dominate the workings of the state. A rhizome analogy is one of the more colourful descriptions: the mushrooms growing in full view above ground represent the official workings and buildings of the state and the dense roots under the surface are the informal networks between state officials and societal clients such as chiefs and 'big-men'.[27] Or, in another version, the state is viewed as merely a shell, thoroughly penetrated by networks governed by societal imperatives.[28] These interpretations have been seen as patrimonial without any pretence of the 'neo', which some have argued undervalues somewhat the still existing formal aspects of many African states.[29] After all, countries like Botswana and Ghana have considerable informal and 'traditional' politics but also have states that tax, legislate and conform to more formal and legal logics, although legal-rational intentions are often hard to distinguish from the patrimonial.[30] Some African countries have survived neo-patrimonial politics without descending into collapse or conflict: hence a differentiated view of neo-patrimonialism over space and time is sensible. This should not be a static conception. In Sierra Leone under Stevens and Momoh, however, the extreme interpretations may well be as close to the actuality as anywhere else on the continent. Zaïre under Mobutu, Uganda under Idi Amin and Liberia under Samuel Doe would be three of the few which may be of a similar excessive ilk. Indeed, the term 'Shadow State' was specifically coined to refer to the manner in which Stevens displaced political activity and resource distribution out of the formal state and into his informal networks over which he had greater control. In this thinking, the alternative notion of building up the capacity of the formal state merely risked the danger of rivals building up power bases within the state ministries and departments.[31]

The system was indeed guided by Stevens' personal attention. The build-up of patron-client networks, with Stevens as ultimate arbiter and dispenser of largesse, began immediately. Stevens saw himself as the people's representative, their patron, and for a considerable time made himself available to anyone. Audiences were almost always obtained, in which Stevens could demonstrate his munificence and reinforce his personal links to the detriment of any intermediaries.[32] Following a trait quite common amongst African leaders, he became known as Pa Siakie, effectively as a father figure for the nation with all the generosity, discipline, respect, benefits and responsibility that this is supposed to entail.[33] Indeed, in amongst the violence, electoral malfeasance and political manipulation, Stevens long maintained his image of a charismatic father figure displaying exactly these sorts of attributes expected from a 'good' chief, who is leading his country and people out of the dangers now clear to all. However, a large part of this image maintenance was achieved through the increasing centralisation of the considerable spoils of the state in the hands of the leader. He endeavoured to ensure that those in positions of authority or with access to potential power bases owed their position in the network to him, and were not loyal to the nation, the region or the party, but personally to him.

Diamonds, which had long been the backbone of Sierra Leone's exports, bringing in 70–80 per cent of export earnings in the first decade of independence, became the cornerstone of Stevens' political strategy. In 1974, the monopoly diamond deal between De Beers and the state, quite lucrative to the latter, was brought to an end. The De Beers-owned Diamond Corporation (DICOR) had been obligated to buy all Sierra Leonean diamonds in exchange for paying a 7.5 per cent levy to the state and offering high prices. While the prices helped to keep down the informal market, smuggling activities also fed through to De Beers via its office in Monrovia across the border. The deal was unilaterally ended when 20 per cent of the market was offered elsewhere.[34] The ensuing lower prices after the ending of the monopoly removed some of the constraints on the informal market.

As a commodity, diamonds are notoriously difficult to control, being small and so easily transported, of high value, in no need of processing, and in the alluvial case taken out of rivers or shallow holes in the ground. However, Stevens' attempts to control both the diminishing formal sector and the flourishing informal channels led to an astonishing collapse in the recorded diamond exports from 2 million carats in 1970 to 595 thousand ten years later, and to a paltry 48,000 carats by 1988.[35] It was not that diamond production fell; it was that the diamond trade was increasingly conducted outside the remit of the state. Equally, it was not that Stevens failed to control the trade in easily portable and concealable diamonds; rather, his efforts at control included his engineering of the shift from formal state channels to informal semi-legal and outright smuggling networks. The simultaneous shift to more small-scale alluvial, in place of industrial, mining also facilitated the informalisation of the trade. Within the state, distribution of dealer licences was then made on political grounds and the politically less threatening Lebanese and Afro-Lebanese entrepreneurs like Tony Yazbeck became the dominant players. Chiefs maintained their importance as gatekeepers in the diamond areas.

The fact that resources like diamonds have proved far more often to be a curse than a blessing in Africa is well-known and the reasons behind it, such as the way in which easy revenue increases the disconnect between elite and society, have been explored.[36] There must, however, still be some political options. The obvious comparison is Botswana which is diamond-rich but considerably more economically successful and politically stable than Sierra Leone. It must be noted, though, that the comparison is not straightforward. Botswana has kimberlite diamonds requiring sophisticated deep mining machinery and the diamond areas, being in a sparsely inhabited region, are easier to control. The country is also almost ethnically homogeneous, giving it a coherency enviable in Sierra Leone.[37]

The allocation of import-export licences and access to foreign currency and loan guarantees became similarly politicised and privatised. For example, rice was imported in large quantities and sold at subsidised levels to potentially difficult urban populations, the armed forces, police and civil service or to pay, for instance, diamond diggers. At the same time, rice was grown and smuggled abroad from the countryside, in particular to Liberia where the Liberian dollar was held in parity to the US dollar. Most food aid, and aid in general, emerging mainly from the US and European Community, was also used as a patronage resource.[38] Directly benefiting from this import and subsidy system were the importation companies in which Stevens and his allies had stakes. Those like Jamil Said Mohammed—who became widely known simply as 'Jamil'—and Yazbeck, with their considerable Lebanese banking connections, proved useful to Stevens. Like Jamil, Nabih Berri, the Amal leader in Lebanon, came from Port Loko.[39] Jamil also had interests in important parastatals and in other key parts of the economy.

Particularly cynical in political terms was the closure of the railways, which, except for a branch line to the Makeni area, served the South and East. Even though the IMF had recommended the closure as the lines were losing money, it was plain to see that the APC government was very keen to implement the policy. The railway was progressively closed down in the early 1970s and the promised upgrading of the roads, particularly to the East, never occurred. Incredibly, the OAU summit hosted at great expense in Freetown in 1980, when Stevens began his year as Chairman of the continental body, almost bankrupted the country. The Le200 million spent on hosting the summit, building the Mammy Yoko Hotel, the Bintumani Hotel Conference Centre and sixty luxury villas above Hill Station, and generally upgrading summit-related infrastructural facilities was twice the original budget and added significantly to the growing debt burden. The Governor of the Bank of Sierra Leone, Sam Bangura, was knowledgeable and critical of the deals made and was killed after being thrown from a high window shortly before the summit. The building housing part of the Bank of Sierra Leone is now named after him.

The result of this shift of revenue and distribution from the formal to the informal and the politicisation of resources, what might be called the privatisation of the state, was a rapidly declining formal sector. In real terms, domestic revenue in 1985–86 stood at just 18 per cent of the 1977–78 figures. Income tax collection had virtually collapsed and the payment of business tax was reported at a rate of 1.7 per cent between 1971 and 1980. By 1991, social spending was at 15 per cent of its value ten years earlier.[40] On the other hand, by the early 1980s Stevens' non-budgeted discretionary spending was estimated at more than 60 per cent of actual budgets.[41] The small manufacturing sector actually managed to shrink in the 1980s and no manufactured goods are reported as being exported after 1980.[42] In a sign of the times, big European companies such as Compagnie Française de l'Afrique Occidentale (CFAO) and Paterson Zochonis, two of the most prominent colonial-era firms, began to pull out.[43] The former company had been trading in Sierra Leone since the late nineteenth century and the latter had been founded in Sierra Leone as far back as 1879. Their legacy does live on, but only on the front of buildings in Freetown. The large CFAO logo still adorns a corner property on Charlotte Street, becoming obscured briefly in the early 2000s by the banner of the rebel political party, the RUFP. The Paterson Zochonis building has become the final destination of *poda poda* buses plying the route between Lumley and the area now termed PZ; bus drivers' assistants can be heard shouting 'PZ' all the way down Wilkinson Road and Siaka Stevens Street.

There were some striking improvements such as roads upgraded and bridges built, for instance the four-lane Congo Cross Bridge and the bridge to replace the ferry across to Aberdeen, both in the west of Freetown. The Chinese built the Siaka Stevens Stadium, now the National

Stadium, in the capital. However, the general deterioration of the roads was clear for all Sierra Leoneans to see. Agriculture and the much-vaunted education system also declined. Rice production fell owing to poor producer prices and cheap imported rice, and many farmers switched to subsistence cultivation. Overall, the tiny growth in agricultural output in the 1980s could not keep pace with population expansion.[44] The pay for teachers and other civil servants decreased to the point that it was no longer a living wage and, by 1989, some teachers had not been paid for twelve months. In the late 1980s, only 30 per cent of children were enrolled in secondary school and just 40 per cent in primary school, well below the sub-Saharan average.[45] Momoh went as far as to declare that education was a privilege not a right. At tertiary level, the colleges lacked basic facilities and scholarships were politicised, both factors in the unrest amongst students. Health care deteriorated and drugs were diverted from hospitals into private clinics and dispensaries.

Stevens did, however, have to contend with the global economic crises of the 1970s from the position of a peripheral and primary commodity-producing state. Sierra Leone was certainly not immune to global economic currents that undermined most Southern post-colonial states. As it was a non-oil producer, the two oil shocks hit the country hard, even if the first was cushioned to some extent by a rise in diamond, coffee and cocoa prices. The oil shock of 1973, caused by the drawing down of production by OPEC countries in response to the US arming of Israel, and leading to a quadrupling of oil prices over twelve months, was not of Stevens' doing. Equally, there was little Stevens could do in 1979 when a similar reduction of oil production caused by the Iranian Revolution led to a two-and-a-half-fold price rise by 1980. The ensuing fall in terms of trade, the global recession, and the declining demand for tropical produce in the West exacerbated the difficulties. The drop in the price of diamonds, coffee and cocoa in the early 1980s compounded the balance-of-payments problems. The closure of the Marampa iron ore mines in 1975 added to the predicament. By the 1980s the economy was in crisis. Dependency theory tells us that these massively fluctuating prices and the peripheral and subservient position of African economies in the world market are the key reasons behind Africa's economic problems.[46] However, Stevens' response to the global crises is at least equally important, particularly when compared with other leaders. Not all African governments resorted to such drastic strategies to prop themselves up in power and in many ways the severe global economic crisis simply unmasked the partly self-inflicted domestic economic crisis.

Stevens also had the challenge of the Cold War era international political terrain. Sierra Leone was certainly not seen as a particularly important asset in the Cold War arena. The colony's importance as a shipping post during World War II did not continue into the post-war superpower environment. When Albert Margai and Stevens were threatened by their own armies, it was to Guinea, not to one of the superpowers, that they turned for military assistance. However, Stevens is a particularly instructive example of what has been termed 'extraversion', in which African leaders are said to have considerable propensity and expertise in the use of the outside world for domestic or personal purposes.[47] A consummate balancer of forces at home, he replicated this expertise on the international stage. Sierra Leone was in thrall to neither superpower bloc, unlike some of its near neighbours: Guinea looking east and Côte d'Ivoire looking west. Instead, Sierra Leone was officially non-aligned and Stevens could play one power off against the other or use all at the same time. The country had embassies in China, the Soviet Union, the USA and Saudi Arabia. As noted above, the ISU was trained by the Cubans, Israelis and British. The Chinese financed sugar cane plantations, the Soviets ran Sierra Fisheries, the World Bank's International Development Association funded agricultural development projects and the US Peace Corps and British VSO supplied numerous volunteers.[48] The evidence of extraversion during Stevens' time follows the usage of the colonial power in the internal struggles of the independence period and will be revisited in the chapters concerning contemporary times.

From 1985, despite his promises of a 'new order' and 'constructive nationalism' and his initial popularity, Momoh found it difficult to make any headway in reforming the state. A Limba from Binkolo in Bombali District in the North, Momoh was born in 1937 and so, at under 50 years of age, was the youngest president to come to power. His military career started in 1958, included training in Nigeria and the UK, and culminated in 1983 in him becoming the first Major General in Sierra Leonean history.[49] Politically, he had been a nominated MP and a member of the cabinet since 1974. Promising to instil military discipline into Sierra Leonean life and to remove those who took and did not contribute, Momoh also came to power at a time when he had the heavy hand of Structural Adjustment Programmes (SAPs) urging him on.

Disappearing fast were the days when superpower blocs could be flagrantly played off and aid conditionalities resisted. Instead, starting as austerity measures in 1977 but increasing considerably as a three-year SAP under Momoh, the liberal economic reform of the IMF and World Bank became the order of the day. Privatisation, removal of subsidies, balancing of the budget, floating of the currency and shrinking the state became policy prerequisites for further aid. In an even worse predicament than many other African countries, Sierra Leone was now in no condition to resist even if it so wanted. Basic essentials such as rice, milk, kerosene and medicine were scarce, there were frequent power cuts in the capital, and the black market thrived. The official rate for the leone was Le6 to U$1 while the black market rate stood at Le25.[50] Equally, Momoh seemed initially keen to risk structural adjustments in an attempt to improve the economy in a way that Stevens thought politically dangerous. In 1986, a raft of conditionalities was accepted including the floating of the leone, further privatisations and the potentially explosive removal of subsidies on rice and petrol. In Africa, most governments had kept the urban populations fed and docile with subsidies, and Stevens and Momoh had only to look across the border to Liberia in 1979 to see the calamitous effects wreaked on the William Tolbert government by an overnight 50 per cent rise in the price of rice. Tolbert survived the riots, again with the help of the Guinean army, but lasted just one more year before being toppled and killed in a military coup.

Initially, some progress was made. International finance came in, changes were made to the export process for diamonds, gold and agriculture, and foreign firms were prioritised. Official diamond exports rose in 1986–87 and subsidies finally ended in 1989–90, albeit with an alarming 180 per cent rise in the price of rice and 300 per cent rise in that of petrol.[51] On the other hand, the SAP policies could also be used as a political stick or carrot vis-à-vis entrenched interests and potential adversaries and power bases from the Stevens era. The more adept African leaders of this time, such as Paul Biya in Cameroon, Jerry Rawlings in Ghana and Stevens in its early stages, did indeed successfully 'adjust to adjustment'.[52] The process does depend, for instance, on who the buyers of privatised state assets are and what deals remain in place after privatisation.[53]

Beyond the urban population in Sierra Leone, other key losers in the Momoh era were the favoured Lebanese from Stevens' time and some others benefiting from the established informal networks, who were replaced with Israeli networks. Indeed, relations between Stevens and Momoh also deteriorated during this period. A coup plot then emerged in March 1987. It is unclear how much Stevens was involved, but those implicated were from the inner workings of his regime, some of whom subsequently fled to London. It is thus evident that Momoh was having some effect on vested interests, but he became less keen after the coup. At the same time, his use of the army to police the State of Economic Emergency declared in 1987 and to evict illicit miners in Operation Clean Sheet in 1990 proved counter-productive and led to greater liaisons between smugglers and soldiers and significant numbers of disgruntled miners. Official diamond exports fell to almost nothing in 1989, aid decreased in the post-Cold War environment and the IMF and World Bank credit was suspended in 1990 when debt servicing ceased.[54]

Momoh became increasingly reliant on the Limba Ekutay association, in particular what was termed the 'Binkolo mafia', a support base centred on his home town which had provided many of the recruits into the Sierra Leone Army (SLA) during the APC years. This very narrow support, however, was not an adequate long-term policy for maintaining power in such a political and economic climate. For instance, James Bambay Kamara, another Limba, became the notorious and powerful head of the police. An intra-party dispute between Kamara and Vice President Minah ended in Kamara's accusation that Minah knew of the 1987 coup but did not report it.[55] Six, including Minah, were subsequently executed for the coup plot. Kamara was in turn executed after his alleged involvement in an APC counter-coup in December 1992 after the APC had been ousted.

By 1991, the SLA was a shadow of its former self alongside the infrastructure of the state. When the RUF invaded from Liberia backed by Charles Taylor and his Liberian rebel forces the SLA was ill-equipped for the task of crushing the rebellion. Under pressure from within, and now in the post-Cold War world from without, for multi-party elections to take place Momoh conducted a referendum and 90 per cent voted for the end of the one-party state. Elections were planned for June 1992, but events moved too fast. Momoh and the APC were removed from office in April of that year in a military coup involving fewer than 100 men led by a young Krio officer, Captain Valentine Strasser. It was an ignominious end to 24 years of APC rule, but one that was in large part self-inflicted.

The argument that Stevens faced such extraordinary domestic and external circumstances that he had to take the extraordinary measures that he did holds only limited merit. It is instructive to any who study the post-Stevens and Momoh era right up to the current day to note that conditions for governance are structurally very difficult in Africa and, as detailed before, particularly so in Sierra Leone. However, as a purportedly rational response, Stevens' method held the seeds of its own destruction, although that came after his death on 29 May 1988. The regime was not exceptionally violent like those of Idi Amin in Uganda or Macias Nguema in Equatorial Guinea, nor was the leader particularly ill-equipped to rule like Samuel Doe in Liberia. However, a state that cannot collect taxes, provide basic amenities to its people or defend its borders, and a government that relies on a clandestine diamond trade, overt ethno-regional resource distribution and, when deemed necessary, coercion—in a time of global austerity and then neo-liberal conditionalities on aid—are entities largely living on borrowed time. The hollowing out and informalisation of the state sufficed in the short term to keep Stevens and Momoh in power, and perhaps they believed in their paternalistic status. There is also no long term without a short term. However, in the long term, the rationality and effectiveness of the model proved extremely and disastrously questionable. In some ways, Stevens had changed Sierra Leone, although in very few ways for the better and often merely to exacerbate the structural problems that already existed.

6

CIVIL WAR AND THE INCENDIARY DEBATES
OVER ITS PROVENANCE, 1991–1996

That the state and armed forces of Sierra Leone were in no condition by the early 1990s to resist any sort of invasion or insurrection is one area of agreement in the debates concerning the civil war. The armed forces had become a largely emasculated link in the APC patronage chain and were essentially an 'army of foot soldiers', largely 'ceremonial' and with a 'practically non-existent' ability to respond to threats.[1] The state had been informalised and shrunk back to such an extent that infrastructure needed by the armed forces in the defence of the country was in a poor condition. The most meagre of incursions into the ill-controlled and forested border areas would have had at least some success. Agreement over the war, however, largely ends there. The origins, players, motivations, format and longevity of the conflict have been the subject of intense debate. Conflicts, particularly those in a domestic setting, almost always produce intense concurrent disagreements amongst the observers who seek to explain them. This is probably a reflection of the intimate and brutal nature of these conflicts, and the deep scars they create. The Sierra Leonean civil war was a particularly nasty conflict with civilians very much in the firing line. Images of violence against civilians using hand-held basic weaponry were sent around the world. As might be expected, the debate on the causes, participants and trajectory of the war generated its share of intense heat.

The war shifted considerably over time in terms of the key players, their alliances, the format of the conflict and its geographical location.

An attempt should thus be made to separate the varying phases. The following analysis will first investigate the initial phase of the war, 1991–96, from its immediate origins prior to 1991 through to the revolutionary United Front (RUF) invasion into Kailahun District, the fluctuating war zone in the South and East, the Valentine Strasser coup of 1992, the emergence of the Kamajor militias, and the mercenary-assisted push back of the RUF. The second phase starts with the 1996 election of Ahmad Tejan Kabbah and the SLPP and the Abidjan Accord, and continues with the period of the RUF-army junta in 1997–98, the ECOMOG (Economic Community of West African States (ECOWAS) Monitoring Group) fight back, and the junta retreat to the North, and finishes with the invasion of Freetown on 6 January 1999. The third phase is the beginning of the end and includes the Lomé Accord, the UN and British deployments in 1999 and 2000 respectively, the RUF and Liberian armed forces incursion into Guinea, UN sanctions on the Liberian President and RUF backer Charles Taylor, and the final peace deals in 2001. Much of the debate will emerge in the discussion of the first phase in Chapter 6, although the importance of the various shifts in the war in the latter two phases, detailed in Chapter 7, will be noted as they impinge on the debates.

It has been a popular notion that the Sierra Leone civil war was either an extension of the Liberian conflict or at least a product of international concerns, primarily those of Taylor and the former Libyan leader Muammar Qaddafi, coinciding with the end of the Cold War. In much the same way, the civil wars in Congo/Zaïre have been portrayed as an extension of the Rwandan conflict and genocide and as international wars due to the eventual presence of considerable numbers of Rwandan, Ugandan, Angolan, Zimbabwean and Namibian troops as well as various peace-keeping forces. Somewhat justifiably, the second Congolese conflict has been described as 'Africa's First World War'.[2] The origins of the Sierra Leonean civil war are also, to some extent, situated outside the borders of Sierra Leone. The trial of a Liberian, Taylor, in The Hague under the auspices of the Sierra Leone Special Court (SLSC) focused minds on the role that he played. The war, like many in Africa in countries such as Somalia, Liberia and Congo/Zaïre, broke out in the aftermath of the end of the Cold War, a few years after the imposition of SAPs and concurrent with shifts towards democratisation. The extent of the international origins thus requires some scrutiny.

The origins of the RUF can be traced back to training camps in the Libyan desert. In the late 1980s, there were a number of Sierra Leoneans, perhaps 35–50—alongside Liberians (including Taylor), Ghanaians and Gambians—who went to Libya for insurgency training.[3] Qaddafi's notions of anti-imperial rebellion had led him to sponsor West Africans who might push this agenda forward. To assume these factors as the key origins would ignore any development of insurrectionary tendencies inside Sierra Leone in the 1970s and 1980s, but it is certainly important that links between Qaddafi, Taylor, the future RUF leader Foday Sankoh and President Blaise Compaoré of Burkina Faso were forged through Libya. According to most accounts, the majority of these Sierra Leoneans had abandoned the idea of violent struggle before the creation of the RUF. However, of those that continued to plough this furrow, three were prominent in the formation of the RUF, and were involved with Taylor and his rebel group, the National Patriotic Front of Liberia (NPFL): Abu Kanu, Rashid Mansaray and Sankoh.

Taylor's invasion of Liberia was launched in December 1989 from Côte d'Ivoire and was in itself international. He began with a small multi-national force, only about 200 strong and significantly non-Liberian, including Sierra Leoneans and Burkinabe, with tacit French backing. In an extremely successful rebellion in territorial terms, by mid-1990 the NPFL had taken over 95 per cent of the country. Taylor benefited from President Samuel Doe's over-reaction to the incursion, targeting the eth-nic Gio and Mano residents of Nimba County, where Taylor had entered the country. Mandingo traders and Doe's fellow Krahns, both perceived beneficiaries of the Doe regime, and those otherwise associated with the regime became the targets of Taylor's forces. His success was underwrit-ten by support from a broader range of people against the decade-long authoritarian rule of Doe. However, by 1991, Taylor's control over the Liberian countryside was threatened by anti-NPFL forces coalescing in Sierra Leone and ECOMOG's first military intervention, to which Sierra Leone was a contributor, also playing the role of a staging post for the predominantly Nigerian force. NPFL support for an RUF invasion in 1991 served to undermine the Sierra Leonean state and any opponents harboured there, and simultaneously created a lucrative avenue to the nearby diamond fields. Taylor would also have calculated that the RUF, given limited international intervention and a disgruntled population particularly in the South and East along the Liberian border, could plau-sibly be expected to reach Freetown and topple the APC government.

Often portrayed as the puppet-master in this corner of West Africa, Taylor has been held responsible for the cause, the instigation and the prolongation of conflict in Liberia, Sierra Leone, the south of Guinea and the west of Côte d'Ivoire. He was the organiser of the initial invasion of Liberia, the driving force behind the NPFL, and a man with phenomenal presidential ambitions and the will to override all other considerations. During the rebellion, Taylor constructed a commercial empire trading largely through Côte d'Ivoire with French companies. At its height, his extravagantly titled 'Greater Liberia' boasted its own currency, TV, radio, newspaper, international airport, deepwater port and administrative capital. The former interim Liberian head of state Amos Sawyer argues that from the very start Taylor's ambitions were grand: 'to restore Liberia's 'days of glory' and its president's place as leader of one of the three power blocs in West Africa, the other two being Nigeria and francophone West Africa'; and 'to be the leader of the Mano basin area', that is, Liberia, Sierra Leone and Guinea.[4] One investigative journalist noted: 'Taylor had a map he carried around with him called Greater Liberia. It included parts of Guinea, diamond fields in Sierra Leone. It wasn't something abstract to him. He had a very clear idea of what he was trying to achieve. He had a grandiose plan, and he almost succeeded.'[5] A former UN representative in Liberia, Jacques Klein, compared Taylor to a Count Dracula-like vampire, who cannot be killed normally but instead requires a stake through his heart.[6]

Taylor came out of the bush in 1996 and won the elections the following year, on the basis that people feared either that he would go back to war if he lost or that no other candidate could effectively control Liberia.[7] His presidency was little different from the past in its reliance on coercion, arbitrary rule and narrow networks of patronage, and continued Liberia's descent into a pariah state. Faced with another rebellion from 2000 onwards, he was eventually cornered in 2003 and agreed to exile in Nigeria. Pressure that was then mounted by Western governments on Nigeria and Liberia to surrender him to the SLSC, and his trial in The Hague for war crimes committed in Sierra Leone—the first international trial of a former senior office holder in a state since the Nuremberg Trials in Germany and the Tokyo trials in Japan in the 1940s—are indicative of the way in which Taylor came to be perceived as the lynchpin of Mano River conflicts.

On 23 March 1991 the RUF, at this point a small group of Sierra Leoneans and others primarily from Liberia and Burkina Faso, invaded from

Liberia into Kailahun District in the remote East of Sierra Leone. There had been cross-border incursions by NPFL rebels before, but this was different as it was declared shortly afterwards on the radio by Sankoh as the start of the RUF rebellion in Sierra Leone. Indeed, assisted by the parlous state of the SLA, the RUF quickly captured most of Kailahun and opened a new front in Pujehun District, again from Liberia. Evidence suggests, however, that despite a Sierra Leonean leadership, the early RUF had many Liberians including three commanders who were captured and paraded by the SLA.[8] Equally, and despite Taylor's assertions during his trial, support came from his Liberian rebel force. There also appeared to be an ongoing connection with Libya and delivery of money from there.[9] The RUF made considerable headway during 1991 and was only seriously beaten back by the Liberians in Sierra Leone who formed the United Liberation Movement of Liberia (ULIMO). Indeed, these Doe loyalists forced the RUF out of Pujehun back into Liberia and followed them there, opening up a front against the NPFL. It would seem that the RUF rebellion was, at least partly and at this stage, a Liberian conflict fought on Sierra Leonean soil.

Indeed, the internationalisation argument can be taken further. First, although many Liberians and Burkinabe were withdrawn in early 1992, the involvement of Liberia and Libya did not peter out for many years.[10] In April 2012, Taylor was convicted in the SLSC of eleven charges of war crimes and crimes against humanity in aiding and abetting the RUF. The judge noted that he had extended 'sustained and significant' support to the RUF and had sold diamonds and bought weapons on its behalf and knew the rebels were committing atrocities. Importantly, though, he stopped short of saying Taylor had effective command and control of the RUF, and so Taylor could not then be held responsible for ordering the crimes.[11] In addition, however, the later roles played by South Africa-based mercenaries, ECOMOG and UN peacekeepers, the British Army and the drawing of Guinea into the latter stages of the conflict kept the level of international military engagement high.

Secondly, and in a non-military sense, the international markets for diamonds, one of the objectives of Taylor and the RUF and a fuel for the war, were at the time much less concerned with the origins of the stones. Some were reported as being bought by Al-Qaeda and others as sold by ECOMOG officers.[12] Former Soviet bloc countries seemed equally unconcerned with the final destination of arms shipments. Finally, the timing of the conflict at the end of the Cold War is not a coincidence. The removal of the Soviet Union as a dispenser of aid and a power against which to play off the West, and the tightening of Western aid conditions and the imposition of SAPs all played a role in further weakening the most crisis-ridden African states at a crucial moment. The new demand for democratisation also laid many African countries open to a very difficult and potentially divisive process, whatever the predicted benefits in the long run.[13] Thus the ability of the state to defend itself, to provide for its citizens through development but more importantly through patronage, and to pacify the marginalised and discontented diminished further as the end of the Cold War drew nearer.[14]

The Sierra Leonean conflict would probably not have happened at this particular point in time had it not been inspired from Liberia and had the end of the Cold War not provoked the downgrading of international aid alongside the old economic and new political conditionalities in Africa. However, there are certainly considerable underlying domestic causes of the conflict which would suggest that outside forces might be seen as only a catalyst or trigger. The conditions in Sierra Leone created by the APC and even going back further in time have been seen as ripe for conflict. One interpretation of conflict stresses the weak state inherited from colonial times, which presents post-colonial leaders with almost intractable problems for which the solutions often lead to conflict. Equally, in this model the weak state is always prone to penetration from outside forces in whatever guise.[15] It is a model with some utility, particularly in Sierra Leone, but is also a rather blunt instrument, and in the Sierra Leonean case the precise conditions that led directly to the war are again subject to debate. On the other hand, the rebels themselves have been seen as the main cause of the conflict, rather than the state. The motivations for fighting and origins of leaders and foot-soldiers and the type of conflict that ensued have been equally contested. Arguments driven by a 'greed' analysis tend to focus on the rebels and particularly their relationship to resources.[16] All of these arguments are persuasive up to a point in the Sierra Leonean arena, but in the end it is more a case of their tending to overlap and interweave.

The condition of the Sierra Leonean state over time has been elaborated in the previous chapters. Not only was the state ill-prepared to counter a rebellion, it had also made many enemies within its own borders, which could potentially fuel the insurrection. Specifically, the downgrading of the formal state had removed facilities, infrastructure, education and opportunities. Ethno-regionalism and manipulation of 'tradition' had made sure that the South and East in particular simmered with resentment. The political violence and brutalisation of the youth provided more animosity.[17] The general shortages and the high-end corruption left many staggered. The distance between the elites and non-elites and the urban and the rural, which had caused periodic trouble in the past, had if anything grown. The decline in state resources then sucked dry the already malfunctioning patron-client system on which people relied either to get on in life or simply for survival. Recent actions by Momoh had also backfired and stirred up bitterness in various important quarters.

However, the part played by each of these factors and sectors of society is a key matter for argument. The debate over whether this was an urban- or a rural-driven conflict is particularly intense. First, it has been suggested that the backbone of the RUF rank and file, and indeed much of the leadership, came from an urban milieu. This interpretation has been used pointedly to explain the brutalities meted out by the RUF in the countryside. Would-be urban insurgents had little success in fomenting rebellion in the cities and so went to the countryside. They were then, to use an inversion of Mao Tse-tung's phrase, 'fish out of water' in this environment and hence could not find sympathy amongst the rural population and resorted to more and more coercive measures.[18] Indeed, in a similar environment to the NPFL, the RUF should have picked up considerable support given the history of where they invaded and the scant resistance the armed forces could muster, and likewise marched to the gates of the capital in six months. Despite early successes in remote Kailahun District, the RUF singularly failed to do this, being driven back into the Gola Forest by late 1991 and only finally reaching Freetown in 1997 when invited by the military junta.

The attempt by the RUF to emulate the NPFL after the initial invasion backfired. The RUF was not helped, as the NPFL had been, by an extreme reaction of government troops which could have provoked a rush to join the insurgents, but the RUF's strategy did include the targeting of government officials, chiefs and sometimes traders. The APC was hated in these parts and Sierra Leoneans in general had sometimes felt aggrieved against their chiefs and reacted accordingly. However, the chiefs' relationship with their subjects was rather more ambiguous than that of the NPFL's targets with Liberians, and the violence, which extended to ordinary civilians, came across to many as simple brutality. This has been blamed on the backing from Taylor, which reduced the need to cultivate the local people, and the excesses of the Liberian and Burkinabe mercenary contingent in the initial invasion force, but the violence continued after they had left in early 1992. RUF atrocities, documented by many organisations and writers and splashed on TV screens across the globe, included rape and killings; the amputation of limbs—'long sleeve' for amputation at the wrist, 'short sleeve' at the elbow; the traumatisation of children by, for instance, forcing them to kill their parents and then conscripting and drugging them in order to kill further; and the wholesale destruction of property. Almost all Sierra Leoneans were affected in some way and child soldiers and amputees became for a time almost a by-word for Sierra Leone.[19] The TRC estimated that 60 per cent of all war atrocities were committed by the RUF as opposed to 17 per cent by the state's armed forces. Of the RUF's total violations where the age of the victim was known, it was estimated that 15 per cent were against children.[20] These tactics had recently been on display in Mozambique, where Renamo rebels eventually won over some support in their fight and subsequent electoral campaign against the Frelimo government. Despite a mixture of recruits and forced conscripts, the RUF won remarkably few civilian hearts and minds in Sierra Leone.

One might see this failure as a result of the 'fish out of water' problem. A compelling historical analysis places Sierra Leone's 'lumpens' at centre stage.[21] On the basis of Karl Marx's notion of the lumpen-proletariat—an unthinking impoverished sector of society whose parochial concerns, he said, had severely hindered revolutions prior to the Russian experience and any possibility of social and political change—the Sierra Leonean version is tracked over time. It is not clear that Marx's notion of lumpen-proletariat can fully apply in Africa, but a type of lumpen history in Sierra Leone is taken through its various stages from the rebellious, anti-social and ill-educated Freetown youth culture of the 1940s, through the addition of politicised college drop-outs in the late 1960s and 1970s who rejected the elite which they had formerly wished to join, and finally to the RUF. Lumpen youths played their roles in the orchestrated APC political violence and anti-APC demonstrations in the 1970s and 1980s.[22] This was a disaffected, semi-criminalised and often under- or unemployed sector of society, which was often politically motivated but equally often co-opted by those in or out of power. Some of these youths had been attracted to the semi-lawless and violent mining and border areas into which the RUF invaded by the opportunities provided by diamond mining and smuggling, and were receptive to the appeal of the rebels.[23] These explanations focus on individual rather than communal motivations for joining the rebels, and they hold some weight considering the RUF's poor relations with local communities and the violent and mercenary activities of the fighters. They also hint at an explanation of the eventual violence directed at city dwellers, politicians, wealthy traders and Lebanese, who had benefited from the system which had rejected or used the disadvantaged who became fighters.

Mercenarism, in the form of looting and mining, was indeed another feature of the RUF. It was also a feature of the other factions in the war. The lumpen analysis seeks to explain not only this ubiquitous activity but also the so-called 'sobel' phenomena. The term 'sobel'—soldier by day, rebel by night—was coined to illustrate the fluid and predatory nature of the conflict and highlight the extensive collaboration between elements of the SLA and of the RUF, two forces supposed to be fighting each other, in widespread looting. A typical arrangement would be, for example, for one side to draw back from a town or mine and allow the other to capture it and loot, then for the 'attacking' side to withdraw and allow the 'defending' side to return; the spoils were then shared. In 1994, after the coup, Strasser admitted that at least 20 per cent of his army was disloyal. Civilians would often regard the SLA and RUF as equally threatening, and sometimes could not tell the difference between the two forces. The similar backgrounds of SLA and RUF recruits can then begin to explain their similar behaviour.[24] This is particularly the case after Momoh and then Strasser rapidly expanded the size of the armed forces with often unsuitable, poorly trained and sometimes underage recruits. For example, in 1991, Captain Prince Benjamin-Hirsch recruited most miners and unemployed youth around Segbwema in Kailahun District into a division, depriving the RUF of exactly its type of recruit in that area.[25]

Mercenarism also fits with a greed analysis of conflict, which is juxtaposed with grievance as a driving force: 'The true cause of much civil war is not the loud discourse of grievance but the silent force of greed.'[26] It also links into one of the underpinning notions of post-Cold War 'New War' theory.[27] Some have stated that there was no rebellion in Sierra Leone and hesitate even to use the word 'rebel' in reference to the RUF, preferring the more economically oriented label 'bandit'.[28] Thus the blame for the war can be placed squarely on resources, in particular diamonds, and those who wanted them.[29] The award-winning Hollywood film *Blood Diamond* also put the stones at the heart of the matter, and the Sierra Leonean Ambassador to the UN stated categorically in 2000:

We have always maintained that the conflict in Sierra Leone is not about ideology, tribal or regional differences. It has nothing to do with the so-called problem of marginalised youths, or, as some political commentators have characterised it, an uprising by rural poor against the urban elite. The root of the conflict is, and remains, diamonds, diamonds and diamonds.[30]

The argument is intellectually based on the idea of rational choice theory and the reasoned cost-benefit analysis of actors. In a converse scenario, rebellions based on grievance are seen as non-starters as they inherently suffer from non-instant gratification and 'free-riders', that is, those who benefit but don't fight.[31]

Although this is a temptingly simple explanation and one that is not without merit in Sierra Leone given the number of times diamonds and looting crop up in the story of the conflict, it is indeed too simple. Rebellions of any hue need financing wherever it comes from, particularly after the Cold War when ideological funding dried up. Crucially, though, it fails to take into account the complexity of the conflict, relying purely on economic rationality to explain intentions, and presents what is largely a false dichotomy.[32] Motivations of looting and grievance are surely inextricably intertwined. A proponent of the 'resource curse' theory noted the limitations of this particular idea when applied to civil wars.[33] Additionally, one of the key drivers of the greed proposition later adapted his theory towards concerns for the 'feasibility' of conflict, including notions of terrain and outside security umbrellas: 'where a rebellion is feasible, it will occur'.[34] Motivation is then 'supplied by whatever agenda happens to be adopted by the first social entrepreneur to occupy the viable niche'.[35] Again, opportunity is clearly important in Sierra Leone, but it is once more a mono-causal thesis.

The leaders of factions should not, however, escape scrutiny under a lumpen rubric. Major Johnny Paul Koroma is often regarded as typical of the 'sobel' phenomenon. The looting of the Sierra Rutile mines in 1995, which his troops were ostensibly guarding, has been attributed to collusion between Koroma and the RUF leadership. He later became leader of the chaotic and brutal military junta in 1997 which notably invited the RUF to share power, gained two seats in the 2002 elections largely on the back of an armed forces vote, and then was indicted by the SLSC before going missing. In the coup of April 1992, the soldiers who ousted Momoh and the APC were all junior officers. The initial leader of the group of around 100 coup-plotters, who came heavily armed straight from the front line to State House, was 26-year-old Lieutenant Solomon Musa, later to be involved in the 1997–98 junta as well. Many others, such as the future military head of state in 1996, SLPP presidential candidate in 2012 and elected president in 2018, Julius Maada Bio, were also lieutenants and chose Captain Strasser as head of the National Provisional Ruling Council (NPRC) partly for his slightly higher rank.[36] Importantly, many were very young and had grown up in Freetown's slums replete with resentment at their position in life and at the APC regime.[37]

Strasser, who was just 27 years old when he assumed power, grew up in the poor East End of Freetown. His way out of poverty was through an APC patron, Thaimu Bangura, who would feature prominently in the 1996 elections, but he hated the elitism of the system as well as the APC.[38] After Strasser's displacement in a palace coup by Maada Bio in January 1996, he moved briefly to the UK initially on a scholarship to Warwick University, but lives at the time of writing in poverty and in poor mental health in one of the villages outside Freetown. The aftermath of the 1992 coup saw widespread looting of the homes of politicians and businessmen, the spoils of which were never accounted for and probably contributed to the post-coup flamboyance of some of the soldiers.[39] The coup itself was initially very popular as it ousted the very unpopular Momoh, it presented a possible if misplaced hope of ending the war either through negotiation or by military efficiency, it brought about the end of shortages mostly due to APC hoarding, and it offered a new beginning. The regular clean-ups in the cities were popular, continuing voluntarily into the 2000s, and state-sponsored street art decorated some of the city's main roads.[40] Benjamin-Hirsch and Paramount Chief Gulama were two different but typical subjects for the large portraits painted on walls. It was not long, however, before disappointment set in. There were no peace negotiations and the war continued, perhaps because the NPRC officers believed the RUF was on the back foot and could now be defeated. Equally, the APC political *modus operandi* gradually returned. Some blamed civilian politicians such as the NPRC Secretary General (and later to become SLPP Minister of Finance and

National Chairman) John Oponjo Benjamin for the decline, but arbitrary military rule, summary executions by the armed forces and the 'sobel' phenomenon also played a part.

It is a considerable stretch to describe all of the leaders above as lumpen—Maada Bio went to start a doctorate in the UK and then became president—although their followers might have been and they certainly were not of the elite at that time. However, above all, Sankoh requires examination. He was a former army corporal with only primary-level education, who was incarcerated in 1971 for his failure to inform the authorities of the Bangura coup attempt. Considering that he and Bangura were from the same district, that Sankoh held a position at SLBS TV, and that he has claimed to have played a large part (however exaggerated) in that coup, the accusation was probably correct. After his release from Pademba Road Prison in 1978 until his departure for Libya, Sankoh earned a living as an itinerant photographer. It is clear that during his experiences in prison and in the 'revolutionary' groups that he attended prior to the RUF and the Libyan trips, Sankoh developed a striking animosity towards the elite.

Sankoh was always considered the leader of the RUF, even during two later periods of imprisonment, up until his eventual death in SLSC custody in July 2003. His education and experience, however, were not ideal for leading a revolutionary or even a political movement, although the loyalty generated amongst the fighters ensured the RUF's survival. He was clearly willing to use child soldiers and terror against civilians as a weapon and was equally ruthless with his comrades. Before the end of 1992, Kanu and Mansaray had been executed by their RUF comrades for alleged battlefield crimes, leaving Sankoh firmly in charge. It is perhaps, though, the virulent strain of animosity towards the elite and the educated which informed his methods within the RUF, and indeed within later coalition governments, and sealed the character of the rebellion. One might see here an extreme version of the gap between a patronising elite and a populace which broadly, although clearly not entirely, shows deference to its purported political and social superiors. Educated 'recruits' were indeed picked up along the way but their effect on the movement was always stifled. It is instructive to compare Taylor with Sankoh: Taylor was of the elite, even if not in its top echelons, and knew how to operate in this arena and bring on board useful political cadres; Sankoh and others in the RUF resented exactly these people.

An incident in 1997 illustrates this and his commanders' attitude. Sankoh was arrested in Nigeria in early 1997 and an attempt to take over the RUF leadership was made by an educated group, including Captain Philip Palmer, a Fourah Bay College engineering graduate and apparently an RUF founder-member; Dr Mohamed Barrie, Chief Medical Officer of the Sierra Leone Ore and Metal Company (SIEROMCO) mine, abducted by the RUF in January 1995; Ibrahim Deen-Jalloh, a lecturer from the rural teacher-training college at Bunumbu; and Fayia Musa, a former Njala College student, recruited in 1991 whilst a teacher in a Kailahun secondary school.[41] Their coup, apparently premised on Sankoh's authoritarianism and unwillingness to abide by the 1996 Abidjan Accord which some of them had taken part in creating, proved short-lived when battlefield commanders arrested several of the leaders. The RUF command was provisionally assumed, in Sankoh's two-year absence, by Sam 'Maskita' Bockarie, a former illicit-diamond miner and hairdresser who had been at Sankoh's side from the start and had, by this point, earned a reputation for brutality. Bockarie was eventually indicted but never tried by the SLSC. His activities continued in Liberia and Côte d'Ivoire for some time after the demobilisation of the RUF, until his death in May 2003.

In a stark contrast to Renamo, a rebel movement with which the RUF is often compared, the RUF failed to establish a political cadre or create any sort of consistent or lucid political message. Renamo was largely a creation of the Rhodesian security forces in the late 1970s and was backed by apartheid South Africa in order to destabilise Mozambique after Zimbabwean independence in 1980. Despite these inauspicious beginnings, it had an apparently deliberate policy to bolster the quality of its political cadres. There was a concerted effort to draw in people with a higher educational level than existing members—'capturing' them during raids on secondary schools—who could contribute to Renamo's political and administrative development. Later, some 100–200 secondary and pre-university-level students were attracted to Renamo with the promise of scholarships.[42] In Renamo's 'liberated' areas, attempts were made to install a more credible administration and Renamo's First Congress in 1989 was a milestone. Renamo then carved out a constituency based on the championing of 'traditional' and religious authorities and antipathy to the southern-dominated Frelimo and its Marxist, secular and modernising political programmes.

The RUF had precious little to compare, 'recruiting' but not construc-
tively using educated personnel and establishing little of permanence in
its 'liberated zones'. It would appear that Sankoh and the whole of the
RUF from top to bottom might be construed as lumpen. The RUF certainly had no convincing text or ideological programme to persuade the
outside world or act as impetus for the combat forces. The RUF manifesto, *The Basic Document of the Revolutionary United Front of Sierra Leone
(RUF/SL): The Second Liberation of Africa*, was released in 1990, but predated the RUF as an organisation and was a redrafted version of a PAN-
AFU document.[43] The second and final publication five years later,
Footpaths to Democracy: Towards a New Sierra Leone, Vol. 1, contained
quotes from the first document alongside an anthem and a lengthy text
attributed to Sankoh. Despite the stirring slogan, 'Arms to the people;
power to the people; and wealth to the people', both publications are
often disparaged as totally unrepresentative of RUF aims. The claims to
follow active conservationism and liberation theology are extraordinary
in the circumstances. According to Eldred Collins—a close aide of
Sankoh through the war, one of the designated RUF officials in the junta
and the aborted post-Lomé Accord coalition, and leader of the political
party in later years—he wanted to explain politics to people and RUF
soldiers, but Sankoh was not interested.[44] However, the sentiments of
anti-urban elitism would certainly have struck a chord within and outside the rebel forces. The promise that 'No more shall the rural countryside be reduced to hewers of wood and drawers of water for urban
Freetown' is particularly specific and poignant. Although during a decade
of conflict the RUF fought against four politically different regimes in
Freetown, the widespread notion of elite exploitation only ever went away
for a brief period at the beginning of the NPRC regime.

Several claims have, though, been made for some sort of RUF ideology, however ill-articulated and unconnected to most people. It was
considered highly controversial when in 1996 some credence was given
to the RUF's revolutionary claims, with the assertion that disaffected
intellectuals who harboured sincere democratic and radical beliefs led
the RUF and that the violence was the product of an intellectual project by a vengeful movement of exiles, the consequences of which had
not been fully thought through.[45] The thesis was in part a response to
an influential 1994 article which highlighted Sierra Leone as an example of a rather vague neo-Malthusian global future where a *pot-pourri*

of factors including environmental degradation, overpopulation and cultural and religious schisms leads inexorably to widespread low-level conflicts.[46] The critics, however, refused to countenance ideological credit being handed to the RUF and the lumpen critique followed soon afterwards. Any serious individuals had been purged from the hierarchy before the fighting started, and the leader and movement that emerged had no ideological motivation.[47]

In subsequent publications, however, the original thoughts on the RUF political project were qualified. It has since been suggested that the RUF was a millenarian sect, created almost by accident, and underpinned by Qaddafi *Green Book* egalitarianism, messianic or charismatic authority and the meritocratic communities of the camps.[48] It is argued that some egalitarian concepts were indeed practised within the RUF.[49] The RUF camps in rural central Sierra Leone 'embodied (through free basic education and medical services) the movement's egalitarian political message'.[50] Indeed, the RUF was a 'populist movement without popular support' and could not have survived in this environment over ten years purely through coercive means.[51] There is a similar and pertinent argument that if it had no ideology at all, it would not have been so angry. Grievances before and during the war fed into a dangerous psychological combination of deliberately inculcated 'shamelessness' within the RUF and the 'threat of shame' when facing civilians or if reintroduced into wider society.[52] In broad brush terms, the RUF's millenarianism and violence might be seen as akin to that of the Khmer Rouge in Cambodia, but without their organisation, efficiency or overt, developed ideology.

To substantiate the distorted ideology argument, much work has been undertaken to assess the attitude of foot-soldiers. Surveys of fighters indicated that combatants shared a single preoccupation, education, and that the war was fuelled more by social factors than the lure of diamonds.[53] There are 'remarkably consistent' data with 'opposed parties (villagers, RUF cadres and [other] fighters …) agreeing on the significance of a combination of poverty and injustice, especially affecting youth'.[54] Of course, these rather singular readings and, from the combatants' point of view, self-justifying assertions do not sit easily with the conflict evidence as related above.

However, despite a common perception that forced conscription was the primary recruitment method of the RUF, some have argued that a reassessment is needed. First, aside from the very young children, of which there were a sizeable number, it is suggested that many joined more or less voluntarily and stayed for economic, educational and socio-political reasons.[55] If it was not entirely voluntary, some may have joined after any other potential occupation had been taken away, or at least when there was no loyalty to central or local government which might have held someone back from joining or receiving protection from an armed opposition. In Mozambique, research has shown that the meaning of 'kidnapped' or 'captured' appears to vary—there were those who 'didn't bother to run away' and still others who 'arranged to be captured'.[56] These were opportunities to fight back against the perfidious authorities, and/or to escape the frustrations and despair of daily life. There were also careers in the RUF awaiting some: Gibril Massaquoi, for example, a teacher in Pujehun District who was abducted by the RUF in 1991 and, albeit with only limited education, rose swiftly in the ranks of the military and then political wings. Pujehun was the site of the Ndorbgowusui revolt in 1983 and was fertile ground for RUF recruiting. Equally, there were many, such as the illicit miners or 'san-san boys', who could see an opportunity when it presented itself. This remains, though, a controversial but at the same time compelling argument, which is not necessarily at odds with the lumpen thesis. Both theses suggest there were considerable grievances at play and that some sort of socio-political motivation existed even if it was ultimately co-opted at some stage by one power structure or another.

More in line with the latter 'ideological' strand of thinking, but again not necessarily contradicting the former lumpen ideas, is the notion that rural preoccupations, rather than urban, were a more significant driver of the conflict. There was indeed a considerable rural presence, which built up in the RUF and whose rural grievances must also be considered when examining the motivations of the foot-soldiers of the RUF.[57] Following on from the notion of some sort of RUF ideology, the RUF was unable to export its egalitarian ideals from its camps to the rural population of central Sierra Leone, but not because RUF fighters were unknowns in the area. It failed because 'it sought—in a spirit of revenge—to obliterate the communities from which its cadres had been excluded'.[58] The RUF's cause was 'vengeful egalitarianism' against the abuses of chiefly patrimonialism.[59] Young fighters were seeking to 'overturn' a lineage-based social order.[60]

Chiefly abuses are central to this argument. The local authority of the chief remained powerful over many aspects of life and in some cases could be of an exclusionary nature.[61] Land and property rights dating back to colonial times are conferred by chiefdom citizenship, which in turn is to some extent controlled by the chief. Marriage presented a further area of contention, as local elites monopolised the market and made excessive claims for 'woman damage', when young men interfered with their wives.[62] Chiefly control over local judicial processes completes the picture. As patronage dried up in a state driven simultaneously by APC and IMF imperatives, it was the youth and itinerant workers without chieftaincy citizenship who could most easily be excluded, downgraded or victimised. No surprise that the riots of 1955–56 occurred or that it was some of these people who joined or were 'recruited' in the countryside by the RUF, the SLA and other factions. Education, employment and the neo-patrimonial forces of the state no longer served to fill that gap. Chiefs newly created by the APC are held up as particularly abusive.[63] There are some who see the influence of sometimes impoverished chiefs as exaggerated or emerging from data that rely too heavily on self-serving evidence given by ex-combatants seeking justifications or local communities seeking development aid.[64] Indeed, it is a mixed picture which varies from region to region and chieftaincy to chieftaincy. During the course of the war, some chiefs were killed, others were replaced by RUF 'chiefs' and many more maintained a presence off and on.[65]

However, in many ways rural grievances stand alongside those of a more urban nature, the end result often being some sort of amalgamation of the two within all of the factions. There is one clear connection where youth from whatever background made their way to the diamond fields and found themselves once more in precarious situations and once more, or for the first time, under chiefly rule. This is somewhat of a blurring of the urban-rural gap, although there are distinctive rural and urban issues even if they become conflated. The gap may be better seen as elite-non-elite or generational. From wherever they came, youths in the RUF have been described as displaying 'a fundamental rejection of Sierra Leone's political structures'.[66] Indeed, a general crisis of youth is an often heard term, although once again this is not the whole answer and it is a notion that needs substantial disaggregating.[67]

An interesting juxtaposition to the rural grievance argument is the case of the 'self-defence' militias that grew from late 1992 onwards. The first of these militias, the Tamaboros and the Kamajors, emerged amongst the Korankos of Koinadugu District in the far north and the

Mendes in Southern Sierra Leone respectively. These units were mostly formed by local chiefs who had maintained their authority, such as Sam Hinga Norman. Hinga Norman had been the arresting officer for Brigadier Lansana in Sierra Leone's first coup in 1967 and subsequently went into exile in Liberia when Stevens returned. He became a Mende chief in Bo District after the NPRC came to power.[68] Hinga Norman then went on to play a large part in the conflict and within the SLPP before being indicted by the SLSC and dying in custody in February 2007. One might have thought he would be a suitable recruit for the RUF, being anti-APC and a Mende, residing in Liberia in the early 1990s, and allegedly sharing a prison cell with Sankoh in the 1970s.[69] Instead, on returning to become chief, he began the formation of a Kamajor militia unit in 1994 in response to attacks by the rejuvenated RUF and by SLA soldiers, both interested in diamonds in the area. The RUF had re-emerged from the forest shortly after the NPRC coup and shocked the country by taking its main diamond town, Koidu in Kono District, in October 1992. The front, if it may be called that, then shifted back and forth, the SLA retaking and once more losing Koidu through 1992 and 1993. By 1994, the RUF was threatening the city of Bo and the main Sierra Leonean highways, began sorties into the North and commenced the taking of foreign hostages.

The Kamajors were a response to this encroachment in the South and were the most successful of the militias. They were based on the myths of 'traditional' hunters' guilds and employed locally feared psychological weapons and protective charms.[70] The spiritual underpinnings of the conflict, where the violence is seen as inextricably linked to the spirit world, show some similarities to Liberia but the degradation and bastardisation of the Poro secret societies and the consumption of human organs were not as marked.[71] It was not, however, just the Kamajors who considered spiritual elements important: all forces were concerned with charms and 'witchcraft' or *juju*—spiritual power associated with 'traditional' beliefs and used with both good and ill intentions—as a means of increasing combat readiness. Indeed, provided the *juju* was strong enough and the process enacted properly, it was a widespread belief that even enemy bullets would lose their effectiveness. It was, though, the Kamajors who kept the 'use of magic at the core of their movement' and used it as a source of military tactics.[72] In a similar vein, a sociocultural explanation of the Sierra Leone conflict focuses on ambiguity and concealment in the

Mende world and how these traits are the result of past violence.[73] Within the RUF, observations have been made of the use of secret knowledge to create social alternatives.[74]

The successful mobilisation and coherency of the Kamajors clearly built on notions of common identity and spirituality, but one might also see the Kamajors and the RUF as thoroughly modern phenomena. While the Kamajors developed from localised ideas of self-defence, there were also interests in diamond mining,[75] child recruitment and attacks on civilians and abuse of captives which increased as their role expanded[76]—the TRC estimated that 6 per cent of all atrocities were committed by militias, predominantly by Kamajors.[77] They were also politically aligned with and favoured by the SLPP after the party won the elections in 1996. Indeed, the use of magic in the war in Sierra Leone has been described as 'appropriate and logical' given that the spiritual realm is widely seen as a 'resource for activity that requires significant power'.[78] It is also unclear to what extent contemporary violence in Sierra Leone can be rooted in the history of certain ethnic groups. Kamajor organisation, however, was so effective as to then be replicated in other regions, producing the Donsos amongst the Konos in the East, and the Gbethis and the Kapras, comprising mainly Temnes, in the North. Important to note, most were built on chiefly and 'traditional' authority.

It would appear that ethnicity played a major role in the conflict. In fact, it was just another factor amongst many and did not play nearly the role it played, for instance, in Liberia. Clearly, the RUF began its days as an anti-APC movement of the South and East, the army was predominantly Northern and the militias identified by ethnicity. However, Sankoh was a Northerner, the Kamajors were set up to counter both the RUF and SLA, and the NPRC military regime was infiltrated by SLPP politicians, like Benjamin, and headed after the January 1996 palace coup by a Mende officer, Maada Bio. The Kamajors predictably sided with the SLPP, but the sobel phenomena and the 1997–98 military junta were strange alliances of army and RUF. It appears that ethnicity mattered, just as it does in politics, but it had many other competing nodes of motivation in the conflict. This rather muddies the waters in the New Wars thesis which emphasises a post-Cold War shift towards identity as a cause of conflict.[79] As has been noted, if ethnicity is such a ready tool for mobilisation, then some African rebels have proved remarkably poor at using their 'ethnic capital'.[80] Importantly for the future, there were never any aims to secede on ethnic or any other grounds. Finally, given the religious tolerance in Sierra Leone, it is no surprise that Islam and Christianity played very little part in the war.

Such were the Kamajors' knowledge of local terrain and their coherence as a fighting force that in 1995–96 the RUF was once more driven back. The Kamajors were considerably aided in this reversal by Strasser's resort to the South African mercenary firm Executive Outcomes, following the March 1995 RUF capture of Mile 38, an important highway town close to the capital. In exchange for future mining concessions, Executive Outcomes arrived with around 300 men, helicopters, troop transporters, considerable weaponry and experience in fighting for both UNITA and MPLA in Angola. In alliance with the SLA and Kamajors, to whom training was also given, and a few Nigerian and Guinean troops already in the country, the war was swiftly brought under control. So much so that elections could be held in February and March 1996 and the peace negotiations started under Maada Bio carried through to the Abidjan Accord signed by Sankoh and the new President Kabbah in November.

There is not one cause of the Sierra Leonean civil war. Indeed, considering the country's compact geography and relatively even population distribution, one might conclude that it is not a prime candidate for conflict, like, for example, Congo/Zaïre.[81] It is quite clear that there were considerable mercenary intentions within the leadership and foot-soldiers of the RUF and other factions—intentions which probably escalated over time—and terrible violence against civilians. There was little official rebel ideology, a poor national army and considerable outside interference. However, a conclusion centred on these factors would ignore a multitude of other reasons why a singularly unconvincing rebel leadership could maintain a rebellion over a decade. Mostly young fighters had national and most likely overwhelmingly local reasons for joining, or not leaving, one of the factions. These might hinge on their experience of marginalisation and brutalisation in urban slums or the diamond areas, at the hands of some gerontocratic chiefs, or with a peculiarly distanced, venal and patronising elite. There was indeed a crisis of the neopatrimonial system and it underpinned much of the resentment, anger and even mercenarism. While colonialism had established the political environment, the APC had contributed considerably to the crisis. Joining a faction gave outlet to frustrations, a way out of an unsatisfactory position in society and the means to redress one's situation. The war itself created further reasons to fight. Importantly, though, secessionism and religion were never motives and the role of ethnicity was blurred and not nearly as significant or deep-seated as in Liberia or Rwanda. There was a lull in the war in 1996 and Sierra Leone returned briefly to more familiar preoccupations, but for all the reasons given above, this was not to be the end.

7

THE ESCALATION AND ENDING
OF THE CIVIL WAR, 1996–2002

There were no illusions that the war was over in 1996, even if there were a few optimistic signs. The country indeed returned briefly to more familiar activities with the elections. There even followed a peace deal. The war, however, shifted once more with another military coup in 1997 and the subsequent junta, a re-location northwards and a highly destructive and horrific invasion of the capital, whilst continuing its overall patterns of violence. Novel in the war were the interventions of states and international organisations, in particular Nigeria, Britain, Guinea and the UN. Indeed these interventions were not only quite extraordinary and sometimes forerunners of their kind in this post-Cold War environment, they also became highly significant in the ebb and flow and the ultimate conclusion of the war.

Strasser instigated the democratisation process, but once it began to emerge that his intention was to lower the age-limits in the constitution and stand, he was removed by Maada Bio. Despite clear misgivings in the military, some of whom were accused of attacking the Interim National Election Commission (INEC) offices in Freetown and the home of its chairman, the former UN Under Secretary General James Jonah, Maada Bio stuck to the task. Notwithstanding this perseverance, and given his instigation of talks with the RUF, it is still not clear to which camp in the military he belonged. However, he was later able to reap some reward as the SLPP presidential candidate in 2012 and 2018 by playing down negative aspects of the coup and the military regime and positioning himself as both a democrat and a bringer of peace. A National Consultative Council (NCC), with good civilian representation, twice agreed—either side of the coup—to forge ahead with the elections. Although the RUF was involved at this time in peace talks, there was certainly no peace accord or RUF political involvement, and there was continuing, albeit lower-level, violence in the countryside. The RUF claimed effective control over parts of the East; any travel by road remained hazardous outside the Western Area; and a November UN estimate revealed that up to 50 per cent of the population, some two million people, had been displaced. Some inside and outside the military were concerned to have 'peace before elections', but the NCC voted with a large majority to go ahead, as planned, on 26 February.

The elections were unsurprisingly flawed, but they did reach some sort of a conclusion.[1] Beyond the assaults on INEC, Kabbah's home was also attacked and the editor of the *For di People* newspaper and later APC Minister of Employment, Youth and Sports, Paul Kamara, was shot and injured. The RUF sent a severe symbolic warning of the dangers of voting by amputating hands, and on the first-round Election Day the rebels attacked Bo and centres close to Makeni and Kenema. Security in the South and East was provided by Kamajors, worrying in itself given the partiality of the militia. In party political terms, however, these polls were more peaceful than Sierra Leone had experienced for a long time. Campaigning was limited to the West, the North and urban centres and pockets of the South and East. For the first time, and largely as a result of the security situation, Sierra Leonean elections were arranged on a proportional representation lists system, although there were separate polls for President and Parliament. A little less than half of the 1.6million registered voters turned out to vote in the first round, a figure, however, higher than expected given the security difficulties.

In an unusual move, the SLPP did not choose a Mende leader. Kabbah was a retired high-ranking UNDP official but he was also a Mandingo who could claim affiliations to the East through his birth in Kailahun District, to the North as he spent his early years in Kambia District, and to the South through his Mende mother and his Sherbro wife, Patricia. He even went to secondary school in Freetown. In ethno-regional terms, Kabbah had almost everything. He was in addition a Muslim. In direct opposition to Kabbah was the returning Northern and Christian veteran, John Karefa-Smart. Although religion is not a significant line of political cleavage in Sierra Leone, if elected Kabbah would be the first Muslim President.[2] On the other hand, both his wife and his running mate, Albert Joe Demby, were Christians. Kabbah had also been a high-ranking civil servant in the SLPP-era Ministry of Trade and Industry. However, the 1967 Beoku-Betts report under the NRC military government described Kabbah as lacking the integrity to hold high office, a point gleefully raised by his opponents. In his autobiography, Kabbah noted that it was a case of mistaken identity.[3] He returned to Sierra Leone in 1992 and became head of the National Advisory Council within the NPRC in 1994. One might also say that he did not have a particularly charismatic touch for a presidential candidate, especially when compared with someone like Stevens.

The first presidential round gave Kabbah 36 per cent and Karefa-Smart 23 per cent, neither approaching the 55 per cent winning lead, and so there had to be a second round run-off between just these two contenders. In almost a mirror image of the presidential voting patterns, the SLPP took 27 of the 68 unreserved parliamentary seats while Karefa-Smart's United National People's Party (UNPP) took 17 seats and Thaimu Bangura's People's Democratic Party (PDP) took 12. Bangura was a former one-party state era APC minister. The usual 12 seats were reserved for the election of Paramount Chiefs. Both the army-backed National Unity Party (NUP) led by the NPRC's Finance Minister John Karimu and the discredited APC under Eddie Turay, later to become Ambassador to the UK under the late-2000s APC government, just crept over the 5 per cent threshold to gain a handful of seats. The Northern vote had shifted to the UNPP and PDP. Karefa-Smart and Bangura, at the head of essentially personalist party vehicles with no organisational history, won 57 and 43 per cent of their total votes in the first round in the Northern Province. The Western Area was the most keenly fought, with the SLPP emerging only marginally ahead. However, it was the failure of either Northern politician to pick up a winning majority in the West, and the division of Northern votes between the UNPP, the PDP and the APC, that did significant damage. The three Northern-based parties split 77 per cent of the Northern vote between them. On the other hand, the SLPP was the sturdiest party and, despite a Mandingo leader, gained 80 per cent in the Southern Province and around 50 per cent in the Eastern Province in both first-round elections.

In the presidential run-off, in a move that mostly reflected political opportunism rather than ethno-regionalism, Bangura, Turay, Karimu and the leader of the Kono party, Abu Aiah Koroma, threw their weight behind Kabbah. Although Karefa-Smart managed 78 per cent in the North, he could not beat Kabbah in the West and Kabbah took 92 per cent in the South and 90 per cent in the East. An increased turnout of around 65 per cent in an improved security situation apparently gave Kabbah victory. However, in a scenario that was to continue to plague subsequent elections, turnouts were over 100 per cent in Kenema and Kailahun Districts and 99.6 per cent in Bo District. There were obvious problems of displaced people but these figures were of course highly suspect. It was then agreed by the candidates and electoral officials that all ballots above the number of registered voters for a district were to be subtracted from Kabbah's total, as each of these districts produced a Kabbah win, and INEC thus deducted 70,000 votes from Kabbah.[4] The SLPP leader still won with 59 per cent of the vote.

Although Karefa-Smart considered that 'very serious violations of the law and the Constitution' had taken place, he announced that he had acceded to Kabbah's victory in the national interest. Notwithstanding the considerable irregularities, Kabbah had won largely through a united Southern and Eastern second round vote compared with a fractured Northern vote. Karefa-Smart's UNPP then proceeded to rip itself apart while Kabbah formed a coalition government and appointed supportive non-SLPP politicians to the cabinet. Bangura became Finance Minister and the former APC-era Attorney General and National Diamond Mining Company Managing Director Abu Koroma took up the post of Minister for Parliamentary and Political Affairs. After the elections, Jonah became Sierra Leone's Ambassador to the UN, and then returned home to be SLPP Finance Minister from 1998 to 2001.

It is indeed interesting that Sierra Leone had returned to business as usual in the electoral period. Ethno-regionalism, frail alliances, rigging and a population very keen to participate in elections despite the dangers had all reappeared in the very unfamiliar surroundings of war. Equally, the political methods of the ensuing Kabbah government, including corruption, cronyism and harassment of opposition voices, did not strike many as significantly greater than what happened under previous regimes. However, the war was not resolved. The final major war-related event of 1996 was the signing of the Abidjan Accord in November in the capital of Côte d'Ivoire. Many are sceptical about Sankoh's commitment to this process and see his strategy of buying time for his rebellion in retreat as similar to that used on many occasions by his mentor, Taylor, in Liberia. His duplicity in securing more funds from Libya, the opinions of some who attended the Abidjan talks on behalf of the RUF and then attempted an internal coup, and the lack of interest exhibited by the three accord guarantors, the OAU, the UN and the Commonwealth, are put forward as evidence of Sankoh's real intentions.[5] Others, however, were convinced that something positive could come out of the process.[6] Remarkably, and in an action for which it would be much criticised later, the British NGO International Alert answered an RUF plea and went into the bush in 1995–96 to provide communication channels, assistance in the articulation of demands, and workshops, advice and documentation.[7]

After provisional ceasefires, agreed by the RUF in March with the NPRC and in April with the SLPP government, had reduced the violence, the Accord stipulated a total cessation of hostilities. It went on to include an amnesty for all belligerents, a demobilisation process for many combatants including part of the SLA, the departure of Executive Outcomes after the deployment of an international monitoring group, a trust fund to assist in the RUF's transformation from military force to political party, a commission for the consolidation of peace, and a social forum. It did not specify any governmental positions for the RUF, probably a reflection of its weakness at this point. Little of the agreement was, however, to transpire and sceptics insist that the departure of the mercenaries was the overriding RUF goal.[8]

However, in the immediate aftermath of Abidjan, there was much about which to be positive. Violence was at a comparatively low level. A deal for half a billion US dollars worth of infrastructure reconstruction had been agreed with international multilateral and bilateral donors. There did not appear to be indications that the coup of 25 May 1997 was about to happen. It was however the nature of the residual violence, mostly skirmishes between Kamajors and the SLA, that held many of the warning signs. Most of the provisions in the Accord were not being implemented, except that in February 1997, under budgetary pressure from the IMF and in the mistaken expectation of the imminent arrival of a UN force, the contract with Executive Outcomes was terminated. The Disarmament, Demobilisation and Reintegration (DDR) programme had barely begun, but importantly there were no provisions at all for the Kamajors in the programme. Hinga Norman, by this point the effective leader of the Kamajors and a powerful player, was appointed

Deputy Defence Minister—Kabbah as President was Defence Minister—and *de facto* head of the amalgamated and now semi-institutionalised Civil Defence Forces (CDF). Vice President Demby had also played a part in the Kamajors.[9] The SLPP had no trust in the SLA and hence the CDF became its security force and was rearmed rather than disarmed. With the threat of DDR hanging over the SLA, relations between the CDF and the SLA slowly worsened.

Reasons for the May 1997 coup are then posited on several factors. First, the small band of soldiers who attacked Pademba Road Prison, released Johnny Paul Koroma and others, armed the freed convicts and took State House gave as their official justification the preferential treatment of an ethnic militia. Imprisoned for coup-plotting in late 1996 but now appointed as coup leader, Koroma asserted that the Kamajors now outnumbered the SLA, and may have seen this development with a sense of shame.[10] A second reason emphasises the junior ranks of the coup-plotters in the coup itself and in the ensuing Armed Forces Ruling Council (AFRC) and how these soldiers had been cut out of the patronage system by the higher ranks.[11] The week-long mayhem following the coup, including looting in what was termed 'Operation Pay Yourself', many deaths and the destruction of the Treasury Building, might be explained by this exclusion. A third reason, which emerged in a critique of the second, assumes that any institutional hierarchy had long since broken down in the SLA and that the coup was another symptom of the sobel phenomenon.[12]

All three explanations most likely hold some weight. The event was probably triggered by some forced retirements of officers in September 1996, by the announcement of a cutback in subsidised rice for the army and by two serious clashes between the SLA and CDF immediately prior to the coup, one in Kenema and one, very importantly, in the Tongo Fields diamond mines. The sobel explanation does, however, have extra value when it is considered that one of the first actions of the AFRC was to invite the RUF to share power. 'Maskita' Bockarie led the RUF to Freetown to become part of the 'People's Army' and Sankoh, in detention in Nigeria for importing guns on his person, was declared AFRC Vice Chairman and Vice President of Sierra Leone in absentia. The AFRC proceeded to rule arbitrarily and with terror. However, just as the 1967 and 1992 military coups had found some support amongst SLPP politicians, political enemies of the SLPP were accused of backing the

AFRC.[13] Other civilians took up governmental positions: for example Alimamy Pallo Bangura, former NPRC Ambassador to the UN and later the presidential candidate for the RUF in 2002, took up the post of Secretary of State for Foreign Affairs; and Victor Foh, later to become Vice President in the APC government, became Chairman of the Board of the national telecommunications company, SIERRATEL.

The AFRC were faced with considerably more and diverse enemies. Outside actors had arrived before when Executive Outcomes were deployed, but the first of several more long-lasting interventions came in the guise of the Nigerians. The small Nigerian force which had arrived beforehand under a bilateral agreement became a much larger ECO-MOG deployment and remained in control of the international airport at Lungi and in other sectors. Ostensibly, ECOMOG was an innovative regional variation on international peacekeeping which was becoming considerably more frequent in the post-Cold War world. In a world dominated by one superpower and a discourse that was beginning to place greater emphasis on 'humanitarian intervention' than on national sovereignty, successive ECOMOG deployments in Liberia, Sierra Leone and Guinea-Bissau were largely unprecedented cases of African states intervening in other African states particularly on the basis of peacekeeping. However, it was clear from the start that ECOMOG and the Nigerian President Sani Abacha had taken a stance against the AFRC and RUF and that this was not to be peacekeeping as such.

The Nigerian position in Sierra Leone is interesting in that it was a decidedly non-democratic military regime coming to the aid of a democratically-elected government against a military junta. The first deployment of ECOMOG in Liberia in 1990 was predominantly Nigerian and was effectively sent to prop up Doe's encircled Liberian government against Taylor's incursion. It was driven by notions of Nigeria as a regional hegemon and self-appointed policeman and by fears of the precedent of rebels being allowed to take power. It was also underscored by the linguistic divide in West Africa. The Francophone states of Burkina Faso, Côte d'Ivoire and, more or less, France supported Taylor's invasion into an Anglophone country, while Anglophone troops from Nigeria and Ghana comprised ECOMOG. There are clear echoes of the Nigerian civil war in the late 1960s when some Francophone states supported the Biafran secession, which would have broken up the Nigerian behemoth, and the UK backed the Federal Government. Indeed, it might also be noted that in countries with politicised militaries such as Nigeria, it is a good idea to have an outlet for armed forces' activity—be it military or economic—and to keep some of them as far away from power as possible. ECOMOG rapidly became peace-enforcers and essentially took sides in the conflict, but fought hard whilst also engaging in looting and earning the moniker 'Every Car Or Moveable Object Gone'. Abacha was only just beginning to withdraw the troops from Liberia, when they were required in larger numbers in Sierra Leone. Reasons for deployment across the border would have been similar to those in Liberia except for the additional need for Abacha to divert international criticism of his regime. In both cases—and notwithstanding the considerable effort, loss of life and eventual outcomes—peacekeeping or rescuing democracy was not really the issue.

Petrol and arms sanctions were placed on the junta by the UN and ECOWAS, the Nigerian navy blocked access to Freetown harbour and Nigerian jets somewhat recklessly bombed military locations in Freetown. The Kamajors, abolished by Koroma and then targeted by the AFRC, were of course also in opposition.[14] Hinga Norman, one of the very few deposed ministers to remain in the country, stayed to organise the CDF. On the evidence of this and other actions, his later SLSC indictment was seen by many Sierra Leoneans and others including the British High Commissioner of the time, Peter Penfold, who worked with him, as unjust.[15] Brave civilian resistance came in demonstrations by a consortium of civil society groups including the Sierra Leone Association of Journalists (SLAJ), whose members had been targeted by the junta, and the Women's Movement for Peace, led by Zainab Bangura, whose political role was set to increase significantly in both societal and governmental spheres.

Finally, strong support for Kabbah and the tabling of sanctions against the junta at the UN came from another new and highly significant international angle: the new Labour government of Tony Blair in the UK.[16] Kabbah appeared at the UN and the Commonwealth Heads of Government Meeting in Edinburgh and the UK supported the government-in-exile in Conakry. The Sandline affair, however, raised the bar. Despite a subsequent British parliamentary inquiry into UN sanctions-busting by the British mercenary firm Sandline and the Canadian mining company DiamondWorks, it was still not clear exactly who was involved in the import of arms and logistics. It also appeared that many, if not all, of the shipments arrived too late or were intended not for the Sierra Leonean CDF but for the Nigerians.[17] However, despite the Legg Report's conclusion that arms had been shipped against UN sanctions which the UK had proposed and that the Foreign and Commonwealth Office was briefed, Penfold was pinpointed as the coordinator. He was retired from service, the blame at the British end effectively being placed squarely on his shoulders. Conversely, in Sierra Leone he was treated as a hero by many and subsequently made a Paramount Chief.[18]

The level of British support in 1997–98 and the subsequent deployment of British troops in 2000 and intense post-war support were, and are, indeed extraordinary. Unlike in World War II when the Freetown deepwater port was essential for shipping, or even, to a lesser extent, in the Cold War when each African country was a gain for East or West, Sierra Leone in the post-Cold War era is not of global strategic importance. Equally, Sierra Leone is not in Britain's backyard as it is in Nigeria's. It is also hard to see where any significant material interests to Britain lay in what were quite expensive and to some extent politically dangerous projects. Reasons for this remarkable involvement then range from the personal through to the political, although somewhat different from the political motives of Nigeria. Much advertised, the personal commitment appears to come from Blair's connection through his father's time as a teacher in Sierra Leone.

Politically, several reasons coalesce. First, the 'ethical foreign policy' of Britain's Foreign Secretary in 1997–8, Robin Cook, fitted with the idea of assisting a democratically elected government, particularly in a former British colony and especially in this post-Cold War climate. Second, there were the stirrings of a more belligerent notion of 'liberal peace', which developed from Sierra Leone and Kosovo to Afghanistan and Iraq, all countries where British forces took part in action. One could argue a crucial role for Sierra Leone in the ramping up of British foreign policy, particularly as both Kosovo and Sierra Leone were portrayed as successful interventions on which future intercessions were partly modelled. Like Nigeria's, Britain's intervention in Sierra Leone was of a decidedly partisan nature. Third, and the closest to a Nigerian view, is the idea that Britain has a significant role to play in global affairs, arising from either the legacy of its imperial past, its military efficiency or its practical need to justify its seat on the UN Security Council, requiring action of this sort. Not long before, in 1993, the then Conservative government's Foreign Secretary, Douglas Hurd, had declared that Britain should continue to 'punch above its weight' in the world. Finally, it has also been noted that 'doing good' in Africa survived or re-emerged as an important strain of thinking or perhaps even an emotional feeling, which even in more straightened times still arguably runs through all major British political parties. In particular under Blair, Africa represented a safe area of policy that appeared to transcend politics and on which the vast majority of politicians and the public could largely, if rather superficially, agree.[19] On the African side, both the British and Nigerian interventions were vital for the Kabbah government. Indeed, after the war, Blair became the second British Paramount Chief in Sierra Leone.

As the Conakry Peace Plan negotiated by ECOWAS in October 1997 began to founder, it was not just Kabbah and British elements who were turning to the idea of removal of the AFRC by force. CDF forces engaged with the 'People's Army' up-country and, in alliance with ECOMOG, now numbering 10,000 Nigerian soldiers under General Maxwell Khobe, struck Freetown and quickly took the city in early February 1998. Koroma, Bockarie and the junta soldiers fled eastwards and northwards, bringing the war and the abuses to locations in the North which had hitherto been relatively quiet. However, Kabbah and his government returned on 10 March and ECOMOG rapidly secured the bulk of the country including the diamond areas. Khobe became another foreign hero and was subsequently made Chief of Defence Staff of what was left of the SLA, while Abacha gave his name to a commercial street in the East End of the capital.

Despite this victory, the war was not finished and there would be one more catastrophic event before the beginning of the end. In Freetown, the SLPP government continued where it had left off, Kabbah seemingly unable or unwilling to keep his officials in check. In addition, on the watch of the SLPP Attorney General and future Vice President Solomon Berewa, 24 soldiers were court-martialled and executed for treason, simultaneously bringing condemnations from abroad and aggravating the difficulties with the SLA. Others, including Sankoh who had been handed over by the Nigerians, the former APC Acting Mayor of Freetown Nancy Steele, the journalist (and later APC Minister of Information) Ibrahim Ben Kargbo, Foh, and several AFRC ministers were sentenced to death and awaited their appeals. Momoh was found not guilty of treason and escaped the death penalty but was found guilty on two charges of conspiracy. In the countryside, rebel forces regrouped under Bockarie in the East and the NPRC and AFRC veteran Solomon Musa in the North. Koroma appears to have been rendered powerless at this point and held by the RUF in Kailahun District. The two groups proceeded to take back Koidu, then Makeni, then Waterloo from the ECOMOG forces now bolstered to 15,000. It appears that Nigerians had joined in the mercenary activities and were digging for diamonds and sometimes selling arms to their opponents.[20] The attack on Koidu captured a large arms stockpile but it was also reported that Ukrainian and South African mercenaries were re-arming and training AFRC and RUF forces, which had in any case left Freetown with considerable amounts of weaponry.[21]

The rebel attack on Freetown on 6 January 1999 could not then have been a complete surprise. Not only were rebel forces moving closer and closer to the capital, striking nearby Hastings in the new year, but Bockarie had already announced 'Operation No Living Thing' on the BBC. This became the moniker of the invasion and the destruction and killing in the ensuing two week battle for Freetown lived up to the name.[22] Starting with attacks before dawn on the East End, the amalgamation of AFRC and RUF forces proceeded to central Freetown and, once more, to Pademba Road Prison, where many had been kept after the demise of the junta.[23] Sankoh, perhaps one of the key RUF reasons for the attack, had been transferred from Pademba Road Prison just prior to the invasion. Most important, on their way through the city, the rebels used various familiar means to inflict terror on the citizens including executions, rape, amputations, the burning of households in their homes, human shields and abductions. To some extent the killings and destruction were targeted at the wealthy, the politically aligned, the educated, police officers and stations, judges, journalists and Nigerians. Much, though, appeared to be arbitrary violence. In their ultimately successful attempt to hold on to West Freetown and fight back across the capital, ECOMOG troops were also involved in many summary executions.

The operation finally brought Sierra Leone to significant world attention. This was because the scale of the extreme violence in a crowded capital eclipsed all previous violence in Sierra Leone, and as such it was also portrayed as yet another example of African savagery. It has been referred to as 'a kind of madness with no other method than to experience a nihilistic frisson'.[24] Indeed, this is the part of the war which is the most diffi-cult to explain in any other terms than a lunatic aberration. As a student noted at the time, if their operation aims to kill every living thing, what are they then going to rule?[25] Overt political ambitions, such as seizing state power or terror as a political weapon, were in evidence but these factors, allied to the mercenary intentions and the feared and drugged child soldiers who knew little other than the RUF, still do not explain the level of indiscriminate violence, much taking place in the impover-ished East End of Freetown. We need to return to the psychological notions of fear, 'shame' and 'shamelessness' on the one hand and revenge and anger towards a system that had betrayed people on the other.[26] Even further, there is the very plausible notion of inculcated 'disgust', wherein perpetrators regarded civilians as dehumanised, as being of less worth or worthless.[27] However bizarre, it has been noted that attackers had a sense that the violence was justified and a feeling of self-righteousness based on previous experiences before and during the war.[28] The world before-hand was grotesquely corrupt, unjust and humiliating to them and, from the confines of their new systematically brutalising enclave world where extreme violence was often rewarded and the dehumanisation of others routine, this was the response.[29]

After two weeks of intense street-fighting, ECOMOG drove the attackers out of Freetown, from where they returned up-country. Kab-bah and his government returned from a second period in exile in Guinea. International efforts switched to a negotiated peace deal. The Bill Clin-ton administration in the US, in particular, but also the British and Nige-rians, were keen for a deal in the aftermath of 6 January and put pressure on a reluctant Kabbah to acquiesce. Clinton sent the Reverend Jesse Jack-son as his high profile envoy. Indeed, despite or perhaps because of Tay-lor's closeness to France, including his visit to Paris in 1998, the US (sometimes in opposition to France in Africa) had begun to court Tay-lor, particularly through Jackson and the Black Congressional Caucus leader Donald Payne, and the pressure for negotiation can also be seen through this lens.[30] Kabbah agreed to the negotiations as he remained desperate for outside help and the Nigerians wanted to pull out. Abacha had died in office in June 1998 and the new military leader, Abdulsalam Abubakar, handed over to an elected president, Olusegun Obasanjo, in May 1999. Stretched finances, the loss of over 800 Nigerian lives, the allegations of smuggling, the unwillingness of other—particularly Francophone—states to contribute, but perhaps most important of all, the imperatives of a democratically elected government more sensitive to public opinion created a poor environment in Nigeria for the continuation of the ECOMOG operation. Kabbah thus needed the UN. Sankoh, still on appeal against a treason conviction, was released to attend the negotiations. Strangely, the former AFRC soldiers were not invited. The result, however, was the Lomé Accord signed in Togo in July 1999.

The Accord included an immediate cessation of hostilities and an amnesty, although an attached UN disclaimer interpreted the amnesty as not applying to war crimes and crimes against humanity. Crucially, the Accord also stipulated power-sharing in a coalition government, with Sankoh becoming Vice President and simultaneously heading the commission overseeing gold and diamond production. Seven other ministerial posts went to the RUF. The Accord brought in more familiar international actors in the form of UN peacekeepers from India, Guinea, Kenya and Zambia as part of the new UN Mission in Sierra Leone (UNAMSIL) under the Indian Major General Vijay Jetley in order to gradually replace ECOMOG troops. A number of Nigerians swapped hats to join UNAMSIL.

The deal was seen as disgraceful in some circles. First, it placed trust in Sankoh once again and many saw his posts, particularly that concerning diamonds, as a recipe for a return to war. Few trusted him not to use this time to rearm and even fewer saw him or the ministers on his side as serious political players or peacemakers. Seen in even the most generous light, Jackson's comparison of Sankoh with Nelson Mandela was at best ill-informed. Second, the amnesty was viewed as scandalous after 6 January and impunity as a serious flaw. Finally, comparisons were made with events elsewhere, particularly with the trials of perpetrators in the former Yugoslavia and the hunt for Slobodan Milošević and Ratko Mladić.[31] Conveniently ignoring the International Criminal Tribunal for Rwanda, some saw racism at work in the international system and others argued that some countries were just geopolitically more important. These arguments hold some weight if commitment to international peacekeeping is the subject, but are less convincing where peace deals and war crimes trials are concerned. Instead, one might see the Lomé Accord as the last gasp of the 1990s inclusive peace deals before war crimes trials became the number one priority in global discourse. These themes will be revisited in the next chapter.

As many predicted, the Accord quickly ran into trouble. Sankoh and the RUF were not able to politically benefit from the governmental opportunity—those who might have used this period to consolidate had long since been removed. The virulent strain of anti-elitism was well-developed in the RUF. Instead, Sankoh used his position to cut informal diamond deals and proved once again duplicitous in his actions. In effect, he was not able to accept the exchange of the physical hold over the diamond areas for the entitlement to market the gems.[32] The SLPP also played a part with its reluctance to let the RUF take up the allotted positions. With disarmament slow and US funding blocked by Republican Party initiatives against the Clinton administration, the RUF attacked and seized the weapons of Kenyan peacekeepers just after they arrived.[33] In May 2000, just as ECOMOG was completing its withdrawal, the rebels took a similar course of action which would have serious repercussions. In Makeni, 500 Zambian peacekeepers were taken hostage and their uniforms and arms used in attacks on other UNAMSIL units. The Zambians only returned to Freetown after a trip to Liberia; Taylor was later to claim in court that this was part of his role in the peace process. UNAMSIL was humiliated and the ructions between Jetley and Khobe were played out in public.[34] At the same time, rumours of an imminent Sankoh coup spread around the capital.

The responses on this occasion were swift. British troops and helicopters arrived in a remarkable unilateral venture which in many ways amplified the efforts of the UK in 1997–98. With a publicised role to evacuate foreign nationals, the mission was in effect designed, despite the absence of a UN mandate, to prop up UNAMSIL and the Kabbah government. The Clinton administration had come round to pro-Kabbah, anti-RUF/Taylor British thinking.[35] In what was dubbed as 'mission creep' the British Army soon became far deeper embroiled. At the same time, crowds rallied by civil society organisations, or in some readings by Kabbah's government, surrounded Sankoh's Freetown house. In the ensuing stand-off, twenty-one civilians were shot dead, the house was ransacked and Sankoh escaped, only to be arrested shortly afterwards and charged with the murder of the demonstrators. After its mauling, the UN seriously reviewed and upgraded the mission. The number of troops was increased rising to over 17,000 by March 2002, equipment was improved and the mission's modus operandi became more aggressive. The Indians withdrew and Jetley was replaced with a more senior officer, the Kenyan Lieutenant General Daniel Opande. Finally, a UN Panel of Experts was set up to investigate the diamond trade in the war and went on to recommend targeted sanctions on the RUF and Liberia, including Taylor, President of Liberia since 1997.

The conflict was mostly over within 12 months of these events but the RUF and a faction of the AFRC, the West Side Boys, both had one more aggressive part to play in the conflict despite the presence of British forces and a revamped UNAMSIL. The interim leadership of the RUF was assumed in Sankoh's absence by a poorly educated former Abidjan street seller, diamond smuggler and battlefield commander from the North, Issa Sesay. In September 2000, Liberian and RUF forces invaded Guinea. A combined force attacked from Kailahun District and Lofa County while the RUF invading from Kambia District reached a third of the way to the Guinean capital, Conakry. The Liberian support for the RUF invasion in 1991 and the attacks on Guinea in 2000 have similar features in that each could be seen as an attempt to topple a hostile regime, in the latter case of President Lansana Conté, and a source of looting. Both were also designed to flush out nascent anti-Taylor rebels. This time it was the Liberians United for Reconciliation and Democracy (LURD) rebels aiming to threaten Taylor's hold on the presidency. After the invasion LURD proceeded to do just that. The Guinean army and air force were, however, to prove a much tougher opponent than the SLA. With backing from the US and UK, the Guineans could deploy helicopter gunships and fighter planes and routed the invaders. Allied with Sierra Leonean Donso militias and LURD fighters, they drove both sets of pro-Taylor forces back over the border, where the Guinean air force bombed camps in Sierra Leone and Liberia.[36]

At around the same time, in August 2000, the West Side Boys captured and held hostage eleven British soldiers in their camp on the Rokel River in the Occra Hills, just outside the Freetown Peninsula. Negotiations progressed falteringly and the rehabilitated Johnny Paul Koroma, in his new role as the post-Lomé Chairman of the Commission for the Consolidation of Peace, distanced himself from the West Side Boys and encouraged loyalist SLA soldiers. British troops had already repulsed RUF attacks on Freetown and Lungi Airport, but sixteen days after the hostage-taking British commandos attacked the West Side Boys camp. Reports noted at least twenty-four rebel deaths plus two hostages killed, one Sierra Leonean and one British. The West Side Boys, who had become a severe irritant to civilian traffic on the main up-country highway and to UNAMSIL in this area, were finished as a going concern. To reinforce the message, Britain doubled its armed forces in Sierra Leone in November and its military prowess was openly displayed in what was advertised as a 'show of strength' by the British Army on beaches in Freetown.

Finally, in March 2001, the UN placed sanctions on Liberia after the Panel of Experts' report named Taylor, despite his protestations, as chief backer of the RUF. The sanctions included a ban on diamond exports, a travel ban on Liberian officials, the grounding of Liberian aircraft and a tightening of the arms embargo. Taylor clearly took this seriously and his response was to distance himself from the RUF. The supply and trade lines had in any case become more hazardous owing to the presence of LURD in Liberian territory adjacent to Kailahun District, but the rapidly diminishing support from Taylor added significantly to the RUF's difficulties.

Weakened by its military defeats and by a variety of more concerted international pressures, and with a seemingly more conciliatory leader in Sesay, the RUF re-entered peace negotiations and began disarmament in earnest in April 2001. Sesay showed a lack of the duplicity which had characterised Sankoh's dealings and seemed serious and influential. Although it was noted by some that he had most likely made his money already and that he had little choice by this time, his eventual indictment and trial by the SLSC seemed to others, including Kabbah, as unfair, or at least sending out the wrong signals elsewhere given his role in the final peacemaking. Remarkably, by January 2002, 72,000 combatants had been registered in the DDR process, of whom 24,000 were RUF and 37,000 were CDF. The UK-led rebuilding of the new Republic of Sierra Leone Armed Forces (RSLAF) was augmented by 2,350 ex-combatants, two-thirds from the RUF and a third from the CDF, who were trained alongside the existing 12,000 troops.[37] A retired British police officer, Keith Biddle, headed the Sierra Leone Police. Despite the continuation of the conflict over the border where Taylor's war against the LURD was intensifying and now drawing in Sierra Leonean fighters under the command of Bockarie, Kabbah could legitimately declare in January 2002 that the war in Sierra Leone was over.

Equally remarkably, it was a partial military solution to a war, a rare ending to a conflict in Africa. The RUF was not in good shape militarily and the party derived from it, the RUFP, proved to be as politically inept as its parent organisation. There was, however, a peace deal and there was the concurrent threat of further violence. If not totally, there were indeed victors in the war, in particular the SLPP, and the ensuing peace reflected this environment. It seems that whatever cause or motivation the RUF fighters had, it ultimately came to nothing for many of them.

The appalling tragedy of the Sierra Leone civil war was built on historical conditions. We should consider the colonial legacy with the accompanying inherited weak state and conservative elite, the co-existence of 'traditional' orders and the 'modern' state, the urban-rural gap, and the concomitant difficulty in establishing accountable, let alone democratic, government. The APC regime then proceeded to exacerbate these structural disconnections and divides. Outside regional and international influences presented at least the triggers. Indeed, we might consider the rebels themselves as a key cause of the outbreak and format of the war. Inevitably all these factors played a part. Despite this being one of the most vicious of African civil wars, none of these factors should be inexplicable, indeed none appeared overnight, and we should always endeavour to trace the historical line of development.

Its final ending, however, owed much to Nigerian, Guinean, British, US and UN action, although much of this was very late. Indeed, one might note the considerable outside involvement in concluding the war and, with a few notable exceptions, the shortage of Sierra Leonean political leadership to this end. Kabbah and his governments, whether at home or in exile, are seen as particularly ineffectual.[38] The long list of foreign 'heroes', from the Britons, Peter Penfold, Tony Blair and Keith Biddle, to the Nigerians, Maxwell Khobe and even Sani Abacha—albeit with a considerable number of foreign 'villains' as well—is testimony to the continued and increasing importance of and, at certain crucial moments, the resort to and use of outsiders for domestic purposes, or 'extraversion'.[39] At the same time, the internationalisation of the war increased significantly towards the end and Sierra Leoneans could in any case exert less and less sway in its unfolding.

On a broader scale, however, there are notions that conflict has historically been a key part of the development process in Europe and elsewhere. Stronger and more coherent European states emerged over time from the need to defend themselves.[40] Equally, only half a century ago, Europe in particular, but also many other parts of the world, were simultaneously subjected to and emerged changed from intense conflict. The

European Union, the UN and decolonisation are seen as emerging out of this violence, and social changes within states attributed in some ways to the conflict legacy are too myriad to mention. Violence could be viewed as 'the social and political pangs of development', which many or perhaps most societies go through, and not always a deviance from progress, as it is usually portrayed.[41] It is one of the few processes of such intensity to have the potential to instigate change.[42] Outsiders clearly offer ways of ending conflict, although very limited possibilities of structural change within this process. However, whether the ensuing longer-term international involvement, coupled with the war and indeed post-war activities, have structurally changed the pre-war political and social environment in Sierra Leone is an area to be investigated in the subsequent chapters.

8

THE POST-CONFLICT DISPENSATION

PLUS ÇA CHANGE? 2002–2007

On 18 January 2002, Sierra Leoneans, including President Kabbah and the RUF interim leader Sesay, and international guests attended a peace ceremony and symbolic bonfire of decommissioned arms from the war. The war had officially ended, or the *war don don* as announced in Krio, and the prescribed disarmament and demobilisation period had for the most part been successfully completed, but there remained many issues. Some of these would be resolved in the national elections scheduled for 14 May. Others, though, from the incarceration of Sankoh to the upcoming Sierra Leone Special Court (SLSC) and Truth and Reconciliation Commission (TRC), would take much longer to be answered. Most, encompassing the state and its relations with the people in the aftermath of the war, remain ongoing problems with which Sierra Leoneans and outside interests continue to wrestle.

Much attention in the immediate aftermath was directed to the elections. The government's 1996 mandate had already been twice extended because of the security situation, and the elections delayed by five months. There were many, including political parties and NGOs, who still had serious reservations about the short timetable, especially given the large numbers of displaced people, the shattered infrastructure and the security conditions.[1] Nevertheless, the election date stood. A District Block System (DBS) was chosen to fit the tight election timetable. Although an improvement on the nationwide lists system of 1996, it still meant district party lists for the allocation of seats and hence no independents. There was no time for a census, so eight seats were allocated for each district no matter the size of the population. Separate polls for President and Parliament and twelve reserved seats for Paramount Chiefs were however maintained. Security was provided by the 17,000 UN troops but in any case, despite inter-party skirmishes, the RUFP leadership's regularly stated rejection of violence in favour of the ballot box proved to be of some substance. Of an estimated total population of 4.8 million, a remarkable 2.34 million registered to vote in the limited time available.

Unlike 1996, this was an election with an incumbent party and president.[2] Hence there was plenty of noise concerning bias. Attacks on the opposition by SLPP supporters, particularly stone-throwing and harassment in the SLPP heartland, were often reported. The most explosive situation occurred on the final day of campaigning and involved a clash of SLPP and RUFP rallies in the centre of Freetown when UNAMSIL had to intervene and some were injured. However, the general level of electoral violence was, if not as low as 1996, still low by comparison with the elections in the 1970s and 1980s. The SLPP enjoyed the benefit of the state machine behind its campaign, and there were many allegations of government facilities being used for SLPP purposes. SLPP advertising hoardings with large full-colour images of their candidate appeared in greater quantity and in more prominent positions. The high-quality image of Kabbah placed on its own at the busy West Freetown junction of Congo Cross was indicative of resources available. Equally telling was a comparison between the quality and dominance of the SLPP banner in the central square of the Northern (and historically APC) town of Port Loko and the dilapidation of the temporary headquarters and advertisements of the APC in the Southern (and historically SLPP) city of Bo. The presidential candidate of the now reinvigorated APC, Ernest Bai Koroma, complained of the use of chiefs and 'secret society' leaders to intimidate APC supporters.[3] Working in the Commission for the Consolidation of Peace and later to become SLPP Minister of Youth and Sports, Dennis Bright emphasised the very important political role of these societies, and the EU recognised that Paramount Chiefs had 'exerted direct or indirect pressure in favour of the ruling party'.[4]

There were also claims that the majority of NEC commissioners were SLPP supporters, or at least under the control of the ruling party owing to the embezzlement indictments hanging over the heads of three of the five commissioners. Inadequate registration facilities and materials in Freetown contributed to a figure of only around 409,000 registered (compared with 295,000 in 1996) in a capital area swollen with displaced people. Despite the 1996 registration being badly affected by the war, the substantial increase in registered voters between 1996 and 2002 in the South and East was also viewed with suspicion. The numbers doubled in Kenema District, and increased more than threefold in Bonthe and fivefold in Moyamba District. The US Embassy was not alone in noting 'the significant numbers of children under the age of 18' who were registered.[5] There was an Exhibition Phase of the Provisional Voter Register, but the NEC Commissioner for the South, where under-age registration was reported to be at its worst, stated that to his knowledge no one had been removed from the list in the whole of his region.[6] Also working in the SLPP's favour, although probably not by design, was the DBS. Having eight MPs for both Western Area East, with 240,000 voters, and the SLPP stronghold Bonthe, with 70,000 voters, invites suspicion. However, the average district size differed less dramatically, around 174,000 in the North and West where the APC was stronger, compared with around 160,000 in the SLPP-dominated South and East.

Election Day showed fewer signs of irregularities. Turnout was nominally 82 per cent, but even given the uncertainty over numbers this was once again an impressive figure. Transfer voting for internally displaced people who had moved since their original registration was allowed but NEC made a sudden policy change while voting was underway, allowing those with valid voter ID cards to vote where they were registered or those with transfer slips to vote at the places whence they had transferred, whether or not their names appeared on the registration lists. This led to some confusion and an uneven application, but not to specifically attributable irregularities. However, the most crucial anomalies appeared after Election Day during the count, with the re-emergence of highly questionable turnout figures in SLPP strongholds. In an unsettling reminder of 1996, unlikely 98 and 94 per cent turnouts were recorded in the Southern district of Bonthe and in the Eastern district of Kenema, which was suspect especially when compared with the 68 per cent and 75 per cent average turnouts in the Northern Province and Western Area. Even more suspect were 104 per cent figures in the districts of Kailahun in the East and Pujehun in the South. Population shifts were blamed, but the excuses were even less convincing than in 1996.

The result was a landslide. In 1996, Kabbah had polled just 36 per cent in the first round and 59 per cent in the two-candidate run-off. In 2002, he doubled his 1996 first-round vote and avoided a second round altogether by polling 70 per cent of the vote, ahead of Ernest Koroma in second place with 22 per cent and Johnny Paul Koroma a distant third with 3 per cent. Most of the South and East fell as expected to Kabbah, but it was the 87 per cent in Kono District which was unusual. Even more so were the 67 per cent in Koinadugu District, the 60 per cent in Kambia District and the 29 per cent in Port Loko District, compared with 4.3, 6.5 and 2.9 per cent respectively in the first-round 1996 elections, which made the largest difference. Kabbah outperformed his party, but the SLPP victory was still a landslide and roughly mirrored the presidential results. The incumbent party took 68 per cent of the nationwide vote, compared with 36 per cent in 1996, and increased its number of seats in Parliament from 27 of 68 to an overwhelming 83 of the 112 available. The SLPP won every seat in the South and East, but like Kabbah made crucial and significant inroads into the North and West. In 1996, the party managed just 4 per cent and 25 per cent of the vote in the North and West, but this time it took six out of eight seats in Koinadugu District (61 per cent of the vote), five out of eight in Kambia District (56 per cent), three out of eight in Port Loko District (26.5 per cent), four out of eight in West-West (45.5 per cent) and five out of eight in West-East (46 per cent). Indeed, the SLPP could almost claim to be a nationwide party, since it gained seats in every district.

A revamped APC managed to win back many of the votes that had temporarily transferred to the UNPP and PDP in 1996, gaining 21.5 per cent of the national vote leading to 27 seats, 22 of 40 in the North and five of 16 in the West. The new Peace and Liberation Party (PLP), led by Johnny Paul Koroma, was the final party to emerge with tangible success as it won two seats in the West district of the Western Area. However, the UNPP, again led by John Karefa-Smart, failed to win a seat, as did Zainab Bangura's new Movement for Progress (MOP) and the RUFP. The latter party, with Pallo Bangura as its presidential candidate, polled just 2.2 per cent nationwide, peaking at 7.8 per cent in Kailahun District but still not enough for a seat. All opposition parties eventually accepted the results although still claiming many irregularities. International observers gave the elections a relatively clean bill of health and the domestic observation was not at all concerned.[7] On this occasion, nothing was done to correct the over-voting, perhaps because the outcome was so overwhelming. Indeed, an assessment of the results would probably be that the landslide vote and the SLPP representation in Parliament were inflated, either by centrally contrived fraud or by mere administrative inadequacies, but not by enough to change the overall SLPP victory.

One might see the return of the APC in its role as the party of the North as the partial restoration of the post-colonial party political order. The party was deliberately painted as the new APC with a brand new and youthful leader in order to nullify the negative connotations with the past, while still maintaining many of the stalwarts of old. Ernest Koroma, often referred to as simply 'Ernest', was not yet 50 and over 20 years Kabbah's junior. He had been the Managing Director of the Reliance Insurance Trust Corporation (Ritcorp) from 1988 to 2002. Koroma was a Christian, a Temne and an APC man from Makeni, but claimed to have had limited connections to the ancien régime. His wife, Sia Nyama, came from Kono and, in an indication of the continued small size and sometimes incestuous closeness of the elite, was the daughter of the SLPP cabinet minister and Kono 'big-man' Abu Aiah Koroma. The resurrection of the APC from its 5 per cent vote in 1996 was indeed remarkable and was testimony to its brand name, the return of members and patronage funds and, to a degree, Koroma's new look. At the same time, the octogenarian Karefa-Smart and his fractured UNPP and the treacherous PDP, which had split in two and whose original leader Thaimu Bangura had passed away in 1999, made rather unpromising Northern opposition material. Cries of *Owei Osei* ('the sun is hot', referring to the APC party symbol), while generally not as ubiquitous as *Wu-teh-teh* ('abundance' or 'a big majority') from SLPP supporters, were often heard in the campaign and the final APC rally in Freetown was indeed impressive and painted the city red.

It is generally thought that Johnny Paul Koroma gained his votes from a curious mixture of armed forces allegiances and born-again Christianity. However, despite his depiction as the 'Angel' of the PLP, it would appear that the bulk of his votes, 16 per cent in the West-West district, came from the large barracks in this area, particularly when it is considered that the PLP won the majority of votes in the leaked results of the special early elections held for election staff, mostly consisting of military and police personnel. On the other hand, the reformist MOP made little headway despite Zainab Bangura's activist record and public face during the Johnny Paul Koroma junta's rule and afterwards with the Campaign for Good Governance, most likely because of the party's reluctance or inability to play the patronage game.[8]

The RUFP, however, is another story altogether. The electoral collapse of the RUFP might simply be explained by its brutal wartime reputation and its vilification inside and outside Sierra Leone. However, the equally brutal and vilified Renamo had performed significantly better in the 1994 Mozambican elections. The collapse is then not as straightforward as one might initially think. There were several short term and long term reasons why the results were so poor. In the short term, despite the wealth of some individuals, the official party was chronically short of funding, many within the party remained under UN sanctions and so unable to travel to raise funds, and 400 RUF cadres were incarcerated in May 2000 after the incident at Sankoh's residency. Eldred Collins was one among several top RUF officials in Freetown who were arrested and he was not released until near the end of 2001.[9] Party supporters became disillusioned with leaders, in particular Sesay, and were attracted by the lure of the other parties. The RUFP had neither the collective will nor the organisation to create a credible patronage machine to match the SLPP or even the APC, the latter notably being a party which had successfully rejuvenated its own machine and overcome its violent image. Ethnic schisms in the RUFP furthered the exodus to the regionally-defined parties.[10] The presidential candidate, Pallo Bangura, even considered changing the name of the party to reduce the adverse publicity, but feared amplifying the North-South schism or 'Northernisation' developing in the party and so increasing the haemorrhage of supporters.[11]

Many ex-combatants did not view Bangura, relatively new to the group, as the rightful RUFP leader. Bangura was an intellectual: he was an alumnus of the School of Oriental and African Studies in London, had been a lecturer at Fourah Bay College and had held ambassadorial and ministerial positions during the military interregnums and in the RUF/SLPP coalition. He could speak articulately and in the language required of a political party leader in front of an international audience. However, anti-intellectualism within the RUF/P was not confined to Sankoh. The leadership mantle clearly belonged to the jailed and increasingly sickly Sankoh, and even Bangura acknowledged that without Sankoh's leadership the 'intense loyalty' and 'personal contact' were much diminished.

Despite fielding a full complement of candidates in ten of the fourteen districts, the RUFP was conspicuous by its absence on the campaign trail. Some candidates were more concerned with establishing themselves in post-conflict life through 'projects' which might attract NGO funding than with anything political.[12] With the party riven by internal but public disputes over leadership and the disappearance of money, and with little communication between leaders and down the hierarchy, the presidential candidate left the capital on just one occasion.[13]

However, the long term trajectory of the group underpinned the more immediate problems. The failure of the RUF leadership to increase political capacity and to prepare for life after conflict is undoubtedly reflected in the failure of the party at the polls. This might be contrasted with the relative success of another military-linked party, the PLP, in putting together some sort of party structure through which it could maintain and even broaden its support.[14] At the same time, international policy towards the RUFP mirrored the predominant view within the country that this was a case of good riddance. In the new post-millennium international environment of post-conflict justice and exclusion and British and US pro-Kabbah, anti-RUF/Taylor thinking, the RUF was certainly not in line for a fund to facilitate its transformation into a political party, as the 1999 Lomé Accord had stipulated and as Renamo had obtained to its benefit in Mozambique. Bangura was well aware of the timing of this election relative to world affairs. He described a new epoch, particularly after the events of 11 September 2001, and the now regular 'references to terrorists and courts, etc'. The forthcoming indictments of the SLSC were in his opinion a 'Sword of Damocles over the RUFP'.[15] The RUFP, though, was utterly ill-equipped and seemed largely unwilling or unable to argue its case.

The SLPP certainly benefited from its opponents' problems and its position as incumbent, but this does not quite explain the extent of the victory, especially when comparison is made with the closeness of previous competitive elections. Equally, ethno-regionalism does not explain the inroads into the North. It is also not attributable to policy: in a refreshingly frank remark, the APC Secretary General admitted that all the manifestos were basically the same.[16] Probably the single most important contributor to the SLPP cause, after its Southern and Eastern strongholds and its position as incumbent, was the uncertain security environment.

It is remarkable that Kabbah's reputation as an indecisive, feeble president was transformed in just one year into that of the nation's saviour. Many viewed Kabbah, rightly or wrongly, as the bringer of peace, of the British Army, of ECOMOG and of the UN, in that order of desirability. His perceived critical connections to the international community, particularly in Britain and within the UN, were seen to have ensured the huge foreign interventions, and would more likely guarantee their return if the need arose in the future: indeed a further example of external reliance and/or usage. Nothing was said internationally to modify this viewpoint and the UN had already commended the government of Sierra Leone for its efforts in ending the war.[17] Kabbah and the party grew increasingly confident with the slogan, 'We promised and we delivered', declared loudly on t-shirts and banners. This could only refer to the end of the war, given their delivery of very little else and despite their taking five years of rule to deliver that achievement. Regardless of its unrealistic title, the SLPP's 'Million Man March' captured the zeitgeist of the 1995 US demonstration of the same name, eclipsed the last rally of the APC, filled the National Stadium to overflowing and showed the confidence of the party. Kabbah's perceived ability to attract international money, again through his connections, may also have contributed. A frank announcement was reported from an SLPP loudspeaker van in Makeni, which declared that if 'Kabbah go' then 'UN go, white man go, money go'.[18] Eight months after the elections, the Minister of Transport and Communications, Prince Harding, was still pushing this message—of connections but also external reliance/usage—when he announced the purchase of a fleet of vehicles by the government, for which 'the President used his United Nations connection to get us a good bargain'.[19]

Many Sierra Leoneans, even those who did not vote SLPP, believed that the war had finally ended and joined in the creation of a distinct air of optimism. For themselves, Kabbah and the SLPP had a majority, a hefty mandate and a prospective honeymoon period which gave them considerable leeway for action. A great deal of expectation was placed personally on Kabbah, seen by some as the honest but popular broker or even reformer at the top of a rather recalcitrant party. This was undoubtedly an unfair expectation of Kabbah given the history of the SLPP before and during the war and the general modus operandi of Sierra Leonean politics, but his popularity led many to believe that he could in some way re-align the wheels of the SLPP juggernaut. Indeed, in his first presidential address on 19 May, Kabbah caused some commotion when he pointedly noted that 'all Sierra Leone is my constituency'.

There are twin political imperatives related to immediate post-conflict environments: to reconcile and to stabilise. Reconciliation comes in many forms but at the top end, it was not considered important by a landslide-enhanced SLPP to embrace opposition. The 'all Sierra Leone is my constituency' mantra did not quite extend to his new cabinet. There was no talk of a 1996-style coalition so unpopular with elements of the SLPP, or a post-conflict government of national unity as was seen a year later in Liberia. SLPP party veterans, or at least those who had been on the political scene for a while, took up most of the positions. Sam Hinga Norman became Minister of Internal Affairs and Solomon Berewa the new Vice President. J.B. Dauda, who in another example of political incestuousness had been an APC Vice President of the one-party era and would later cross the floor once more to become Foreign Minister in the APC government of the early 2010s, was promoted to Minister of Finance. In 2005, the former NPRC Chairman John Benjamin took over from Dauda in the Finance Ministry when Dauda declared his intention to stand as SLPP presidential candidate—Kabbah was constitutionally required to step down after finishing his second term. There was new blood in the form of Eke Halloway and Dennis Bright, but continuity was more noticeable. Instead, one might prioritise stability and, just as in the justifications for one-party rule, it could be considered that a strong and popular government making focused decisions is the way forward. Certainly, the path towards political stability, and indeed to some extent reconciliation, has to be not only underpinned by security but also illuminated with the signs of economic recovery. The latter priorities were the advertised intentions of the SLPP government.

However, there was a further political imperative unrelated to the post-conflict environment. In a scenario familiar in post-colonial Sierra Leone and indeed Africa, the ruling party needs to stay in power and its main method is through patronage and in particular by nourishing its ethno-regional base. There is less chance of this happening in a coalition and in theory more chance with tried and trusted ministers. Further, the patronage imperative paradoxically feeds stability for some while eating into the imperative to stabilise by economically developing on a national scale. The resulting possibility of stability is then influenced more by the width of the patronage net than by the national development drive, or at least there is an intertwining of the two processes. One might consider two of the main drivers of the conflict to have been the shrinking and skewed patronage net and severe economic and infrastructural deterioration. Finally, and again interlinked with patronage and the notion of 'eating', there is the idea that it is 'our time to chop'.[20] Those in power know that their democratic time is limited and hence they must feather their own nests and those of their followers while conditions remain. Simultaneously explaining incestuous politics and patronage obligations, the SLPP politician S.B. Marah took up a ministerial position in the mid-1970s APC government that had imprisoned him and violently harassed his own party, noting that 'in Africa to be in opposition is alright, but if you really want to help your people you have to come to the government side of parliament'.[21] However, while the expectation, or even obligation, of those in power to disburse the wealth to family, community and ethnic group highlights the continued reciprocity in the process and the part played by the general public, the temptation to keep siphoned resources purely to oneself in a manner illegitimate in even a neo-patrimonial system is clearly great. The SLPP, like the APC before, faced decisions over the hierarchy of all these imperatives.

Security was maintained by UNAMSIL until its military withdrawal in 2006 and replacement with the civilian mission, the United Nations Integrated Peacebuilding Office in Sierra Leone (UNIPSIL). There were many fears concerning the 're-trained' RSLAF and police force, particularly reinforced by the security forces vote for Johnny Paul Koroma. The British-led International Military Advisory and Training Team (IMATT) did make considerable strides in training the RSLAF, particularly in the recruiting of new officers and the depoliticising and subordination to civilian control of the force. Sierra Leonean soldiers were deployed as part of a UN mission to Sudan in 2009. In Sierra Leone, however, the new army was not working from scratch as in Liberia, and vested political and economic interests remained at all grades. New 'ghost' soldiers continued to appear on the payroll and fears lingered of a return to business as usual when IMATT finally follows up on its drawdown from executive to advisory role and withdraws entirely.[22]

The Sierra Leone Police (SLP) benefited from much-needed new equipment and a reform process headed, from 1999 until he stepped down in 2003, by the retired British police officer Keith Biddle. It was indeed an institution that had arisen from the ashes of the war and is to some extent depoliticised and functioning better under a new cohort of officers.[23] SLP officers were deployed in Sudan. The SSD had somewhat renewed itself in the eyes of the public after its combat operations during the war, in particular during the 1999 Freetown invasion, but its transformation into the Operational Support Division (OSD) and the substantial rearming of the SLP begged the question of what the police were for: combat, coercion, or community service and development.[24] It was also feared that Biddle and his Sierra Leonean successors had not quite made the envisioned progress towards 'A Force for Good', particularly given widespread public perceptions of a still corrupt institution,[25] the visible return of bribes at roadblocks and stories of police collusion in robberies and of continued political bias. The presence of the SLP, as opposed to the chiefdom or Native Administration Police, in rural areas has been described as still very thin.[26] At the same time the latent organisational structures of ex-combatants presented another security concern. Some were still disengaged and nursed profound distrust of the political system while simultaneously beginning to coalesce in urban areas as petty traders and *okada* or motorbike taxi drivers, and as a militia for hire by the political parties.[27]

The end of the war brought a huge spike in economic growth which then settled down to a healthy but not particularly elevating 5 to 7 per cent per annum. Concurrently with another diamond rush post-war, official diamond exports rose from US$10 million in 2000 to US$160 million in 2005. The government, however, conceded that, despite the Kimberley Process Certification Scheme established in 2003, 10–15 per cent was still smuggled, while others put this figure closer to 50 per cent.[28] Between 60 and 70 per cent of the government budget came from international aid. Indeed, aid was led by the British government Department for International Development (DFID) within its unprecedented ten-year agreement with the Sierra Leonean government in 2002. This commitment continued the considerable involvement of the British Labour government, from its support of Kabbah in the days of the AFRC junta through to the military intervention of 2000 and the establishment of IMATT. It also aimed to hold the government to a series of benchmarks and indicators of 'governance reform'.

The DFID initiative was indeed extraordinary, but it fitted into the prevailing international discourse of 'liberal peace'.[29] While democratisation, accountability, promotion of civil society, economic liberalisation and good governance remained high on the bill, pro-poor strategies had been given greater weight within an overall notion that peace, democracy and free markets are a feasible combination which is transferable to a post-conflict environment. The Millennium Development Goals (MDGs) underpinned the pro-poor strategy and SAPs were being replaced by Poverty Reduction Strategy Papers (PRSPs), advertised as a more tailored and more negotiated process than before. Where the state had been part of the problem in the Washington Consensus of the 1980s and 1990s, it was now part of the solution within the Post-Washington Consensus. Even though some saw little change from one consensus to another given the underpinning liberal ideal, state reform was indeed given high priority by donors in Sierra Leone and added an extra significant imperative to the SLPP agenda: satisfying the donors.

In line with liberal state rebuilding, two high profile reform processes were, respectively, continued and implemented during this second SLPP term of office: the Anti-Corruption Commission (ACC) and Decentralisation. In the first eighteen months after its establishment in 2000, the ACC brought just seven cases to court, in which only one person was found guilty. In that case the Agriculture Minister, Harry Will, was given a lenient fine and the judge concerned was subsequently jailed for receiving bribes. At the time of the elections there were other cases outstanding, including that of Transport Minister, Momoh Pujeh, accused of smuggling diamonds. He was later found guilty before appealing against the verdict and winning, then becoming the Minority Leader in Parliament after the APC victory in 2007, before passing away while in office in 2012. No further high profile cases were brought to court under the SLPP. Ibrahim Okere-Adams, the Fisheries Minister and a Temne with important Northern support in a disproportionately Southern administration, was charged in 2005 but remained in the cabinet and did not make it to court. The ACC head, Valentine Collier, was replaced soon afterwards by Henry Joko-Smart, a relative by marriage of the president. While the Commonwealth Secretariat contributed two non-Sierra Leonean judges in 2003, all prosecutions still needed the go-ahead of the Attorney General who doubled as the SLPP Minister of Justice.

The difficulty in reading the performance of the ACC is in knowing the reasons behind the charging of individuals. On the one hand it could be genuine governmental commitment or institutional autonomy. There was after all enough corruption to keep the ACC busy. It was discovered that only 5 per cent of essential drugs made the journey from the Central Medical Stores to the Primary Health Units. Of 236 listed senior civil servants in 2007, only 125 were found to be at their posts.[30] On the other hand, it may be the case that scapegoats are required in order to satisfy donors—the main contributor, the DFID, temporarily withdrew funding in 2007. Equally, one might easily see a correlation with pre-war commissions. The bodies instigated domestically by Sierra Leonean military governments in the late 1960s failed to instil structural change, either through a lack of seriousness—the Dove-Edwin Commission was supposed to have mistaken Kabbah for someone else—or more likely through facing too many vested interests and the ambivalence towards corruption that is inherent in a patron-client system. The charges brought forward by Stevens' various commissions were mostly used politically. There is enough evidence of timing, obfuscation and curious decisions in today's ACC to suggest that all the drivers and obstacles noted above may be at play at different times.

The return of local councils in 2004 after a hiatus of 32 years was a significant event. The rural political battleground between chieftaincies and councils began anew. Equally, the Western donor viewpoint on the liberal notion of decentralised democracy by comparison with the less liberal institution of chieftaincy was brought under scrutiny. It had already been tested. In the aftermath of the war, the DFID organised a survey of public attitudes to chieftaincy which showed that the institution was still legitimate but that reform was required to ensure better accountability and eliminate certain grievances, particularly among the youth, which it was noted bore comparison with those expressed in the 1955–56 riots.[31] The DFID and the state were however simultaneously faced with a dilemma now remarkably familiar in Sierra Leonean colonial and postcolonial history, that stabilisation of the countryside was urgently needed and the chiefs were best placed to do this. The SLPP clearly saw an opportunity to reinvigorate its chiefly political bases and was also very keen.

Indeed, many chieftaincies were smoothly restored as the chiefs had either been present on and off, stayed and fought the armed threats, or been replaced by rebel 'chiefs' who largely stood down. Of 149 Paramount Chiefs, 63 had died or been killed and thus gave way to successors elected by their peers in late 2002 and early 2003.[32] People had generally maintained respect for the traditional roles, although some evidence suggests that the judicial aspect suffered most and that alternative dispute mechanisms created by donors were becoming more trusted.[33] The notion that people shop around for justice is far from unknown. Customary authority seemed still to be valued for its role as 'a defence against the abuse of bureaucratic power'.[34] The resulting funding of the restoration of chieftaincies without reform, however, risked the return of some pre-war problems.[35] Chieftaincy legislation by government does remain ongoing but is largely conservative.[36] The funding, however, also diverted significantly from the liberal aims of the donor community, some of whom took a very dim view, seeing the DFID programme as a shot in the arm at a vital time for what they perceived as a moribund and anachronistic institution.[37]

Conversely, fitting snugly into the liberal canon was the decentralisation process. Intended to increase accountability, representation, pro-poor policies and service delivery and decrease the intense centralisation on the executive in pre-war Sierra Leone, the process was supported by the World Bank and UNDP. One City, five Town and 13 District Councils were re-created in 2004 and elections successfully held.[38] In a sharp contrast to most other reforms, decentralisation happened and happened quickly, most likely because the SLPP saw the process as a twin-track development of councils and chieftaincies and also did not want to lose the electoral momentum of 2002. Indeed, in the May 2004 elections, the APC overwhelmingly took Freetown but failed to dent the 70 per cent nationwide vote for the SLPP. The coercion of independent candidates to withdraw from running against the SLPP in Bo, Kenema and Freetown, and the greater than 100 per cent turnouts in the South, were also sharp reminders of 1996 and 2002.[39]

In addition, in the rush to implement, any reforms to the previous local government format, such as limitations to chiefly representation, any special allowances for representation such as those enacted for women, youth and the disabled in Uganda, or non-partisan polls as in Ghanaian local elections, were not pursued. Equally, the division of labour between councils and chiefdoms was not fully clarified. The councils were financially, and therefore potentially politically, dependent—on the one hand on Freetown, which supplied revenue transfers, and on the other on the chiefs, who collected local taxes—and rivalries soon built up.[40] Disbursal of donor funds could then be delivered at Council level or through Ward Development Committees which were supposed to be participatory but often became dominated by the existing power structures or else dwindled away.[41] Chiefs' control over land presented another obstacle to council authority. Despite the democratic credentials and greater access to donor revenue of the councils and the poor record of some chiefs, the battle of the councils for legitimacy with respect to the chieftaincies could only be a very long one.[42] The compromise reached whereby councils were ranked as the highest authority but chiefs ranked above councillors in any given chiefdom is indicative of the field of contention.[43] The evident victory of the chiefdoms over councils in Stevens' abolition of the latter in 1972 is a salutary reminder of the political battlefield in the countryside for stability, representation and patronage.

Despite its flaws, decentralisation was a success story by comparison with other political reforms. Indeed, it has been noted that there is consensus over this reconfiguration amongst political parties, in particular the SLPP and APC, but that at the same time it has benefited exactly these two parties.[44] However, foot dragging on most public sector reform was widespread and began to irritate donors. An independent review for the DFID in 2005 found that the 2002 agreement had not prompted faster progress and the World Bank concluded for the same year that, while Sierra Leone was performing better at public financial management, it ranked poorly on transparency, corruption and rule-based governance.[45] Finally, in 2007 the DFID suspended budget support. Despite the accompanying announcement that this was a benchmarks-based decision, 2007 was also election year. The SLPP accusation of an attempt at regime change by suspending funds just before elections was to live with the DFID for years to come.[46]

Sierra Leone, along with a handful of other countries, was in many ways a guinea pig for liberal state-rebuilding after conflict in the early 2000s. State-building and the donor-government relationship are investigated further in the next two chapters. It also held the same status, alongside an even smaller number of cases, in terms of post-conflict justice. Sierra Leone had not one, but two bodies established to discharge justice: the SLSC and the TRC. The SLSC is a hybrid court model described as the second generation of international criminal justice.[47] Established by a treaty between the Government of Sierra Leone and the UN in January 2002, it was designed to prosecute a much more limited number of cases than the International Criminal Tribunals for Rwanda and Yugoslavia; to be cheaper, relying to an extent on less expensive Sierra Leonean staff; to combine international and Sierra Leonean law; and to subsist on voluntary contributions.[48] It has also been noted that another reason for a hybrid model is that it is an alternative to the International Criminal Court (ICC), towards which the US is not partial. Over time, the US provided around half of the voluntary contributions and all of the three Chief Prosecutors were Americans. In 2003, the court indicted thirteen individuals: five, including Sankoh, Sesay and Bockarie from the RUF; four, including Johnny Paul Koroma from the AFRC and West Side Boys; three, including Hinga Norman from the Kamajors; and, in a slightly later unveiling, the Liberian President (until 2003) Charles Taylor.

The SLSC was indeed novel and part of the new wave of criminal courts established mostly during the 2000s. Treating the turn of the millennium as a fulcrum, one can detect the balance beginning to change. During most of the 1990s, stress was placed on negotiation. Cambodia, Mozambique, Angola, Sierra Leone and Liberia, until the late 1990s or the turn of the millennium, were all approached from the point of view of persuading all groups to the table: to include rather than to exclude. The intervention in Somalia in 1992 can be seen as one event that bucked this trend, but that case can be viewed as an anomaly in 1990s discourse. The ICC, constituted in 1998, ratified by a 60th state in 2002 and beginning its first case in 2006; the Yugoslav and Rwandan tribunals established in the mid-1990s, but gaining momentum through the first decade of the 21st century; the SLSC in 2002 and the considerable pressure put on both Liberia and Nigeria to send Taylor back from exile and to trial; and further international courts in East Timor, Cambodia and Lebanon in the 2000s, all point to the change in thinking towards the judicial and retributional. *Gacaca* courts, established in 2002 in post-genocide Rwanda, were billed as a 'traditional' halfway house between reconciliatory processes and retributive justice, but were criticised (or praised) as doing mostly the latter.[49] Pointedly, the UN Secretary General Kofi Annan stated in 2004 that we should 'reject any amnesty for genocide, war crimes or crimes against humanity … and ensure that no such amnesty previously granted is a bar to prosecution before any UN-created or assisted court'.[50] Impunity, then, became the number-one enemy. From entirely different perspectives, one observer asserted that there had been 'a millennial shift from appeasement to justice', while another claimed an 'international law fundamentalism' to be now at work.[51]

This discursive shift has not, however, been universally applied. At the time of writing all cases brought in front of the ICC have been African. Selective justice has so far ruled out anyone from powerful nations at any tribunal. At the SLSC, President Compaoré of Burkina Faso and Qaddafi of Libya were not indicted as their assistance had passed through Taylor, but this is a fine point. President Kabbah, who as Defence Minister was Hinga Norman's superior, was also not indicted as there was said to be not enough evidence and Hinga Norman had declared he was not taking orders from Kabbah; again a fine point. Indeed, given Taylor's final verdict of guilty of 'aiding and abetting', this charge could be laid at the door of the UK, US and France in the Mano River region. One view is that the primary imperative of the SLSC's international backers for the establishment of the court and for its particular selection of indictees was to assist 'regime change in Liberia and regime consolidation in Sierra Leone'.[52] Equally, many conflicts around the world have not been subjected to trials at all, either because it would be politically inexpedient on the part of global powers to do so, or—often—because it would be utterly counterproductive for the peace process. Israel is an example of the former reason and Liberia, in both the 1989–97 and 2000–2003 periods, is a case in point for the latter. Retrospectively, the implications for South Africa or Northern Ireland need no elaboration. Where a judicial solution has been attempted, as in Sudan and Uganda through the ICC, it is far from clear that it is more beneficial than peace deals and amnesties for conflict resolution or long term stability. The digging in of Laurent Gbagbo in Côte d'Ivoire and Qaddafi in Libya in 2011 followed the threat of and a referral to the ICC, respectively. There is also an inherent danger of isolating individuals as the main or only cause of the war, which has then seemingly been dealt with.

We can, though, safely say that the SLSC was extremely fortunate in that the RUF was militarily disintegrating by the end of the war, had never had a political wing, and was deeply unpopular. The same applies to other factions with the partial exception of the Kamajors. Taylor was soon to go into exile. Hence, there were limited repercussions on the peace deal or post-conflict stability, although in 2006 Taylor was flown from exile in Nigeria to Monrovia to Freetown to The Hague—the final flight made in order to reduce the destabilisation. Crucially, though, repercussions are not or would not be limited in almost all other scenarios, where rebel forces tend to maintain some coherency and support based on perceived or probably real injustices of the past.

The trials fell behind schedule but over time were concluded: the AFRC, West Side Boys and Kamajors trials in 2007, the RUF trials in

2009 and that of Taylor in 2012. All nine who completed their trials were found guilty of war crimes or crimes against humanity; in the case of Taylor only of 'aiding and abetting' and 'planning'. However, there were several, arguably the biggest Sierra Leonean fish, who did not face trial. Sankoh and Hinga Norman died in custody in July 2003 and February 2007 respectively. Johnny Paul Koroma went missing shortly before his indictment and shortly after his alleged involvement in a failed coup plot. His whereabouts and status remain unknown, although rumours and allegations raised in Taylor's trial point towards execution with involvement of Taylor. Finally, Bockarie was killed in Liberia shortly after his indictment in May 2003.

For several years, until Taylor was arrested, it was viewed that the only high profile indictee in custody was the relatively popular Hinga Norman. Taylor thus came to be considered indicted combatant number one. He was served his indictment during peace talks in Ghana in June 2003— no matter that this was an embarrassment to the hosts and the Nigerians, that an emboldened LURD withdrew from the talks, and that the Ghanaians allowed Taylor to return home. Further, once Taylor went into exile in Nigeria in August 2003 with an agreement that he could stay there as long as he did not interfere in Nigerian or Liberian politics, the imperative coming from the US and EU was to bring him to trial. With no systematically documented evidence of a breach of conditions, but with heavy pressure applied, Taylor was finally brought to the SLSC. The fact that a future bloodbath in another capital city will probably not now be avoided, as no-one will trust an exile agreement, was brushed aside in the headlong rush for justice.

The immediate political repercussions in Sierra Leone were indeed limited, but not absent.[53] For a while, Johnny Paul Koroma, with his continued support in the armed forces, presented a potential security threat. Taylor's trial created occasional international media coverage, particularly when the British 'supermodel' Naomi Campbell and the American actress Mia Farrow both gave evidence.[54] More telling were the lack of impact and the limited interest generated in Sierra Leone by the final verdict. The key repercussion, however, involved the Kamajor indictees, in particular Hinga Norman. There was a latent security threat here as well. However, most importantly, the death of Hinga Norman and the run-up to the Kamajors verdict in August 2007 coincided with the period before and during the campaign for the national elections. A major contributor to the relative success of Charles Margai and his SLPP-break-away party, the People's Movement for Democratic Change (PMDC), was the feeling that the SLPP had betrayed all three Kamajors and had effectively murdered Hinga Norman, the man who had done most to fight for the SLPP cause but was seen as a rival by Kabbah. Margai made significant political capital of his one-time association with Hinga Norman and his public backing for the PMDC, and partly for this reason took ten seats and many votes off the SLPP in its strongholds and held considerable sway in the presidential run-off. Further elaboration of the 2007 elections is undertaken in the next chapter.

In its endeavour to prosecute any people involved in war crimes, the SLSC had charged some who were seen by probably over half the population as heroes, not villains. Civil wars are indeed brutal and messy affairs and it might be noted that universalising black and white legal prescriptions and the criminalisation of all combatants alleged to have been involved in abuses are ill-suited solutions to mostly domestic political and social struggles. The purportedly apolitical legalist discourse often became political also: following former US president George W. Bush's assertions of a clear distinction between good and evil on many occasions after 11 September 2001, his notion was repeated by the first SLSC Chief Prosecutor, David Crane.[55] In his view, 'the good guys (Kabbah and the British government) won'.[56] The president of the SLSC, Geoffrey Robertson, was removed from the trials in 2004, as he had pre-empted the court in already denouncing the RUF for 'grotesque crimes against humanity' in his book.[57] The civil war was presented as a fight between apolitical criminals, which to some extent in the Sierra Leonean case can be argued, but Crane appears to have been wholly taken with the notion of conflict due to individual criminal gain and the blood diamond story.[58] Thus, in the depoliticising process a whole tranche of underpinning political questions is missed and the concerns that justice affects politics and politics affects justice are entirely overlooked. On an international scale, if it is thought that the limited repercussions in Sierra Leone are transferable elsewhere, then there may be difficult times ahead. Giving overriding priority to the rights of individuals in a law court may well involve the sacrifice of the greater welfare of all.[59]

Somewhat strangely, Sierra Leone also had a TRC, which followed the lead of the South African TRC in the 1990s. Although the latter was criticised, the South African chairman, Archbishop Desmond Tutu, emphasised religious redemption married with supposed 'traditional' African notions of *ubuntu* (restoration to the community) rather than punishment.[60] Established in 2002 and submitting its report in 2004, the Sierra Leonean TRC aimed to simultaneously document the war and reconcile those who did not appear in front of the SLSC. However, it was overshadowed by the SLSC and perpetrators' fears of being turned over to its big brother undermined the TRC and led many to stay away.[61] On the other hand, it stuck to its brief and provided a historical account and accompanying recommendations, unlike the Liberian TRC which in 2009 published long lists of perpetrators who should be tried or banned from office, notoriously including President Johnson-Sirleaf in the latter section.[62] Many recommendations were thrown into the long grass in Sierra Leone and the TRC was criticised for letting people down by not producing tangible results. However, one recommendation which was partially fulfilled was that concerning reparations: by the end of 2010, 13,000 victims had received micro-grants. Equally and somewhat similarly to the South African case, evidence emerged that, while the Sierra Leonean TRC may have been short on the revelation of truth, it did serve to some extent as a ritual of repentance and forgiveness, which may have laid some foundations for reconciliation. Part of this process may have played a role in the restoration of some chiefly authority over youth and is further elaborated in the next chapter.[63]

It is not clear whether Sierra Leoneans wanted or needed either a judicial or official reconciliatory process. It has been noted instead that 'social forgetting' has long been a cornerstone of reintegration and healing in Sierra Leone.[64] In Liberia, 'forgetting' has also been employed as a useful short-term conflict-resolution strategy.[65] There were also local Sierra Leonean reconciliatory processes which went some way towards reintegration of ex-combatants and displaced people.[66] Across the continent, *mato oput* emerged in Northern Uganda as a means of reconciliation purported to be culturally sensitive, although as in South Africa, there are questions about the representativeness of this notion. Equally, 'traditional' reconciliation may be problematic owing to arbitrariness, harshness and a proliferation of processes and, on the other hand, their ceasing to be traditional and flexible when codified—a context reminiscent of colonial times.[67]

The SLSC is, however, criticised as failing to adjust to local culture: the court was severely hampered by 'different ideas of social space and time, of causation, agency, responsibility, evidence, truth and truth-telling from those employed by international criminal courts'.[68] One report notes the early loss of public support for the SLSC, partly due to the perception of 'limited Sierra Leonean input'.[69] There was little Sierra Leonean law brought to bear. Finally, although it cost far less overall than other tribunals, the price per trial by the end of 2011 was actually akin to that of the other courts.[70] The SLSC is criticised from without for its spending of US$26million per annum over a decade on nine individuals, while being described from within as not so much 'lean and mean' as 'anorexic'.[71] As the prosecutions were largely arbitrary, expensive, subservient to the interest of powerful people, and irrelevant, destabilising or lacking meaning in the domestic environment, perhaps the end result of the SLSC—and even the TRC—is more akin to that of a side show rather than anything that has profoundly shaken the Sierra Leonean body politic.

The key gain from the period 2002–7 was clearly the maintenance of a reasonable level of security. Despite continuing problems within the security services, the withdrawal of UNAMSIL and rather lacklustre political and economic progress, there did not seem to be any tendency towards a resumption of conflict. This is of course extremely important and more likely points to a population tired of conflict, a society knitting itself back together and the disintegration of combatant factions, rather than most governmental or international actions, even though some reforms, such as those in the security sector, have been broadly advantageous. Indeed, nothing unduly momentous occurred during the SLPP's second term of office. Despite the war, structural change was not obvious at this stage. Indeed, one could easily see the return of the pre-war patron-client system in government, elections, councils, chieftaincies and the ACC, even if the SLPP was watched closely by the large international community on the ground. Sierra Leoneans had to wait until 2007 for the national elections to produce results which were historic, even on an African continental scale. In many ways, the actions (or often inaction) of the SLPP after the war, especially in its leaning towards the narrowly corrupt at the expense of the developmental or even patrimonial, contributed significantly to the events of 2007. At the same time, tentative shifts in society were beginning to appear, the profundity of which will be examined in the next two chapters.

9

POLITICAL SHIFTS IN SIERRA LEONE

ELECTIONS, LIBERAL REFORM, SOCIETY
AND THE NEW MULTIPOLAR WORLD, 2007–12

In many ways, the period after the end of the civil war and, in particular, the years after the momentous 2007 elections encapsulate the ongoing patterns of continuity and change in Sierra Leonean politics. The historic defeat of the SLPP at the ballot box and the re-emergence of the APC in power suggest some forms of democratic consolidation but simultaneously, and paradoxically, the continuance of old patterns of politics. The successes and failures of liberal reform also point to a Sierra Leonean state that is either partly transforming or simply adapting to a new set of outside pressures. While the RSLAF deploys in Sudan, the police force at home reverts to its old *modus operandi*. The notion that the war has changed Sierra Leone is common currency but there is contradictory evidence. Finally, the new multipolar world including the huge new presence of China and India and many others in Africa presents new landscapes and possibilities. It is this mixed picture that the chapter aims to capture.

Even without the turnover in power, the 2007 election would have been a milestone as it came after five years of peace and was the third national multi-party election in a row.[1] With the turnover, 2007 became a historic year. Although this was the second exchange of power through the ballot box in Sierra Leone, these are still uncommon occurrences in Africa. Almost non-existent in the Cold War era, the number of turnovers has increased since 1989—for example Benin in 1991, 1996 and 2006, Zambia in 1991 and 2011, Senegal in 2000 and 2012, Malawi in 1994 and 2004, Kenya in 2002, Nigeria in 2015, The Gambia in 2016, Liberia in 2018—but they remain relatively rare and confined to a few countries. More common is the predominant party system of Botswana, Tanzania and Cameroon where the opposition might feasibly win one day but such a day seems a long way off.[2] One pattern that seems to have emerged is the frequency of a turnover following the stepping down, for whatever reason, of a president.[3] Given that Jerry Rawlings and John Kufuor constitutionally stepped down preceding the first two turnovers in Ghana and Daniel arap Moi, Mathieu Kérékou and Ellen Johnson Sirleaf did similarly in Kenya and Benin respectively, the likelihood of defeat of the incumbent party's new candidate appears to be greater on these occasions. Reasons for an enhanced possibility of change may include the political space created by the president's departure, difficulties of succession and disruption to networks of patronage. Sierra Leone approached the 2007 elections in exactly this environment, with Kabbah vacating the top position and the incumbent SLPP presenting Vice President Solomon Berewa as its presidential candidate.

Berewa, known also as 'Solo B', is a Christian and a Mende from Bo District. He served as Attorney General and Minister of Justice in the first Kabbah government and Vice President in the second. The notable event of the former period was the court-martial and execution of twenty-four AFRC soldiers. Berewa ran with the Foreign Minister Momodu Koroma who had useful Northern connections, being born in Tonkolili District and having mixed Temne and Mende parentage. Ernest Koroma returned as the leader of the APC after winning a gruelling courtroom battle with the 1996 APC presidential candidate, Eddie Turay, the son of the former President, Jengo Stevens, the former Foreign Minister, Abdul Karim Koroma or AKK, Abdul Serry-Kamal and other heavyweights for the leadership of the party. Importantly, his running mate, Samuel Sam-Sumana, hailed from Kono District, although his emergence as a virtual unknown owed much to his party contributions, reported to be considerable. Many such donations to both parties originate in the diaspora, particularly in the UK and US.

Other parties such as the UNPP and PLP re-emerged from 2002 but were largely ineffective, the latter emasculated without the missing Johnny Paul Koroma. The PDP, predictably, and the RUFP, less predictably, allied themselves with the APC. The real test for the two-party system came from a new party with an old political player at its head. The PMDC was formed by Charles Margai after his defeat in the race for the SLPP presidential candidacy. The issue of succession became one of prime importance early on. As he came from the Margai family dynasty and was the son and nephew respectively of the first two Prime Ministers, Albert and Milton Margai, his SLPP and Southern credentials were clear. Further, he was elected as an SLPP MP in 1977 but could not take up his seat as he was jailed for a year; he returned to the law profession and did not join the APC under one-party rule; he was key in reviving the SLPP in 1991, and he held ministerial posts in the SLPP government between 1998 and 2002. However, this was not the first time he had lost the contest for the SLPP presidential candidacy and left for another party. In 1996, when he lost the nomination to Kabbah, Margai defected to the army-backed NUP.

In probably the fairest elections in Sierra Leone since the 1960s, campaigning was open and vigorous. The DBS was replaced with the familiar first-past-the-post system in 112 single member constituencies, although with a redistribution of seats to better reflect the population. The West gained five seats and the East three, while the North lost one and the South seven. Five years after the end of the war, the importance of security as a vote-winner had all but gone. There was, however, as in 2002 an incumbent party in government. Indeed, the SLPP benefited from state and donor resources which the APC and PMDC could not begin to match and the voter roll appeared suspiciously inflated in certain SLPP strongholds. A few journalists were intimidated. Violence, mostly but not entirely associated with the SLPP, crept further back into the proceedings, particularly as the tensions increased between the first and second rounds. In the earlier part of the campaign, there was violence in Pujehun and Kono Districts and an alleged assassination attempt on Koroma led to the beating by Koroma's security of the SLPP and former NPRC man, Tom Nyuma. In the later part, a confrontation between APC and SLPP supporters in Freetown was curbed by the police, Koroma and Margai were stopped from campaigning in Kailahun and Kenema Districts, and Margai and the APC Secretary General Victor Foh were harassed in Pujehun.[4] Both leading parties employed informal 'task forces' raised from latent wartime command structures for protection, intimidation and sometimes logistics.[5]

However, on 11 August, in another show of electoral enthusiasm, nearly two million voters went to the polls in a 76 per cent turnout. Remarkably, the APC retook or held on to all the Western Area and the vast majority of the North, and made small inroads into Moyamba and Kono Districts, more than doubling its parliamentary tally to fifty-nine seats and gaining a slim majority. The APC share of the vote went from 51 per cent and 30 per cent in the North and West in 2002 to 70.5 and 55.5 per cent respectively in 2007. In the North, the SLPP managed just one seat in Kambia District and two seats in Koinadugu District, down from a total of eighteen in the North in 2002. The incumbent party's share fell from 93 per cent in both the South and East in 2002 to 45 and 67 per cent respectively in 2007. The SLPP took the entire East except for the one seat that went to the APC in Kono District, but only 14 of 25 in the South. The final tally of the SLPP was almost halved to 43 seats. Crucially, ten Southern seats went to the PMDC, including all three in Bonthe District, a further three each in Bo and Pujehun Districts and one in Moyamba District, inflicting considerable damage on the SLPP in the process. No other parties or independents were successful. As is common in Sierra Leone, the presidential results emerged in a strikingly similar pattern to the parliamentary. Koroma gathered 44 per cent, doubling his 2002 performance and winning in all Northern and Western Districts, against Berewa's 38 per cent, necessitating a run-off between these two contenders. Berewa won all Southern and Eastern Districts with the exception of the loss of Bonthe to Margai. However, Margai's overall 14 per cent, gathered largely from the South but also to a lesser degree from Kenema District in the East, seriously dented Berewa's margins of victory in SLPP heartlands.

The presidential run-off was a fraught affair. In a move almost identical to Thaimu Bangura's actions in 1996 and recalling floor-crossing by Marah, Dauda, Margai himself and many others, Margai threw his hat in with a strange bedfellow and supported Koroma, thus bucking ethno-regional imperatives. There was also sporadic violence and serious attempts at rigging. The returns from 477 out of 6,156 polling stations, nearly 8 per cent of the total, were found once again to have more ballots cast then registered voters. Of these, 426 were in the South and East, many in Kailahun District, suggesting a significant effort by the ruling party to use its heartlands to stuff ballot boxes. The process for manufacturing greater turnouts at particular locations is obviously opaque but one method appeared to be a conspiracy of local notables and 'traditional' leaders, the local populace and party observers and NEC officials at the polling station.[6] In a sharp distinction to the way over-voting was handled in 1996 and 2002, all 477 results were invalidated by the National Electoral Commission (NEC). Some, particularly within the SLPP, saw the actions of the Commissioner, Christiana Thorpe, as partial to the opposition despite her being appointed by an SLPP administration.[7] Indeed, the Commissioners of the Eastern and Southern Provinces resigned after the run-off. Others—including, at least in public, Kabbah—saw a Commissioner trying to do her job. Thorpe then moved swiftly to announce the national results before the SLPP could stop her.

Koroma thus emerged victorious from the 7 September polls with 55 per cent of the vote in a high turnout of 68 per cent which did not include the invalidated votes. His votes came from 85 per cent in the North, 69 per cent in the West, and a remarkable increase in the South and East from 9.5 per cent and 16 per cent in the first round to 28 per cent and 22 per cent in the run-off. His worst performance of just 7 per cent was in Pujehun District which had experienced considerable violence during the previous APC regime, but he managed 41 per cent in Bonthe District, 41.5 per cent in Kono District and even 25 per cent in Berewa's home district of Bo.

There had been small early signs that the turnover was possible, if not probable. In a throwback to the notion of 'SLPP na face, APC na heart' in the 1960s, 'watermelon politics'—SLPP green on the outside and APC red on the inside—became common parlance. The queues for funding outside Berewa's West Freetown house were noted as an example of the phenomenon, but one might also say that if the phrase is in widespread use in common language, then something is afoot. Indeed, several popular musicians such as Daddy Saj and Emmerson had captured the zeitgeist before the elections. Emmerson released the songs *Borbor Bele* and *Tu Fut Arata*, both examples of accessible pop-reggae which did not specifically mention SLPP but did target, respectively, those with large bellies who had 'eaten' too much and the rats with two feet.

Explanation of these conditions and electoral results needs to be sought from several angles. First, the effects of the invalidations and Margai's rather opportunistic support for Koroma are clearly important in the presidential run-off. If it is considered that the votes cast at 426 stations invalidated in the South and East were mostly lost Berewa votes, then the 51 others were potentially Koroma votes. Thus Berewa was deprived of the votes of around 60 per cent of the registered electorate, allowing for a realistic turnout and some votes for Koroma, in the balance of 375 polling stations: perhaps in the vicinity of 60–70,000 votes. In addition, Berewa gained disproportionately in Kailahun and Kenema Districts in the East from first to second round but both Berewa and Koroma won just over 50,000 extra votes in the South, which to some extent would be attributable to the mixed results of the Margai effect. Koroma led Berewa by 160,756 votes. The combined result of a counterfactual calculation based on rough assumptions, i.e. adding some 60–70,000 votes to Berewa's total and transferring 50,000 votes from Koroma to Berewa, may thus have been crucial, although neither factor on its own would have been enough. It is, though, a counterfactual and serves only to note the effect of this particular penalty for rigging and the supposed effects of the support for Koroma from Margai.

Probably more important are the political failures and successes of the three parties and their leaders. Noted in the last chapter was the considerable political capital that Margai was able to accumulate based on the SLPP 'betrayal' of Kamajors put on trial at the SLSC and the death in an SLSC jail of Hinga Norman. Kabbah's relationship with Hinga Norman had faltered many years before and the latter had instructed followers to vote for the PMDC before his death. It is also no coincidence that one of the other Kamajors on trial came from Bonthe District where both the PMDC and Margai were most successful.[8] He also benefited from his name and gained some support from professionals and students tired of the two-party system and the two parties on offer. Berewa was seen as uncharismatic compared with the other two main candidates. At various times, the SLPP resorted to blaming the international community for suspending aid, backing Thorpe and pushing for regime change. In contrast, the APC had rallied from its courtroom battles at exactly the right time. The previously disaffected Turay was awarded the post of High Commissioner to the UK and Serry-Kamal the positions of Attorney General and Minister of Justice after the elections.

It was often noted that the SLPP had become complacent and assumed the continuation of its support from 2002. In many ways, the SLPP lost the election rather than the APC winning it. This notion of complacency can, though, be broken down in two interlinking ways: concerning national development and related to specific benefits for its main supporters. The formal record of the SLPP government was perceived by many as leaving a lot to be desired. Despite the support of the DFID, which by this point had suspended budget support and the building of some schools, roads and medical establishments, many thought that not enough benefit had reached the average person. In this interpretation the SLPP was seen as too corrupt, and corruption was thought to have increased since 2002.[9] The whereabouts of the proceeds from a gift shipment of rice from Libya exercised the media in the run up to the election.[10] In addition, the SLPP's attempts to broadcast its achievements were lacklustre. For instance, a radio station, a key method of information dissemination in Sierra Leone, was set up by the SLPP six months after the APC station, and just one month before the first election. Berewa chose not to appear at all in Sierra Leone's historic first presidential debate. The spectre of *Borbor Bele* loomed over the elections. It has been noted that these concerns might be more applicable in urban settings, particularly amongst the youth, and perhaps mostly in Freetown, but it would still have had an effect.[11] Indeed, the Western Area is where the SLPP slumped worst, from nine seats in 2002 to zero in 2007, although historically the capital is more pro-APC. The Senegalese elections of 2000 are comparable elections in which maginalised urban youth with a long history of involvement in Senegalese politics were seen as instrumental in the turnover of power from Abdou Diouf to Abdoulaye Wade. There remains, though, a question as to whether urban youths in Sierra Leone and in Senegal are looking to fundamentally re-construct the system or to simply insert themselves into the patronage net.

Probably more important, given the appearance of Margai on the political scene, was the complacency towards traditional SLPP supporters. Patronage only works as a model for staying in power if it is sufficiently disbursed. Given a neo-patrimonial model of reciprocity or a model which notes the father figure role of African leaders—of a figure who can be ostentatious and feed himself but can only maintain legitimacy by also feeding his family, meaning his political supporters—the SLPP was instead probably seen not as too corrupt but as too narrowly corrupt.[12] Too much was 'chopped' or 'eaten' at the top and did not find its way through the informal networks or through formal channels in the direction of the heartlands. The SLPP had not honoured its obligations. Berewa's gatekeeper position with regard to the channelling of aid and the award of contracts to deliver the aid was seen before the election as a distinct patrimonial advantage, but the beneficiaries were clearly too few. As an indication of the party's lack of concern, whether in developmental or patrimonial terms, the road to the South and East, through the regional capitals of Bo and Kenema, was in just as poor condition as it had been in 2002, and the road to Kailahun District in the far East remained in an appalling state. The succession from Kabbah to Berewa, and indeed Kabbah's less than enthusiastic support including his backing of Thorpe, thus provided the opportunity for a turnover. The SLPP was then found wanting in many ways, even in its own ethno-regional backyard, a state of affairs that was successfully exploited by the APC and PMDC.

Given the immensity of this electoral moment, the notion of democratic consolidation rears its head. In a thin version of consolidation, two turnovers were enough for Sierra Leone to pass, although the two occasions are decades apart and the first turnover was postponed for a year.[13] However, there are many more nuanced definitions which require institutional and attitudinal considerations.[14] Institutionally, Sierra Leone still struggles at election times and in providing democratic accountability in between. In 2007 there were simultaneous steps forward and backward, particularly as regards violence and rigging. It is, though, the notion of elite and public perceptions that is most vexing. Democracy in Sierra Leone is indeed nearly the only game in town: there is not too much likelihood of a shift in regime type, although Mali in 2012 is a good example of a military coup and conflict in a relatively stable democracy. There is broad elite acceptance and public enthusiasm, but this was also the case in 1967.

A key question is whether one can consider a democracy that is underpinned not by policy but by patronage and ethno-regionalism, and where communal bloc votes are commonplace, as consolidated, and this depends entirely on the criteria for measurement. As noted before, there is considerable tension between the ideas of a requirement of economic, educational and class development before democratisation and the currently more prominent liberal thinking that the opposite is true—that democracy can firstly be pushed by domestic and foreign actors and then deliver development.[15] How much democratisation in Africa was driven from outside and how much was an organic internal process is then pertinent to the ownership, the sustainability and the substance of the resulting democracy. Both drivers were present in Sierra Leone: there was push from outside and inside. However, despite the increasing influence of internal drivers with usage over time and the emergence of democratic 'rituals', the development and class factors are still largely not in existence in Sierra Leone.[16]

One conclusion is that we are seeing a 'thin' procedural version of democracy rather than a 'thick' liberal notion. On the other hand, Sierra Leone could be seen as cultivating its own version of 'communal democracy' unrelated to considerations of class and societal wealth. If anything, democracy is a concept with many definitions, histories and contemporary actualities.[17] The democratic project is indeed 'everywhere emergent and incomplete' and the West may only claim a 'historical priority', not a 'monopoly of its current or future forms or definitions'.[18] Still, one would be bound to question the long-term stability of a democratic system built on such foundations as in Sierra Leone and indeed in many other African states. Whether democracy now delivers development is yet another question related to its sustainability. All of these questions of democratic consolidation continued into the elections of 2012 and 2018, covered in the next chapter.

In the aftermath, the defeated Berewa stepped down from the leadership of the SLPP. Whatever Margai's reasons for making the leap towards the APC camp, which despite having its beginnings in the first campaign is most likely simply political opportunism, the PMDC was rewarded with cabinet posts in a coalition government. Margai did not take up a post but, amongst other placements, Health and Sanitation went to Soccoh Kabia, son of the renowned Mende Chief Ella Koblo Gulama, and Captain Benjamin Davies became Minister of Lands, Country Planning and the Environment. In addition, while many APC cadres such as Ibrahim Ben Kargbo, Alpha Kanu and Serry-Kamal took up cabinet posts, some further leavening of the veteran APC bread was introduced through the appointment of the activist Zainab Bangura as Minister of Foreign Affairs and the Krio accountant David Carew as Minister of Finance.

Once again, some saw a potentially reforming president at the top of a more or less recalcitrant and unreconstructed party. Indeed, the ensuing five years of the APC term were strewn with evidence that could be interpreted as change and evidence that could just as easily be interpreted as conservation of the status quo. For a start, the introduction of new PMDC and non-APC faces into cabinet was an interesting development, even if towards the end of the term the PMDC presence had dwindled to two members and shortly before the election, Kabia defected to the APC. At the same time, Koroma was regularly accused of appointing Northerners to state positions, for instance replacing J.D. Rogers with Sheku Sambadeen Sesay as Governor of the Bank of Sierra Leone, or of reviving some form of Ekutay. Somewhat conversely and more unusual were the indictment and prosecution by the ACC of two cabinet ministers and the APC Mayor of Freetown. Two important actions allowed the ACC greater rein. First, legislation was passed to give the ACC direct arrest and prosecutorial powers, thus sidestepping the Attorney General. Second, Joko-Smart was replaced as head by the lawyer, Abdul Tejan-Cole, seen by many as a clean pair of hands. Although Tejan-Cole was to dramatically resign in May 2010 and be replaced by the former SLSC Deputy Prosecutor, Joseph Kamara, the prosecution of the two cabinet ministers had by then already started.

The first prosecution was that of Sheku Tejan Koroma, a PMDC appointee who replaced Kabia in the Health Ministry. He was suspended from his post in November 2009, less than nine months after taking over, and found guilty of abuse of office March of the following year. The second was of someone much closer to the core of the party: the Minister of Fisheries and Marine Resources, Afsatu Kabba. She was indicted and sacked in March 2010 and found guilty of misappropriation of public funds and abuse of office in the following October. Although the head of the National Revenue Authority, Alieu Sesay, was acquitted in June 2011, the sitting Freetown Mayor, Herbert George-Williams, was subsequently arrested in November and found guilty on corruption charges. As before in Sierra Leone, from the 1960s right through to the 2010s, one might read a number of motivations into these prosecutions, sackings and indeed failures to prosecute. Donor and domestic discourse demanded action and Tejan-Cole used the new powers relatively effectively. Equally, Tejan Koroma was not a party insider, but then Kabba was. Rumours circulated about APC intra-party squabbles that led to Kabba's 'sacrifice', but it is nonetheless remarkable that some heads rolled.

Other initiatives and reforms continued sporadically. The Attitudinal and Behavioural Change Secretariat was established but the Executive Director and National Coordinator were subsequently convicted of corruption by the ACC. More substantially, electricity was targeted and the mothballed pre-war Bumbuna Dam and Hydroelectric Project in Tonkolili District were finally brought on stream although still requiring major capacity and distribution work. Two sizeable and much-trumpeted policy initiatives emerged from the Ministries of Health and Agriculture in 2010: respectively, the provision of free healthcare for pregnant and breast-feeding women and children under five and a smallholder marketing programme. In the case of the former, and despite the absence of a Health Minister in the wake of the sacking of Tejan Koroma, the initiative was rolled out on time on Independence Day. Results by mid-2011, under the ministry leadership of Zainab Bangura until her departure for a UN job in 2012, seemed to indicate that some health care was being delivered free, but that a minimum standard of care was not being similarly delivered. Indeed, no clinics anywhere met the minimum standard set out in the initiative.[19] In addition, scandals hit the news in 2011 involving the disappearance of UNICEF-procured drugs and in early 2013 with the ACC indictment of twenty-nine of the country's top health officials, including the Chief Medical Officer, Dr Kisito Daoh, who was later acquitted of the charge of embezzlement of over US$1million of vaccine funds.[20] The policy must though have had some popularity as the SLPP later put forward a 2012 campaign policy of extending free health care up to the age of eighteen.

On the state reform side, the Public Sector Reform Unit (PSRU) was charged with such key duties as the cleaning of state payrolls. Reporting directly to the President after 2007, the PSRU had some success in the cleaning of payrolls and the expunging of 'ghost workers'. Of 17,500 civil servants, not including teachers, on the books in 2007, there was documentation for just 6,500. The total number was reduced to 13,000 after the DFID-funded payroll clean-up, saving Le500m (around US$130,000) per month. However, the payroll cleaning for teachers proved significantly more difficult and the DFID eventually withdrew funding.[21] The Ministry of Health was particularly targeted for reform in order to deliver the healthcare initiative. Donor-funded training, refurbishment and the doubling or significant increases of salaries resulted in small improvements but nothing like what had been expected.[22] A large EU-funded 'carrot and stick' initiative then began across the board in 2011 with the 'carrot' of higher salaries and the 'stick' of retrenchment.[23]

Equally, the continuing decentralisation programme had its fair share of ups and downs. In 2010 the APC government reintroduced District Officers, which was seen by many not so much as a bureaucratic exercise as a political manoeuvre. Some read the reintroduction as a sign that the APC was worried about the autonomy of Local Councils, thus showing—along with regular elections, the distribution of central resources to councils administered largely according to the rules and often improved local service delivery—the effectiveness of decentralisation.[24] However, lack of local capacity, lack of interest shown by parts of central government more focused on chieftaincy, the bulk of international resources still moving through government and NGOs, regional disparities, and patronage voting were problems that had clearly not gone away.[25] The relationship of councils with chiefs was still sometimes fraught, particularly over tax collection, or just as often interwoven, with chiefs' backing or being elected as councillors and mayors.[26] Centralisation of power in the executive as against the councils and indeed the still-under-resourced and mostly rather dormant Parliament remains evident.[27]

Disorder and violence emerged sporadically to threaten the political calm. As the PMDC faded into the background, the political dispensation returned to its more familiar two-party configuration. The PMDC performed poorly in the 2008 local elections. There were also a few skirmishes and intimidation of candidates to make them withdraw.[28] However, in March 2009, after clashes during a by-election for a council seat in Pujehun District, two days of disturbances erupted in Freetown. The SLPP headquarters was ransacked and partially burnt by APC supporters and seventeen were injured. The presence at the scene of OSD presidential bodyguard and the former AFRC military supervisor Idrissa Kamara, also known as 'Leather Boot', was indicative of continued political party involvement with police and ex-combatants. Kamara was sacked, both party radio stations suspended and a commission of inquiry instigated. More inter-party violence ensued in the 'non-partisan' Paramount Chief elections of December 2009 and January 2010, in September 2011 in Koidu and Bo towns and in January 2012 at another by-election in Freetown.[29] The diamond areas and other mining regions remained generally unstable. A peaceful demonstration near an industrial diamond mine in Kono District in December 2007 turned riotous, resulting in two deaths, many injuries, a commission of inquiry and new governmental guidelines on corporate social responsibility.[30] In April 2012, two days of rioting in Bumbuna related to a pay dispute at the iron ore mines drew a violent response from police and left one dead and several injured.[31]

In addition to the problems of control, reform and the need to respond to donor pressure in this direction, Koroma and the APC government were hit with the global recession. Although Sierra Leone had nothing like the dramatic global slump, GDP growth did fall below 5 per cent per annum for the first time since 2000, bottoming out at 3.2 per cent in 2009 and recovering to around 5 per cent in 2010 and 2011. Countering the global trends was the gradual coming on stream of larger quantities of mining revenue. Diamonds were still the mainstay of the Sierra Leonean economy, contributing 60–80 per cent of exports at the end of the 2000s (depending on prices), but revenue from bauxite, rutile, gold and particularly iron ore rose. It is often suggested in a direct comparison with Botswana that formal control over diamonds should be somewhat easier given the latter-day government-sponsored shifts from artisanal to industrial mining. Problems associated with security, as noted above, and the further removal of livelihoods of predominantly younger miners may, however, be another effect of this shift.[32]

Remarkably, however, heavy demand in Asia allowed iron ore to be mined once again at Marampa in Port Loko District and a new operation opened in Tonkolili District in 2011. Revenue was often estimated in billions of dollars and high double-digit GDP growth predicted. Oil was also potentially on the horizon after the deepwater discovery in 2009. Of course, much depended on the vagaries of production and demand in the global market, particularly in China and India. Chapter 10 continues this story. In turn, any benefit to Sierra Leoneans would depend on what happened to the new revenues at state level: national development, patronage resources and individual bank accounts all vie for priority. The agreements made with African Minerals and London Mining for the two large iron ore concessions quickly raised eyebrows because of the poor terms and the rumours of backhanders paid into APC party coffers. The London Mining deal was indeed renegotiated as it did not conform to the 2009 Mines and Minerals Act, but not so the African Minerals deal as it predated the act. Much would hinge on whether the various organs of state were able to direct resources into areas that are the officially intended end points. The mixed record of the Sierra Leonean state on this account and in its reforms and initiatives under Koroma and ten years into the historic ten-year DFID agreement requires explanation.

In Sierra Leone, the differences in functioning capacity within departments and ministries and between the state organs are striking. While some parts such as the donor-targeted Finance Ministry, from 2009 to 2012 under the leadership of Samura Kamara, performed their official functions relatively well, the National Revenue Authority and the Ministry of Education—both also important to donors—left much to be desired. Across the board, one can readily find continuing evidence of incompetence, unwillingness to work, deliberate obfuscation, and blatant corruption and intimidation. Within better functioning organs, it is often noted that the department or ministry is effectively run by a small number of high-level officials. Probably only in single figures in a given institution, they are frequently seconded non-Sierra Leoneans or from the sizeable, educated and often experienced Sierra Leonean diaspora, and sometimes on significantly higher wages. The former Finance Minister Kamara (and later Foreign Minister and APC presidential candidate in 2018) was sometimes seen as one who wholeheartedly aligned with the largely donor-inspired reforms in his ministry. When it was put to him that Britain was playing a big role in shaping the character and nature of the country, Kamara instantly responded that he would like Britain to play an even bigger role, although this can be read as ideological, pragmatic, or both.[33]

One might first see the use of small numbers of dedicated individuals as a pragmatic solution for donors and government with finite budgets to quickly improve state organs that have been grossly underperforming for decades. Indeed, as noted above, the large healthcare initiative was rolled out on time. In the decade post-2002, the country saw the second fastest improvements in the world on the UN Human Development Index and the third largest improvement in governance in Africa on the Mo Ibrahim Index.[34] Welcome though these advertised figures were, they built from a very low post-conflict base on the back of buoyant commodity prices, remained comparatively poor and are contestable owing to an inadequacy of data. The methods, in addition, beg several questions. On a practical level, there is most likely a finite time in which these individuals can continue to operate at such intensity and be paid so highly. On a longer term basis, success rests on the assumption that the ethic will trickle down to the rest of the institution. Finally, it is a very targeted strategy which leaves other ministries and departments in its wake, leading to partial reform or the creation of 'liberal bubbles'.[35] In some ways it aligns with the 'Drivers of Change' notion, which has been popular and well-known in donor circles and focuses on identifying champions of change and analysing their relations to informal and formal institutions.[36]

It is, as well, a largely donor-driven and very hands-on process in a small post-conflict country where donor influence is greater. Many considered that, despite Koroma's personal attention to the healthcare initiative and his ambitious announcement that it would be completed by Independence Day, the original notion, planning and push came from donors and primarily one key evangelist for this policy within one of the agencies. In a strategy that might be termed 'lighthouse politics', Koroma was considered to be the 'lighthouse' or the ultimate champion who could shine his political light on a policy and drive it through; donors' work is to regulate the light as it moved on from one point to the next.[37] One conclusion is that where more has been achieved under the APC, government ownership of policy on the other hand was as limited as it was in the SLPP era. The focus on high profile policies also puts incredible strain on the limited capacity of state institutions for the purpose of single initiatives. The chances of these policies being properly implemented and, crucially, maintained are rather circumscribed.[38] In a display of hard-headed pragmatism, one donor agency worker engaged in capacity-building noted that their main impact would probably not be in capacity-building, but only in a 'democratic' sense, that is, pushing through policies which may give Sierra Leoneans different reasons for determining which way to vote.[39]

There is also a wider argument that the concerns across the board are primarily those of the donors which, despite some variation in emphasis, are all current liberal concerns aligned with democratisation, accountability, promotion of civil society, economic liberalisation, good governance and the MDGs. The problems of liberal peace-building are of course not confined to Sierra Leone or even to Africa: it has been criticised for viewing Africa as a *terra nullius* with no domestic politics, and described generally as a chimera and its results as 'poverty with rights'.[40] Indeed, the programmes of economic and political liberalisation, the MDGs and aid in general have sometimes been seen as ahistorical in their claims to deliver development.[41] China, South Korea and indeed Europe come to mind. The notion of Sierra Leone and other poor countries as guinea pigs in a mostly well-intentioned but ideological experiment also raises its head. Solutions to the problems, however, often focus on the appropriateness of the architecture, tools and complementarity of international peace-building.[42] The intention is to improve on current paradigms of international intervention, to formulate a blueprint for peace-building, or even to envisage a hybrid participatory 'everyday post-liberal peace' that might embrace engagements between liberal states and non-liberal alternatives.[43] Despite some alterations, such as the return of the state, the 'drivers of change' initiative, the amalgamation of development with security, and the building of politics into development policy, any notion that there may be other non-liberal solutions is considered far less at policy level.[44] A more recent radical donor-sponsored intellectual effort— 'Going with the Grain'—has had much more limited circulation, at least in Sierra Leone.[45] Informal and 'traditional' institutions do figure in some donor thinking, although the tensions with the main policies are abundantly clear.[46]

Probably most importantly, it can be argued that the key reason for the problems of capacity and corruption and the very partial success of the proffered solutions is that some or many at various levels do not buy into reform of the state or even the idea of the Sierra Leonean state as it stands. Considered at the level of those who work in the lower ranks of the state and the population in general, and returning to the notions of reciprocity and obligation, this is a workforce immersed in patron-clientelism whose first priority is to village, chief, 'secret society', family, kith and kin rather than the state. Nepotism, diversion of resources and low levels of productivity can be explained by workers with moral communal obligations below to those they support and loyalties above to those who orchestrated their post in the first place. Indeed, the ones not fulfilling their obligations are considered those very much in the wrong.[47] In the upper echelons, the priorities are similar but on a grander scale involving national politics. These officials are torn between their obligations to their own people and to the state and donors, particularly as it effects their political aspirations. Thus, reform may or may not happen in a given ministry depending on this ever-evolving calculation. This is then 'a hybrid mix of tentative liberal institutions embedded within the local context of personalised exchange and affection.'[48] The only strata partially insulated from these obligations are the technocrats noted above.[49] However, tellingly, one certainty is that the year in advance of elections will always be a time when donor influence dramatically decreases and the reform bus can be parked as politicians turn all their attention to patronage.

Given its ambitious and wide-ranging aims, the main thrust of the liberal reform process is thus not for a quick fix but instead, whether intentionally or not and whether sufficiently resourced or not, for social change.[50] Whether trying to shift legitimacy from chiefs to councils, encouraging accountability through civil society rather than patronage networks and ethnic associations, furthering the transfer of priorities from community to capital, or endeavouring to make ministries function as they were designed, it is a shift in public thinking that is needed. The shift is required away from communalist obligations and 'traditional' structures towards individualist thinking and respect for a 'modern' state and 'modern' societal structures: the creation of *homo economicus*, an ideal of a liberal capitalist economic being, and *homo democraticus*, a similar democratic being.[51] Of course, all societies are in constant flux and there are some who believe that in the aftermath of the war, Sierra Leonean society is in an especially dense period of flux.[52] One compelling view is that war is one of the very few processes which can revolutionise social relationships, sometimes in positive ways.[53] In particular, some analysts, buoyed by the analysis of the war centred on chiefs, see this as a historic moment to modernise governance.[54] The state also has its own Attitudinal and Behavioural Change Secretariat, which is somewhat comparable at least in outlook with the efforts of other African states—now and in the past, military, one-party and democratic, socialist, Marxist and capitalist—to address these issues.

The first question, however, given the historic resilience of Sierra Leonean and indeed other African societies, is whether and how much social change can be pushed from either outside or inside. Equally, there is the further conundrum of whether the imported liberal measures are more or less likely to have greater success than other, often more authoritarian ideologies and methods of the past. Sensibly, there are some calls to manage expectations or accept that 'states producing a minimum of security and essential public goods may be both a feasible and a desirable outcome in the universe of fragile states'.[55] The use of the phrases 'second best solutions' and 'good enough governance' has been noted as an increasingly frequent occurrence in the donor community.[56] The final question, of course, is whether this sort of liberal modernising social change is desirable at all, or whether 'going with the grain' is potentially a more plausible developmental and political path, although one could easily detect a certain strain of that expediency throughout Sierra Leone's troubled political history.

Some have grappled with possible evidence of social change in Sierra Leone and where society is heading. Understandably, it is a difficult issue in the donor community as it is in many ways comparable to the last major outside effort to change Sierra Leoneans during the colonial era. Any allusion to neo-colonialism, social engineering or a new 'civilising mission' is not at all attractive in the current age.[57] Instead, there is often an assumption that either Sierra Leone will change to fit the prescriptions in a linear modernising fashion as is supposed to have happened in the West or, similarly, that Sierra Leone is already rapidly changing and liberal policies act merely as encouragement. In many ways, though, it is not so removed from the colonial-era ideas of sociocultural evolution and stages of development, or Cold War-era modernisation theories. Setting aside the notion of time and the historical *longue durée* of social change anywhere in the world—time periods far longer than the ten years (plus) of the DFID deal, a situation indeed recognised by some donor staff—there is evidence put forward for this sort of structural change. The growth of women's and youth groups outside of Freetown which may challenge the state in a peaceful and democratic manner is seen as indicative of a civil society away from the conventions of ethnicity or patronage. The democratic challenge on chieftaincy from councils, voting partly based on policy performance, and a state that functions however partially in a modern state-like fashion are seen as further indicators.

On the other hand, there is the influential hand and financial input of donors in all these processes and Sierra Leonean acquiescence may equally be seen as a new form of 'extraversion'.[58] One might suggest that there must be consequences of the large donor presence but that many of the consequences will most likely be unexpected. To illustrate how the scenario may not unfold exactly as some have thought, the story of a Paramount Chief's recent successful election campaign is pertinent. Having established his lineage credentials, the candidate then had to convince people that he was the right choice to bring development to this rural chieftaincy. He also noted that it was no longer like in his grandfather's day when one could just turn up at a village with a white envelope (of cash) for the chief. Utterly different now, he had to turn up with five white envelopes: one for the chief, one for the elders, one for the chief's staff, one for the women's group, and one for the youth group.[59] Change can thus be detected in an emphasis on development and a reorganisation of the patronage net to benefit those not conventionally in such a position of influence.[60] Continuity, though, is evident in the continued legitimacy of 'traditional' structures and the *modus operandi* of campaigning. Thus, imperatives 'meet and are negotiated, leading variously to repulsion, modification or acceptance, and hybridity'. This is often in unexpected ways that defy the breakdown into modern and traditional. These 'hybridities' have then been viewed sometimes as 'relatively benevolent' and at other times as 'much darker'.[61]

Some studies support a sense of change but with similar contradictions. Following from the idea of a 'crisis of youth' that has fomented conflicts of varying sorts in Sierra Leone, intergenerational struggles are viewed as key. Youth movements and the fluctuating threat to and co-option in the post-colonial order are not unusual in Africa and the example of Senegal in the 1980s through to the present day bears comparison.[62] There does indeed appear to be a current level of youth empowerment in Sierra Leone through representation in local government and youth associations. At the same time, the established older elites have also moved to co-opt and subvert any redistribution of power, and chiefs still maintain authority and legitimacy, albeit partially circumscribed. For their part, donors provide the discourse and the funds to assist the youth, supported by the analysis that chiefly offences against youths were a key driver of the war, but simultaneously risk accentuating the divide and potential for conflict between generations.[63] One survey in 2008 in Kono District, however, noted an end to unquestioning deference towards chiefs and elders but also revealed a greater youth satisfaction with chiefs, particularly those newly elected, even if they are still chosen only by their peers and for life.[64] At the same time, others have noted a dwindling in the influence of secret societies with respect to chiefs, due to urbanisation and Islam, or even predicted a decline in the belief in *juju* given its failure to protect during the war, all of which complicates the picture further.[65]

Youth organisation can be seen in the Cassette Sellers Association (CSA), the Bike Riders Association (BRA) and various advocacy groups in the diamond areas. Despite some successes in asserting autonomy and rallying behind non-sectional causes, the CSA executive committee still consisted of older men, the BRA engaged in a patronage struggle with 'big men' in Bo, and the Movement of Concerned Kono Youth (MOCKY) became a victim of its own success when its leaders were co-opted into local and national politics. Successors of MOCKY have continued to challenge the state, the chiefs and the mining companies and garnered international attention using donor support, modern media techniques and mobile phone technology.[66] However, the question of whether individuals within an organisation or the organisation itself are cause-driven or looking to penetrate patronage networks from a position of strength has not gone away. Civil society has many such problems of autonomy, funding, co-option and purpose.[67] In another scenario, diminishing returns from artisanal diamond mining and increases in food prices appear to be fuelling a drift back to farming or at least a shift in the balance of priority towards farming amongst those who have long engaged in both and used diamond, or indeed artisanal gold, revenues to invest in agriculture, trading ventures, cooperatives and farming associations.[68]

Challenging the patriarchal hierarchy has thrown up similar nuances. Across Africa, some have noted the exponential increase of women's groups in the post-Cold War era. More autonomous and wide-ranging than during the one-party regimes, women's groups are sometimes portrayed as the largest organised sector in society.[69] There are now African female Nobel Prize winners—the late Kenyan activist and politician Wangari Maathai—and presidents who are also Nobel Prize winners—Ellen Johnson-Sirleaf in neighbouring Liberia. Rwanda has the highest proportion of women in parliament in the world. However, women's groups face similar problems as youth groups in that they can be co-opted into patronage and ethnic networks or may rely completely on funding from outside. Indeed, the international women's empowerment agenda can obfuscate rather than illuminate efforts to understand change in African societies. The celebrated Rwandan statistic can just as easily be explained by patronage or a tactic to keep donors on the side of a regime with a very poor record in other areas. The documentary *Pray the Devil Back to Hell*, which played its part in the award of two Nobel Peace Prizes in Liberia, is to some extent an interesting look at a cross-ethnic, cross-religious women's movement but also an exercise in wishful thinking about a certain type of female empowerment.[70]

The challenges for the many women's groups in Sierra Leone are similar to elsewhere in Africa and to domestic youth groups, and are particularly reflected in the cases of chieftaincy and female circumcision or female genital mutilation (FC/FGM). Creating some friction, Customary Law is still accepted and recognised under the law in Sierra Leone. In this case, while the Constitution guarantees equality on the basis of sex, Customary Law varies across the country: there are fully-fledged female chiefs and Paramount Chiefs allowed in the South, but only junior chiefs of the female population in the North and areas of the East.[71] The court cases pursued up to state level by two women in 2010 concerning the matter of eligibility for contesting chieftaincies in Kailahun and Kono Districts put state and customary laws in contention with uncertain results. Given that the Constitution makes it legal to discriminate where Customary Law dictates so, one case was accepted and the other rejected.[72] Needless to say, the lines of the 'modern' and 'traditional' are thus again remarkably blurred, and politicians are usually keen to sidestep this particular hot potato. Rural women do seem to play at times a generally enhanced role, but whether the driver is from within or without is again unclear.[73]

The issue of FC/FGM exercises many donor agencies, much as it did colonial authorities, as it is seen as a contravention of several purportedly universal human rights.[74] It is, however, prevalent in nearly thirty African countries. The practice is controlled by women, aligned with rituals of adulthood and bound up in beliefs of honour, shame, purity, cleanliness and the good of the community.[75] In Sierra Leone it affects the vast majority of women, it is an important ritual of the Bondo Society and it is patronised by politicians.[76] Indeed, before becoming long-time SLPP Minister of Social Welfare, Gender and Children's Affairs in 1998, Shirley Gbujama threatened to 'sew up the mouths' of those who agitated against FC/FGM.[77] In February 2009, four female journalists reporting for UN Radio on the 'International Day of Zero Tolerance to Female Circumcision' were paraded naked through the streets of Kenema by other women for talking about FC/FGM on air.[78] Legally, a bill outlawing FC/FGM was withdrawn at the last minute in 2007 and has not been reintroduced, although in 2012 eight of the country's fourteen districts signed a Memorandum of Understanding criminalising FC/FGM for children. This does not mean that rural women's groups are ineffective, as noted above. Indeed, the war again created flux with an increase of female-headed households, and there is donor money available. The agenda of women's groups, however, may not always align with that of the donors.

There is another tentative sense of change in the air regarding international relations. The rapid rise of China and India as trade partners in Africa has produced much agonising in Western circles. There is considerable concern that Western influence in Africa and indeed the ability to push forward liberal reforms have now been diminished to be replaced by Chinese and Indian laissez faire, non-intrusive, partnership-style relations. Allied to the concern over criticisms of the efficacy of reform and a 2010s shift towards value for money and increased linkages to trade, some see diminishing Western interest in liberal peacebuilding, although a 'crisis of confidence' is probably a more apt description.[79] Predictions for this new multipolar world, then, range from seeing it as old wine in a new bottle to seeing it as something quite new. On the one hand, either Africa will be once more a bystander in an external struggle over raw materials and political hegemony and fall prey to a neo-imperial scramble for Africa, or African expertise in the processes of 'extraversion' will once again allow elites to control exchanges with the outside world and seal the political status quo.[80] On the other hand, the shift from a bipolar to a unipolar world at the end of the Cold War saw considerable shifts in Africa: the shift from unipolar to multipolar in global interaction with Africa may act similarly, either to reverse the post-Cold War changes or to create a new environment, particularly given Africa's unprecedented quarter of a century of semi-democracy.[81]

At present, Sierra Leone does not have quite the same high profile penetration of Chinese and Indian companies as countries like Angola and the DRC, but the Chinese are visible, particularly in road-building, mining, health and hotels.[82] Indeed, Chinese road improvements in Freetown and across the long-neglected mountain pass towards the interior became highly visible from 2010. Chinese immigration does not appear to be at the level of countries like Zambia, but at the same time the long-standing 'foreign' community in Sierra Leone, the Lebanese, can now finally obtain Sierra Leonean citizenship.

Other very recent international issues have not passed Sierra Leone by. Leasing of land to foreign firms, or 'land grabbing' as it has also been named, is a feature all over the fertile parts of Africa. The APC government's keenness to parcel out land, of which it claimed a rather unrealistic 85 per cent was not used, led to several large leases. It has been noted that state regulatory weaknesses, poor land inventories, and often ill-informed chiefs as custodians of the land have led to opacity and potentially great unfairness in the deals.[83] In addition, while Sierra Leone is not a key node on the main drug routes from South America via West Africa to Europe, it is not unaffected. A large shipment of cocaine was stopped at Lungi Airport in 2008.

Sierra Leone does, however, stand to benefit from the sometimes voracious Asian demand for its mineral products and to some extent its food products, and, as noted above, Western donors are concerned. There is little indication at the moment that Sierra Leone will turn away from liberal reform packages or Western aid; estimated in 2013 at around US$450m per annum but increasing significantly afterwards during the Ebola epidemic, which is covered in Chapter 10. The former Senegalese President Abdoulaye Wade wrote that 'China's approach to our needs is simply better adapted than the slow and sometimes patronising post-colonial approach of European investors, donor organisations and NGOs' and that 'the Chinese model for stimulating rapid economic development has much to teach Africa', but it is not too much of a surprise, given Sierra Leonean history, that none of this rhetoric is yet to emerge from a Sierra Leonean government.[84]

Sierra Leone thus approached the November 2012 elections (covered in the next chapter) in a period of relative calm but with innumerable issues of statehood, governance, nationhood, societal norms and foreign relations still open to interpretations of continuity and change. While it appears that the war and international funds may have shifted society and government to some degree, the question of how structural these changes are and how long they will last lingers on. Sierra Leoneans of all backgrounds may indeed be more demanding of the various authorities, hence increasing accountability, but this may often still occur within familiar parameters of 'tradition', patronage and obligation. Democracy is a case in point, where the electoral turnover was remarkable but delivered much within the confines of familiar voter rationales. Equally, while the 'transformed' APC seemed to deliver more national benefits, its cadres were quite aware that to win again, they also needed to play the more important game of patronage and ethno-regionalism. To some degree, the state-societal disconnections and divides continue to morph and even connect but not disappear, neo-patrimonialism is reinvented for the twenty-first century, and the distinction between modern and traditional loses meaning. Hence there still appears today the unceasing supply of apparently contradictory news stories, concerning corruption and anti-corruption, democracy and rigging, youth empowerment and youth marginalisation, and councils and 'traditional' authority.

More prosaically, there were also new SLPP opposition leaders—the former military head of state, Julius Maada Bio, as presidential candidate with Kadi Sesay as his running mate—and an incumbent party and president with a new track record. This would be a two-horse race and it appeared that the APC had done enough, in terms of development and patronage, to be re-elected. Despite foot-dragging and continuing gross levels of corruption, Sierra Leone had kept its head above water in a global recession, there were new revenue streams and some reform had occurred. In a democratic sense, one might conclude that Sierra Leone was inching its way forward. Despite the well-founded fears of inter-party violence and rigging, the struggling state institutions and the virtual certainty that the incumbent party would abuse its position for the benefits of patronage in a starkly divided country, none suggested that the elections would not go ahead or indeed that further national conflict was just around the corner.

10

MULTIPLE CRISES AND RESPONSES

EBOLA, IRON ORE AND HARD TIMES, 2012–2018

It is remarkable how much changed over the six-year period of 2012–2018. The political and economic auspices looked as promising towards the end of 2012 as at any other time since the 1960s. A third post-conflict election was conducted in November 2012, this time with minimal violence or attempts at fraud and an APC victory; investment was emerging from all angles including a large Chinese input, and iron ore prices were beginning to take off, stratospherically some thought, thanks to the Asian demand. However, within a little over three years of the mines commencing (and re-commencing) to export iron ore in 2011, the prices had collapsed, the mines had closed, and the Ebola epidemic was approaching crisis proportions. By the time of the run-up to the delayed elections in March 2018, with the economy in a parlous state, Koroma due to step down and the SLPP divided, Sierra Leone was once more at a crossroads. Remarkably, a second turnover of power at the ballot box in just over a decade ensued and the SLPP emerged as presidential if not parliamentary winners, but it was not without controversy. The chapter investigates these events and show how Sierra Leoneans and internationals have responded, and how these processes fit into the patterns of Sierra Leonean history.

First in this period, however, came the 2012 elections.[1] The line-up in the 17 November presidential, parliamentary and local council elections was a familiar one. The APC returned with Koroma and Sam-Sumana.

There were rumours of a new vice presidential candidate, particularly as Sam-Sumana's support in Kono had never seemed solid and he had become embroiled in corruption scandals, even though the ACC eventually exonerated him.[2] High profile floor-crossers included the former SLPP Finance Minister J.B. Dauda, who became APC Foreign Minister, and, shortly before the elections, Tom Nyuma, the former NPRC officer, Kailahun District Council Chairperson and 'big man'; the defeated but second-placed contender for SLPP flag-bearer, Usman Boie Kamara; SLPP Western Area regional chairman Lansana Fadika; and Soccoh Kabia, one of the last PMDC members of the cabinet. The opposition was fronted by the former NPRC head of state Maada Bio, but not until after a difficult internal election within a party in some disarray. The SLPP chose Kadi Sesay to be the first woman to stand for a major party as vice presidential candidate. Sesay is a former chairperson of the National Commission for Democracy and Human Rights (NCDHR), an erstwhile SLPP Minister of Trade and Industry, a Temne and Northerner from Moyamba District, and a Muslim. None of the others, including Charles Margai and the PMDC, the UNPP, PLP or RUFP, were remotely placed to win anything in either the presidential or parliamentary races.

The NEC was still headed by Christiana Thorpe after her bruising fight in the 2007 elections and with continued accusations of pro-APC bias.[3] The new biometric voter registration system was introduced, but the electoral body once again had a rough ride, coming into trouble over its hike in nomination fees and its initial miscalculation of the total percentage of the presidential votes. To avoid clashes, a campaign calendar was also introduced wherein each of the parties was given three days in a month to campaign in any given district, during which no other parties could appear on the streets. No unauthorised vehicles were allowed on the streets on Election Day. The Sierra Leone Broadcasting Corporation (SLBC) had been formed from the amalgamation of UN radio and the old state service in 2010 and added to the list of officially independent media outlets. The Independent Radio Network (IRN), formed in 2002, continued its work of disseminating information and monitoring. The elections were observed once again by the domestic coalition, NEW, and by the AU, the Carter Center, the Commonwealth, ECOWAS and the EU, amongst others.

In campaigning, Maada Bio endeavoured to play down abuses under the NPRC, including the execution of the APC-era head of police, Bambay Kamara, and twenty-seven others in 1992, as well as the alleged sale of Sierra Leonean passports to Hong Kong nationals. Instead, he positioned himself as a strongman, but also as both a democrat—portrayed as 'Terminator of One Party Rule' and 'Father of Democracy' on posters—and a bringer of peace.[4] To support this image, he drew upon his actions in toppling the APC in 1992, allowing democratic elections to then unseat the military, and talking to the RUF in 1996.[5] How much credence Maada Bio was given for any of these rather sweeping and contentious claims was open to debate. More concretely, he promised to provide free secondary education and expand the free healthcare initiative, although in the latter case this was a tacit admission that Koroma's policy had support. Being a Mende and a Southerner, Maada Bio could reasonably rely on strong backing in these parts.

Koroma made much of his incumbency. His campaign emphasised his role in government, especially concerning the infrastructure programmes, even if some appeared to have stalled or to be progressing very slowly. The slogan 'Action Pass Intention' endeavoured to indicate the difference between an action-oriented APC and an intention-driven SLPP. References were made to letting the 'Pa' continue his job. In a populist move, footballs were distributed at rallies. At the same time, the campaign and strategies were clearly very well-funded, and there was a particularly concerted effort to make inroads into the East. The most tense area was indeed the East where there was resentment of the moneyed APC presence in SLPP strongholds, the several chiefs campaigning for the incumbent party, and the local defections to APC were resented. A senior SLPP official noted that 'months if not years before the elections, Koroma had been going around the country performing acts of kindness far in excess of what was accepted as normal'.[6] A flashpoint in Kenema District in election week was narrowly avoided after the SLPP accused the APC of smuggling guns in baskets of dried fish.[7]

Remarkably, this was the most peaceful and clean election in decades. There had been electoral violence in by-elections and chieftaincy elections in 2009, 2010 and 2011, as well as further violence in January 2012 at another by-election in Freetown. Despite considerable fears, however, there were only minor incidents during the build-up to the national elections, and they were small-scale and very localised incidents that did occur do not suggest a high level of central planning. Ultimately, the time immediately preceding and during the election was calm. It may be that the campaign calendar and local mediation initiatives under the Political Parties Registration Commission (PPRC) were a success, or that violence was no longer deemed an efficient vote-collecting strategy. More likely, perhaps, is that violence became increasingly inefficient as the elections drew nearer and the results became less clouded, particularly given that violence was very much present until January of election year then abated rapidly.

Equally, beyond the flagrant abuse of government resources, outright fraud was significantly reduced. There were claims by the SLPP of electoral irregularities, including faked results forms, pre-marked ballot papers, ballot stuffing and over-voting in Kono, the West and the North. However, despite these claims, and the very large turnout of 87.3 per cent (which had raised some suspicions), the NEC only found four instances of the formerly commonplace over-voting in the results from the 173 polling stations that they investigated. It seems likely that the biometric registration could only have had an effect on the more brazen types of fraud in the registration period. The precedent of the annulments of 2007, and once again the reduced competition, is perhaps where one should turn to help explain the change in ballot box fraud in 2012. Notwithstanding, SLPP complaints taken through the courts continued deep into 2013.

Koroma emerged as winner of the presidential contest with 58.7 per cent of the vote, which meant that there was no need for a run-off. Maada Bio came a relatively poor second with 37.4 per cent of the vote. Importantly, while sweeping the North and West much as expected, Koroma took Kono District with 58.2 per cent and made inroads into opposition territory in the Eastern Districts of Kailahun (22.6 per cent) and Kenema (18.7 per cent) and the Southern District of Bo (16.7 per cent). This time, these inroads were made without the help of Margai, who came a distant third with just 1.3 per cent of the national vote. The parliamentary and Local Council elections followed suit. The APC took all parliamentary seats in the North and West, and the SLPP took all seats, bar one in Moyamba District, in the South. Again, in what will be seen as a successful campaign by the APC, the East returned the most unusual figures, with the incumbent party gaining ground in Kailahun and Kono Districts. The APC took one seat in Kailahun, but a very healthy six out of eight in Kono.

Beyond the clear ethno-regional patterns in the vote, which occasional policy pronouncements and SLPP appeals to women did not greatly perturb, the APC victories might also be attributed to the efficient use of considerable incumbent patronage resources on the campaign trail, and, to some degree, to the record of the party in office: while it was not outstanding, there were concrete improvements to which reference could be made. Improved roads and electricity supply, particularly in Freetown, were useful, but these improvements also extended outside APC heartlands. Travel to Bo and Kenema was by this point considerably quicker than it had been for many years, and there were visible signs of work on the Kailahun road. That being said, considerable APC effort in the East was indeed rewarded with success in the swing district of Kono, but with few returns in Kailahun and Kenema. On the other hand, the SLPP was unable to counter APC advantages with any great campaigning message or personality politics.

One might conclude that these elections were another step on the path to democratic consolidation and stability. Indeed, a relatively calm and clean election is very much to be desired. One could begin to tentatively question violence and blatant fraud as two of the ever-present rituals of Sierra Leonean democracy, although 2018 was to add more evidence to this enquiry. The notion that the opposition might accept the results was not emerging, and cries of fraud, whatever their legitimacy, continued. The 2018 polls are analysed later in this chapter.

President Koroma noted in his 2013 New Year address that:

we conducted four elections on a single day that were acclaimed by the whole world as meeting international standards of a free, fair, credible and transparent election; our economy was lauded as the second hottest economy in the whole world; our nation was acclaimed as amongst the safest on earth, and in December we were awarded the Millennium Challenge Corporation Award for good governance, promoting rights and investing in people.[8]

He went on to say that 'we achieved a lot in our Agenda for Change.' The devil, of course, is in the detail and, while Koroma might in some ways be very broadly correct in his assertions, the manner and extent to which Sierra Leone is changing—including those parts that are changing faster than, and in different directions to, other parts—is the real stuff of the future for Sierra Leone. Equally, this upbeat tone was maintained during the following year with some interesting effects, but it was soon tempered by the ensuing crises.

Indeed, there was a real sense of optimism, some of it rather starry-eyed, from within the APC after the election. Buoyed by needs in Asia, as noted in Chapter 9, iron ore prices rose dramatically, and in 2011 iron ore extraction began in Tonkolili and recommenced after a 35-year hiatus at Marampa. Revenue in the billions of dollars and double-digit GDP growth for years to come were estimated: in November 2011, both the Finance Minister Samura Kamara and the IMF went on record to predict a 50 per cent GDP growth just for 2012.[9] In fact, GDP growth did rise from its steady increases of around 5 per cent over the previous eight years to 15.2 per cent in 2012, and 20.7 per cent in 2013, and by early 2014 Sierra Leone had become the sixth-largest exporter of iron ore to China. Although this was not as high as predicted, it was substantial nonetheless and enough to produce a shift in governmental thinking.

One key indication was a detectably more muscular approach by the government in its foreign relations.[10] As noted earlier, the Sierra Leonean government has only usually been resistant to donor overtures on an ad hoc basis, and the relationship has only come unstuck in recent times when government compliance with reform has been deemed too limited, such as when budget assistance was suspended in 2007. Indeed, one study found that actors from both sides depicted the relationship as 'strong', 'positive', 'permissive', 'influential' (vis-à-vis donors) and 'appreciative' (vis-à-vis government).[11] Hence, it is a shift when government changes tack. This shift coincided almost exactly with confidence underpinned in the short term by iron ore prices, and in the longer term by the Chinese presence, the latter described at the time as 'unquestionably of extreme importance', particularly in infrastructure projects.[12]

Donors were already noting a 'hardening' in the government stance in 2011, and spoke of government being 'tough' in the ensuing few years. One donor official reported that in 2011 a government minister told Western donors that in two years' time he would no longer be talking to them, and thought that they might indeed be 'going home'.[13] Noticeably, the breakdown in relations with the UN head, Michael von der Schulenburg, led to his ousting from the post in 2012, which was thought by some as attributable to the confidence in government.[14] Spending increased, and ambitious road and energy projects were started, partly financed through loans, which led to an increase of 33 per cent in external debt between 2011 and 2013. The government also secured a US$315 million loan for a controversial new airport at Mamamah, to be constructed on the main Freetown–Masiaka road and thus more accessible than Lungi International Airport.[15] However, this was wholly opposed by Western donors including the World Bank and the IMF.[16]

The sense that global commodity prices can dictate the inner machinations of an African government brings the discussion back to dependency theory. However, the manner in which the government responds is not, once again, catered for by this theory, which locates causal factors in the international realm. One might say that the Sierra Leonean government response was significant, but not as hard line, for instance, as Ethiopia or Zimbabwe, and that the probable reasons for its activities in this period range widely from a disagreement (the UN head), through to electoral and developmental incentives (infrastructure), as well as legacy politics and interactional opportunities (the airport). The effects of the subsequent collapse in iron prices and the Ebola crisis then brings one back full circle to a further consideration of dependency and African agency.

In fact, by late 2014, this government confidence was almost entirely shattered. The slowdown in the Chinese and Indian economies pulled the plug on iron ore demand and the bottom fell out of the market. Both mines that had re-opened in 2011 were closed by early 2015. It was not, however, just iron ore prices that forced the closures. It was also the Ebola epidemic, which crippled Sierra Leone, Liberia and Guinea for eighteen months from mid-2014 onward. The disease spread rapidly and was retrospectively attributed to a case in Guinea near the intersection of its very porous and heavily used borders with Sierra Leone and Liberia in December 2013. The disease came to light in Guinea in March 2014, and the first known death in Sierra Leone occurred in Kailahun in May. Although Sierra Leone closed its borders in June, the death rate accelerated in the South and East of the country. The first case was reported in Freetown in July, and there were cases in all districts of the country by October. In the same month, the number of cases peaked at nearly 3,000, and in December the death rate reached its highest point of almost 1,200 deaths.

This was very much a human catastrophe. By the time the last case was recorded in Sierra Leone in January 2016, over 14,000 Sierra Leoneans had contracted the disease and nearly 4,000 had died. Schools, farms and businesses had been closed or under-used for long periods and the economy was reeling, shrinking by over 20 per cent in 2015.[17] The sickness, confinements and quarantines of whole areas were harrowing, and the fatalities and hardships were also immense in their proportions. In addition, given that the disease could be spread through bodily fluids, any physical contact with an infected person became highly dangerous. Thus, the societal toll also included everyday interactions. Gone were the tactile greetings, conversations and care-giving of most Sierra Leoneans, and gone or strictly policed were the majority of visits, gatherings, bars, clubs, cafés, local cinemas and places of worship that were the stuff of everyday life before the epidemic.

The response of the international community, of the Sierra Leonean government, and of ordinary Sierra Leoneans to the Ebola crisis requires some discussion.[18] Initially, the response from the internationals bodies and the government was underwhelming, characterised in one report as 'confusion, chaos and denial'.[19] Both parties faced considerable criticism for not reacting fast enough or appropriately. Médecins sans Frontières (MSF) were particularly scathing about the initial international response, noting in June 2014 that the epidemic in the three countries was already 'out of control', and yet MSF were 'the only aid organisation treating people affected by the virus'.[20] In August, the World Health Organisation (WHO) declared a Public Health Emergency of International Concern, but MSF remained critical of the slow arrival of resources on the ground.[21]

On the part of the Sierra Leonean government, the National Ebola Task Force was set up as early as March 2014. However, the dysfunctionality of this group, and of its second iteration established in July, the Ebola Operations Centre, was clear, with reports of a lack of strategic planning, serious infighting within the Ministry of Health, which was swiftly overwhelmed, and by arguments over money. The Ebola Audit Report grabbed the headlines when it was published in February 2015, as it noted that 30 per cent of the 84bn leones (US$18m) was not accounted for, funds which had come primarily from institutions and individual donations, as well as tax revenue that the government had set aside from May until October 2014. Non-payment of hazard workers and hospital staff caused protests and strikes.[22] A Presidential Task Force on Ebola was launched at the end of July and the Minister of Health was sacked. Although, in early September, when health workers and supplies finally began to arrive in significant quantities, they still found that there was limited coordination at national or international level.[23]

However, faced with a crisis of growing proportions, October saw a step change in both national and international responses. The UK took over the lead international role and, in mid-October, the National Ebola

Response Centre (NERC) was opened. On the Sierra Leonean side, the Chief Executive Officer role was handed to the seconded Minister of Defence, Retired Major Pallo Conteh, who directly briefed the President as well as the main international element of the NERC, comprised of the UK, UN and US. The British Army, RSLAF and the DFID played major roles in leading organisation and implementation. Indeed, RSLAF was generally praised, while the police were not broadly trusted and therefore side-lined, giving an indication of the successes and failures of IMATT, which by this point still functioned but had slimmed down to the International Security Advisory Team (ISAT).[24] Once the NERC had overcome initial tensions, the all-important coordination and policy decisions came from a close relationship between the DFID and President Koroma, who was seen as having a detailed handle on the response. In a notable display of authority, the major policy decision of imposing and enforcing large-scale quarantines was pushed through by Koroma against UK advice.[25] Many see this phase as by far the most successful part of the official response in Sierra Leone.

This would, however, leave ordinary Sierra Leoneans out of the discussion. Indeed, their role has generated as much debate as the role of the government and international institutions. Many reports and commentaries noted Sierra Leonean cultural practices as a large part of the problem in the spread of such a communicable disease. The custom of returning to a native village to die and be buried near ancestors; the close attention and care given to family members when sick; reliance on 'traditional' medicine and healers; burial and funeral practices such as the washing of the dead; and fear and misperceptions were all raised as significant contributors to the spread. For instance, the first cases in Sierra Leone were traced back to the funeral of a 'traditional' healer and, in November 2014, WHO staff estimated that 80 per cent of cases in Sierra Leone were linked to burial and funeral practices.[26] Equally, the riots in Kenema in July 2014 were accompanied by lurid stories of the use of blood for cannibalistic rituals, and widespread rumours that APC had caused the disease in order to decimate SLPP strongholds in the East.[27] The idea that 'free health care is free die' was heard in Kroo Bay in Freetown: people were not going to hospital because they might catch Ebola, but also because they didn't trust hospitals.[28] Some Sierra Leoneans were being portrayed as resistant to the Ebola response.[29] Finally, and from the opposite angle, a common phrase, '*Papa don cam fo save pikin*', meaning 'Father has come back to save his children', highlights a continued reliance on outsiders.

Another side to this narrative sees ordinary Sierra Leoneans in a different light. One argument dismisses cultural explanations for resistance to Ebola responses, and instead places the onus on contrasting historical state–society relations in Guinea and Sierra Leone; for example, Guinea had more resistance, and historically Guinean state institutions have poorer relations with local institutions such as chieftaincy.[30] This argument, however, risks exaggerating the purportedly closer relations in Sierra Leone. Another prominent argument presents Sierra Leoneans, their chiefs and secret societies performing extraordinarily brave actions and creating imaginative innovations in times of extreme difficulty and limited international as well as governmental support. Evidence is put forward of Sierra Leoneans learning fast in the face of adversity and lack of advice, yet these lessons and innovations were also ignored by officialdom. Remarkable stories emerged of how some communities began organising their own effective and safe burial teams, quarantines, by-laws, and protective clothing. Customs were altered to fit the emergency.[31] Latterly in the Ebola epidemic, it is suggested that communities and responders' approaches did converge, as both sides began 'thinking like an epidemiologist and like a villager'.[32]

These variant narratives of the roles of international, national and local actors raise important issues for this book. One might argue that any country faced with such an outbreak would need international help. However, the level of resources supplied by international bodies and the international lead in the organisation to counter the Ebola epidemic, even if heavily criticised, shows the dependence of Sierra Leone on the outside world. One might also note that some national leaders, including Koroma and Conteh, stepped up to the plate, but one would also have to acknowledge the impediments placed in the way of organisation by in-fighting and corrupt practices by other figures often at or near the national level. Finally, one could remark on the resilience of Sierra Leonean local and 'traditional' practices in the face of crisis, even while some helped and others hindered the fight against Ebola. The response at a local level emphasised that chieftaincy structures as well as the Poro and Bundu societies still, in many cases, function and hold legitimacy in the eyes of the populace, more so than most national institutions. Following on, there remains a legitimacy gap between local and national, and the national still struggles to get its message heard. Herein lies the continued debate on the future of Sierra Leonean governance.[33] One might finally note that, just like the war, all Sierra Leoneans were affected in some way—by the end this was once again a collectively experienced crisis.

It took until 17 March 2016 for WHO to declare Sierra Leone Ebola-free. However, the agreement between Koroma and the UK DFID minister, Justine Greening, to establish a two-year Post-Ebola Recovery period according to plans developed by the DFID had already been enacted in June 2015. In many ways, the new plan was based on the strategies used to combat Ebola, utilising a highly centralised team to focus narrowly on what was urgently required. The rationale was explained as the need to strike while the iron is hot and to use the period to push through as much as possible, before the onset of campaigning for the 2018 elections and potentially before the government turned to the Chinese.[34] The method, following on from NERC, was the creation of the Delivery Team in State House: essentially two parallel groups, one governmental and one advisory, the latter rather expensively assembled and comprising about 25 members from two consultancy firms employed by the DFID—McKinsey and Adam Smith International—and the (then) Africa Governance Initiative (AGI), an NGO established in 2008 by Tony Blair. The centralisation of command, the geographic location of the Delivery Team in State House and the intimate connections with the President, certainly had their benefits. The plan built on strong UK–Sierra Leone relationships which had been developing since the start of the Blair and Kabbah governments in the 1990s, and strengthening during the Ebola epidemic, particularly between Koroma and the DFID and the UK High Commissioner, Peter West (2013–16).

However, there were considerable criticisms. First, the centralisation in State House excluded some within the government, in particular in the ministries and departments and to some extent in the donor community. This was a plan dominated by the President and the DFID. On the one hand, there was considerable disgruntlement in the government from perceived losers in the new arrangements, and it was noted that the President had needed to bring complaining ministers back in line.[35] It was suggested by one donor head that donor access was 'perhaps too easy', and by a critical government official that it was an 'open door' and 'unlimited'.[36] The second phase of the Post-Ebola Recovery in 2016–17 came under the title of the 'President's Recovery Priorities', with billboards and government vehicles sporting the President's Recovery logo on them. It also looks rather similar to the 'lighthouse politics', 'liberal bubbles' and the reliance on small numbers of people to push reform as discussed in Chapter 8. On the other hand, the DFID in 2015 was variously seen as 'arrogant', 'bullying', 'resented' and not a 'team-player', as well as having 'solved' the Ebola crisis, thus legitimated to take the same approach into the future. The Delivery Team was known by government and donor officials as the 'DFID's Delivery Team'.[37] Although by mid-2016 donor–donor relations had significantly improved, some donors continued to ignore, or only work when necessary with, the Post-Ebola Recovery programme. Secondly, in policy terms, it was argued that the Post-Ebola Recovery priorities were not actually focused, but too broad in that there were, by the halfway point, forty-five initiatives and over 150 sub-initiatives, including such large projects as community health workers.[38]

The end of the Post-Ebola recovery period coincided with the ratcheting up of the campaign for the 2018 elections. Crucially, President Koroma was constitutionally obliged to step down after his two terms. As in 2007, this left a partial vacuum at the very top and opened up the process to more possibilities. Given the poor state of the economy as well in the post-Ebola and post-iron ore high prices environment, the opposition could conclude that it had a good chance at the polls. Initially, there was an unofficial campaign which suggested that the constitution might be changed to allow 'more time' for Koroma, particularly as his programme had been derailed by Ebola, but perhaps sensing his legacy in jeopardy, Koroma did not follow up. The election date was in any case scheduled outside the constitutional limit of five years and three months, but it was set to go ahead on 7 March 2018.

There were, however, problems for both of the main political parties. At the top, the APC had to choose its new leader, and a raft of top politicians lined up to contend, including Vice-President, Victor Foh; Justice Minister, Joseph Kamara; former Ambassador to China, Alimamy Petito Koroma; APC stalwart, Alpha Kanu; Minister of Mines, Minkailu Mansaray; former Finance Minister, Kaifala Marah; and Foreign Minister, Samura Kamara. At the same time, the SLPP was also in flux. The party was still not over its schisms dating back to the last election. This time, the main contenders included Maada Bio, despite his electoral defeat in 2012, a former UN Under-Secretary-General, Kandeh Kolleh Yumkella or KKY, and the SLPP and NPRC veteran, John Oponjo Benjamin. This looked to be a close-run fight, and the hostility between the contenders seemed to be handing the APC a victory, until Yumkella suddenly 'suspended' his bid in July 2017, blaming harassment, violence, as well as a lack of internal democracy, and began talking instead of a grand coalition.[39] This left Maada Bio as clear frontrunner in the SLPP, but also opened up the system to the possibility of a credible third party.

In the end, a surprise package of Samura Kamara and Chernor Maju Bah emerged as the APC presidential candidacy. Maju Bah was the Deputy Speaker of Parliament, a Muslim, a Fula and an MP in Freetown, hence a plausible choice as a running mate. Kamara was an outlier in the race for presidential candidacy and many assumed he had been selected by President Koroma, resulting in an unsuccessful court case on the grounds of both undemocratic election and dual citizenship.[40] Kamara could, however, point to his leadership in two key ministries—Finance and Foreign Affairs—and his economics background outside the country and inside government during the previous SLPP administration. He is a Temne and a Catholic, although his parents were Muslim. He also had to face up to Maada Bio, whose details appear above, and Mohamed Juldeh Jalloh, a Muslim and a Fula from Kono, again a plausible selection.

However, there would not just be a credible third party to upset the equilibrium, but a fourth as well. Yumkella did indeed return with a new party, the National Grand Coalition (NGC). Until 2015, he had enjoyed an illustrious career mostly outside Sierra Leone, serving as a UN Under-Secretary-General and as Director-General of the UN Industrial Development Organization, and painted himself as progressive and internationally-connected. He is a Muslim and a Susu from Kambia District. Yumkella was clearly feared enough by the APC for the party to file an unsuccessful court case against him, alleging he had dual citizenship.[41] In addition, another returnee surfaced in the form of Sam-Sumana. He had been expelled from the APC in 2015 for allegedly creating his own party, and then shortly after dismissed from the vice-presidential position after seeking asylum in the US embassy, the latter action by the APC was subsequently declared illegal by an ECOWAS court just three months before the elections.[42] Sam-Sumana is also a Muslim but crucially comes from the key district of Kono. His new-founded Coalition for Change (C4C) enjoyed an immediate and potentially sizeable regional base.

Added this time to the usual campaign methods of personal appearances, mass rallies, billboards, newspapers, radio and handouts, was a greater emphasis on social media and house-to-house campaigning. Demonstrating the potential of social media, a lot of fake news was generated and spread. For instance, close to the polls, 'news' that UN peacekeepers were about to be deployed spread across WhatsApp along with old photos. The Police Inspector-General subsequently released a formal statement to the contrary. With 75 per cent of the vote counted, and the leading candidates almost even, a story emerged that Maada Bio had won with an implausible 56.3 per cent. Internet usage remains low and predominantly urban but, as with newspapers with similar low circulation, the stories were rapidly shared and became well-known, although to what effect in 2018 is questionable.[43] House-to-house campaigning dominated the period between elections when rallies were conspicuous by their absence. In addition, task forces were re-assembled and violence, while not ubiquitous, re-emerged, particularly in the interim period and immediately after the announcement of the final results, and it involved supporters of both parties and 'regional' rhetoric from some politicians.[44] Contents of the campaigns are discussed below in explanations for the results.

Once more, a campaign calendar for the political parties was established and no unauthorised vehicles were allowed on the streets on Election Day. Biometric voter registration was used for the second time. At NEC, Christiana Thorpe stepped down as head, and long-time elections administrator, Mohamed N'fah-Alie Conteh, was appointed by the APC government in her place. The number of observing organisations was reduced from 2012, but still included the domestic coalition, NEW, the AU, the Commonwealth, ECOWAS and the EU. There was the usual buoyant media with the significant escalation of the use of social media, as noted above. After an earlier war of words with Koroma, Emmerson was once again active with new songs satirising politicians, including mockery of Kamara by using a voice sample of one of his less inspiring moments.[45]

The results were extremely close between the two frontrunners, but were complicated by the significant gains of the next two candidates. A high turnout of 84.2 per cent of registered voters gave Maada Bio a slight lead in the presidential race with 43.3 per cent against Kamara's total of 42.7 per cent.[46] Predictably, Maada Bio won overwhelmingly in all of the

South plus Kenema and Kailahun in the East, and Kamara came first by some margin in all of the North, excepting Kambia but including the new districts of Falaba and Karene, plus Western Area Rural and Urban. Yumkella came third with 6.9 per cent and Sam-Sumana fourth with 3.5 per cent. These were not high totals and certainly disappointing for Yumkella, but they remained crucial for the run-off that now had to occur between the two frontrunners. Only one other candidate broke the 1 per cent barrier, and then only by a slim margin. Sam-Sumana won in Kono and took over 80 per cent of his total there, amounting to more than 70,000 votes in the district. Yumkella accumulated over 38 per cent of his vote, nearly 67,000, in Kambia and neighbouring Port Loko Districts, but importantly took over 48,000 in his combined total in Western Area Urban and Rural. In comparison, the difference between Maada Bio and Kamara was less than 15,000 votes.

Remarkably, Parliament has also seen some perturbations on past history. Whilst Kamara was emerging as runner-up, the APC maintained its position as the largest party in the chamber. The SLPP had forty-nine seats, APC had sixty-eight, C4C had eight, and NGC had four. There were three independent members and fourteen Paramount Chiefs (the two extra representing the two new districts). As expected, the SLPP won the vast majority of the South and East, and the APC did the same in the North, but there were anomalies. Unusually, independents took seats in SLPP territory in Kailahun and Pujehun, and the SLPP won one seat in APC territory in Tonkolili. In addition, the APC took its usual one seat in the Southern district of Moyamba, and the APC won all seats in the reorganised North-West, except one seat in Falaba. Most striking, APC amassed seven seats to the SLPP's one in Western Area Rural and eighteen seats to the SLPP's two in Western Area Urban. All C4C seats were won in Kono and all NGC seats in Kambia, with the APC taking the remainders in each district. There were a total of 115 men and seventeen women elected in non-chieftaincy seats.

Before the run-off could take place on 27 March, the process was temporarily halted by allegations of electoral fraud. In a complicated series of events, an interim injunction was granted, after a former APC MP applied three days before the run-off date, and then rescinded two days later.[47] By this point, it was too late for 27th to be Election Day, and the run-off was put back to 31st. This was not, however, the end of fraud allegations and court cases which both re-emerged after the run-off. In the meantime, Yumkella and the NGC refused to back either candidate, and Sam-Sumana rather ineffectually flirted with the APC camp just two days before the run-off.[48]

In another high turnout of 81.1 per cent, Maada Bio won the run-off by a small margin with 51.8 per cent of the votes cast, a matter of 92,235 votes. Importantly, Maada Bio comfortably won Kono. Sam-Sumana's supporters were clearly more convinced of their grievances and allegiances than their leader—Kamara's vote increased by only around 6,000 votes whereas Maada Bio's increased by over 60,000, in the third lowest district turnout of 69.3 per cent. However, there were other shifts. Kamara gained around 20,000 extra votes in Western Area Urban, but Maada Bio performed better, winning around 33,000 further votes. Meanwhile in Kambia, which had the second lowest turnout at 65.7 per cent, Kamara's addition of around 27,000 votes to his first round total was not significantly far ahead of Maada Bio's additional 19,000.

Explaining the electoral defeat of an incumbent government is always complex. Explaining the third such defeat in Sierra Leone history—the second in just over a decade—is more complex still, with the additional caveat that the incumbent party in 2018 lost the presidency but not the Parliament. In 2018, the incumbent APC certainly had a record in government. On the plus side, Ebola had been defeated and Koroma was seen as having played his part. Infrastructure continued to appear, most noticeably in the Chinese-built second road out of Freetown over the mountain pass, which cut time getting in and out of the west of the capital enormously. There was the promise of the new airport and a 62km toll road from the outskirts of the capital past the proposed airport and on to Masiaka. As Freetown is electorally important, these actual and proposed schemes were useful for electoral support. Indeed, the APC continued to perform well in the capital.

However, across the country many were feeling the hard times and prices of basics, including petrol and electricity, had risen. The government was fiscally in dire straits and less popular, even though it could hardly be blamed for the effects that the Ebola epidemic and poor iron ore prices had on the economy. Floods, however, which took the lives of hundreds outside Freetown in August 2017, could be blamed by some on government mismanagement of land after the construction of the mountain pass road. Indeed, roads are certainly not everything, and there was little else to celebrate. Further, corruption scandals continued to plague the government. Ebola had indeed been defeated, but the unaccounted billions of leones identified by the Ebola Audit Report remained unexplained. In August 2017, less than six months before the elections, two Assistants to the President and a Minister of State in the Vice President's Office were sacked for their part in selling government Hajj scholarships designed for those who cannot afford to undertake the journey to Mecca.[49]

Maada Bio and the SLPP took some advantage from the economic malaise and corruption scandals, but it was not through any finely calibrated and differentiated manifesto. Maada Bio's campaign was almost as lacklustre as that of Kamara's. Indeed, the slogan *Paopa*, meaning 'by any means necessary', proved controversial. However, there were other important dynamics, particularly as the run-off came in sight. The first round presidential poll was close, and showed that the SLPP had overall gained ground on the APC since 2012, but in the run-off there were sizeable votes from two other players over which to compete. Given the shifts from the first round to the run-off, Maada Bio's choice of a Kono man for running mate, rather than a Freetown man as Kamara had chosen, was perhaps more astute. Probably more tellingly, just over half of Kono voters chose Sam-Sumana in the first round, and it seems that almost all of them transferred to Maada Bio in the run-off. The dismissal of Sam-Sumana from the APC and the vice-presidential post in 2015 was far from irrelevant in voters' calculations. Similarly, the allegations aimed at Yumkella by the APC (which were dismissed by the court during the campaign) most likely ate into the number of votes that switched from Yumkella to Kamara. In this Northern district, Maada Bio almost kept pace with Kamara from the first round to the run-off.

With regards to symbolism, the SLPP were smarter. One might juxtapose SLPP usage of Palm Sunday—the SLPP symbol remains a palm tree—to Kamara's appearances in a bow-tie. Equally, Maada Bio, whilst still emphasising discipline, seemed to get beyond his military past and in softly-spoken tones endeavoured to present another image of himself. He had, in the period since the last election, studied in the UK for an unfinished PhD in politics. In the first ever Sierra Leonean presidential debate with all leading candidates staged on 15 February, Yumkella insisted on speaking in Krio.[50] This was most likely to show authenticity from a man who had spent so long abroad, and was deemed by some as the winner, but importantly many placed Maada Bio ahead of Kamara.

Maada Bio talked about his policy of free education even though this was already an APC initiative—conceivably it was the partial implementation by the APC which allowed Maada Bio the political space. In the final calculation, Kamara emphasised continuity—*De Pa Don Wok* or 'Koroma has been working'—in an unhealthy economic environment, and Maada Bio was the change candidate—a 'New Direction'—in a close race where he gained a small but propitious lead in the first round; change had certainly been in the air in the region following the recent electoral overturns of power in Ghana and Liberia.

One would have thought that the parliamentary results would have followed suit as has been the case in all other elections, and the fact they did not warrant an explanation. Certainly, the first-past-the-post system played a significant part and benefitted the APC in Freetown. Despite polling around a third of votes in both Western Urban and Western Rural, this translated into only two out of twenty seats in Western Urban, and one out of eight in Western Rural. Proportionally, this would have been nine SLPP seats.[51] The SLPP also lost out to three independents in its heartlands. A small number of additional seats may have accrued to APC after the creation of the two new districts, although this could also have simply redressed a previous imbalance.[52] Taking these factors into account begins to even up the numbers of seats. The result, of course, sets a new precedent for Sierra Leone in that the President's party does not have a majority in parliament, and the outcomes are not predictable. Indeed, in the immediate aftermath of the election, there were ugly scenes in government when all APC MPs left Parliament in protest after court injunctions led to an order of expulsion for several of their number. Importantly, the election of the Speaker occurred straight afterwards and, despite the APC majority, the SLPP veteran, Abbas Bundu, was elected.[53]

However, there still remains the issue of whether we can trust any of these results. After the run-off, the APC filed a petition alleging that the run-off election was fraudulent.[54] The rush to swear in Maada Bio as President—in a hotel foyer immediately after NEC had declared the results on 4 April—is suggestive of an effort to head off any petition. Over-voting was certainly detected, and once again in the first round, the results in 221 polling stations (accounting for 1.9 per cent of the polling stations) were declared void. These were from all over the country, with the districts of Port Loko, Kambia, Kenema and Western Area

Urban most affected. As always, this hides very high vote levels that are just below 100 per cent, and some alleged that there were many more stations over the maximum limit, predominantly in the South.[55] Allegations of irregularities in the result data entry, reconciliation of result forms, mixing of ballot boxes, and intimidation of party polling agents also emerged.[56] Added to the problems concerning the voting register during registration and the election, there was sufficient evidence to raise doubts. It must also be noted that in a considerable turnaround from past events (but similar to Liberia in 2017) it was the opposition which was alleged to have cheated. However, concerning the first round, the Commonwealth Observer Group Chair and former President of Ghana, John Dramani Mahama, noted that 'Our overall conclusion is that the voting, closing and counting processes at the polling stations were credible and transparent', and the EU observed 'well-conducted elections … although the campaign was marred by intimidation', particularly by security services, including a raid on the SLPP situation room and Maada Bio's home on Election Day.[57] Some within the APC, however, went on to publicly accuse Mahama of bias.[58]

It could be noted that the APC, with all the advantages of incumbency, had been outflanked in every quarter even concerning irregularities, and to others that the APC had finally lost an election that they themselves had organised. Intra-party rivalry was a key factor, with the defections of Yumkella and Sam-Sumana as well as the inclinations of their supporters proving to be highly important. Koroma's 'selection' of Kamara as APC presidential candidate led many to question his wisdom. Indeed, a series of mistakes by APC, from their presidential candidate selection, to the treatment of Sam-Sumana, to the court case against Yumkella, to a particularly uninspiring campaign, added to the sense of economic malaise and political stagnancy and provided the impetus for change. Maada Bio and the SLPP played a slightly better game in campaigning, strategising and bringing people from outside their heartlands onside.

Again, one conclusion might be that these elections were yet again another step on the path to democratic consolidation and stability, given another overturn in power. This occurred only in the presidency, but that is where most of the power lies. However, one might take a more nuanced look at precedents or rituals of Sierra Leonean democracy which appear to be emerging. On the one hand, a version of democracy is embedding where the electorate is enthusiastic and knowledgeable. It is also a version underpinned by fragile institutions and firmly entrenched in patronage, chieftaincy and ethno-regionalism, which shows only slight perturbations over time: it took the conclusion of a war to give Kabbah 70 per cent of the vote. In addition, some violence and fraud re-emerged after 2012 and the opposition, once again, did not accept the results. Elections, of course, are not everything. However, their twists and turns remain, in Sierra Leone's case, remarkably good indicators of the general shifts and continuities in politics, government, state and society.

Finally, a note on the comparison of the three opposition party victories is necessary. There are many factors that are different in the three outcomes, for example in 1967, as opposed to 2007 and 2018, there was no violence, and an incumbent leader and chieftaincy elections proved crucial. However, there were similarities in that there were significant economic problems before each election, a level of complacency and key mistakes by incumbent political parties, and better organisation from the main opposition, as one might expect. Electoral irregularities were also ever-present, although latterly becoming more varied. Crucially, however, was the presence in each case of other serious political forces—independents in 1967, the PMDC in 2007, and NGC and C4C in 2018—which served to upset the delicate balance of Sierra Leonean electoral politics.

It is too early to measure the record of Maada Bio's government in this book. However, two key events immediately after the inauguration are worth noting. The parliamentary difficulties, which are noted above, might be viewed on the one hand as an indicator of the difficulties to come but, on the other hand, as a sign of parliament becoming more important than it has been since the 1960s. The second can also be read in two ways. The new cabinet showed a number of returnees from previous SLPP governments, briefly including Charles Margai, but it was the appointment, for the first time since the colonial era, of a Chief Minister which raised eyebrows. Tasked with coordinating the government, this might be seen as a continuation of ideas that Tony Blair's AGI and the DFID had promoted in the period after the Ebola epidemic. It also proved controversial in that the position was said to be too large and too powerful, and unclear in its role next to that of the Vice-President and Chief of Staff.[59] Those interested in history will also note that the National Cleaning Day introduced by the NPRC was re-introduced by a former member of the NPRC, Maada Bio. No doubt, the new SLPP government faced the most difficult challenge of any incoming dispensation since its predecessor in 2002. Much was blamed by the SLPP on the outgoing APC, but many factors, such as the Ebola epidemic, iron ore prices and the global downturn, were not the fault of the APC; any party would have been hard-pressed to handle these crises. In this environment, the success or otherwise of any of the new programmes will be challenged and remains, of course, to be seen.

The underlying themes and patterns underpinning the narrative of this book continue, then, to shift and turn, but remain, to a considerable degree, in place. 'Traditional' authorities and practices took centre stage in the Ebola epidemic where they were either blamed for the spread of the virus or praised as a significant component of the fight against it. The urban–rural divide has not gone away. Democratisation continues apace, and, although steps forward have been made, in particular the 2018 opposition victory, there are new scenarios such as in the opposition majority parliament, and there are backward steps in terms of the contestation of election campaigns and results. The direction of travel thus remains opaque and the creation of a new type of democracy persists as an idea. International forces continue to buffet Sierra Leone in familiar and novel ways. The Chinese arrive, iron ore prices go up precipitously and fall alarmingly, Ebola emerges and is beaten, and the Western presence is substantially increased during the epidemic and in its aftermath. The pros and cons of these interventions and the advantages and disadvantages to either the Sierra Leonean government or its people are many. Finally, the issue of structural or procedural change is left for consideration in the following and conclusive chapter.

11

CONCLUSION

No-one would deny that Sierra Leone has been through practically the full range of statehood experiences, and that its history and politics have tested the analytical powers of generations of scholars to the full. The absence of radical ideological politics at state level and, despite some agitation in academia, its rarity at any level is perhaps the only missing ingredient. Its people have been and are still the main bearers of this extreme range of experiences. Sierra Leone has also remarkably found itself fluctuating between an existence, like much of Africa, at the global periphery and being thrust into the limelight at the centre of international interest in failing states, diamonds, conflict, post-conflict reconstruction, epidemics, and the idea of liberal peace.

The story of Sierra Leone can be found, in part, elsewhere in Africa, whilst at the same time having a number of unique features of its own. Comparable colonial legacies and the controversy around this matter emerge from north to south and east to west on the continent. There are differences over style from officially sanctioned British indirect rule to the supposedly widely divergent French and Portuguese direct rule which, in the final analysis given the lack of resources, looked remarkably similar. Partial or complete settler rule in South Africa, Rhodesia, Kenya and Angola also led to perturbations in colonial methods. In addition, there were differences in the reliance on coercion, with the Congo under Leopold II of Belgium standing out. However, all were economically extractive but at the same time concerned with their various versions of the 'civilising mission'. All were equally circumscribed in each of these projects by a heavy reliance on local African political hierarchies to maintain control and achieve at least some acquiescence to colonial imperatives. Colonial power did indeed reconfigure local hierarchies, particularly as it added the colonial state into the mix and made some forms of capitalist and governmental penetration, but many local features such as political and social practices remained or were even strengthened. Chieftaincy, 'traditional' spiritual beliefs, judicial and land practices, and social hierarchies were often changed only in that they were re-organised, categorised and codified by the colonial state.

Colonialism in Sierra Leone fell very much into the British indirect methodology, with local power and legitimacy remaining in the chieftaincies and 'secret societies', even though distortion and manipulation of chieftaincy and coercion were also conspicuous. There are perhaps two key differences from other British African colonies. One comes with the longer duration of colonialism and the Creole population, a historical variation that Sierra Leone shares to the same extent with few other African states, most pertinently with Liberia and Angola. Indeed, a tentative argument is made in this book that the combination of chiefly power and Krio paternalism led, from 1951 onward, to peculiarly conservative national political dispensations. Ties to Britain remain, there are no radical governments and, in an indication of the continued importance of 'tradition', Paramount Chiefs maintain their fourteen (once twelve) seats in Parliament. Despite the patron-client relations building between the centre and the provinces during colonial times and shifting into the postcolonial era, it is argued here that there has also developed an accompanying extended gap between urban and rural, or perhaps more accurately between elites and non-elites. The other key difference concerns the discovery of diamonds in 1930. The repercussions of Sierra Leone's simultaneous reliance on, and struggle to, control diamonds include those associated with the resource curse as well as issues of 'traditional' and state authority, all of which are still felt today.

Most of the decolonisation in Africa occurred in the first half of the 1960s, when nationalist demands coincided with the desires of all imperialists barring the right-wing regimes in Portugal and Spain to get out. Sierra Leone was no different. It is also a good example of an elite and a former colonial power with similar attitudes on how the relationship should continue and how Sierra Leone should be ruled. There was very limited confrontation by comparison with Ghana or neighbouring

Guinea. Indeed, Sierra Leone then fitted into a group of broadly capitalist and Western-leaning African states, including such countries as Kenya and Sierra Leone's near neighbour Côte d'Ivoire, that sought state-led development but not to the same extent as the socialist countries. All these governments, no matter their hue, would later be classified as more or less neo-patrimonial, with a political culture that built on pre-colonial and colonial legacies of reciprocity and patron-clientelism. Equally, in what was later labelled as extraversion, all would use outside support, either putting all their eggs into one basket or playing off East and West, much as Sierra Leonean governments have endeavoured to do.

Just as the colonial authorities in Sierra Leone were forced to rely on more legitimate local structures, so it was the same for the post-colonial governments across the continent. The difference in Sierra Leone is the particular response of the immediate post-colonial SLPP and APC regimes. The SLPP under Milton Margai was not just reliant on chiefs but built on chiefly families. His half-brother, Albert, took the SLPP into the realm of ethno-regional power, shifting the SLPP southward and eastward. The twelve months in 1967–68 then became the year when problems crystallised: Siaka Stevens and the APC were elected, removed by the military, exiled and then reinstated by junior military officers, all during this small time period. Given the further precariousness of the political environment, Stevens responded with a cult of personality, a one-party state, an extreme version of neo-patrimonialism that veered into straightforward patrimonialism, a 'Shadow State' that endeavoured to control illegal and legal markets through informal networks with Stevens at the head, and a steadily increasing layer of coercion. The severity of the accompanying economic and infrastructural decline from a relative high, particularly in educational terms, puts most other Cold War era African neo-patrimonial one-party and military regimes, apart from Mobutu's Zaïre, into the shade. The 1970s was a time of global economic treachery—but Stevens' model was even less equipped to emerge from this trough than most other African states.

In many ways, it was the actions of Stevens within the confines of a colonial legacy that made conflict more likely. There are, of course, other factors which go to explain the 1991 outbreak of fighting, its timing and its various formats. Sierra Leone is unfortunately far from the only African state to have descended into civil conflict, particularly in the decade after the end of the Cold War. Indeed, the end of the Cold War, with the concurrent withdrawal and increasingly conditional nature of aid and the availability of small arms, has been identified as a common factor over all of Africa to explain the timing and format of what have been described as 'New Wars'. In this formulation of a post-Cold War world, ideology is now much less the issue at stake and identity, commodities and the post-modernisation of conflict have emerged to take its place. The emphasis is sometimes placed on international and regional factors as in the DRC, on specific actors and commodities as in Liberia, on marginalisation as in Uganda, on democratisation as in Congo-Brazzaville, on clan identity as in Somalia or on ethnicity as in Rwanda and Burundi. A heady cocktail of these factors is often proffered. The inadequacies of the neo-patrimonial state and its elites are sometimes put close to centre stage in explanations.

Sierra Leone was also centre stage in these post-Cold War debates because of its televised and seemingly senseless brutality. The notion of identity conflict does not have great traction in the Sierra Leonean civil war, but other factors do come together. One might explain the timing through international interference via Libya and Liberia and the repercussions of the end of the Cold War on an already reeling state. One could account for its longevity in terms of the fuel provided by diamonds and looting. The format might be explained by the brutalisation of youth during the APC years and the recruitment of such elements into the conflict and by the emergence of a peculiar brand of cynical war-time leadership, particularly embodied by Foday Sankoh of the RUF. Motivations for fighting, however, are legion and, despite much heated debate, can be said to hinge around the variety of grievances of urban and rural youth under state and local 'traditional' authorities. Of course, this is also a spectacular failure of the neo-patrimonial state as a strategy to compensate for the imbalances in legitimacy between state and society handed down from the juxtaposition of pre-colonial practices and the imposed colonial state. The resolution of the conflict, however, had much to do with outside actors. Despite bravery at certain crucial times from Sierra Leoneans, it appears that the concerns of Nigeria, Liberia, Guinea, the UK and the USA had most effect on the peace process rather than the endeavours of the Sierra Leone government, armed forces or rebels.

Most African states have been subjected to the imposition of liberal reforms. Those that have largely escaped are the very few with long-term healthy economic records, such as Botswana, and the slightly greater number with commodities, usually oil, which allow leeway, such as Equatorial Guinea. All, though, have been subject to, and are not immune to, post-Cold War global liberalising discourse. Liberal economic solutions since the 1980s and liberal political formulations since the start of the 1990s were imposed on the vast majority of African states which, owing to their economic woes, were unable to resist. The impositions were designed to correct perceived internal, not external, failings, such as the bloated and corrupt state, interference in the market by the same state, and finally the unaccountable and undemocratic governments. It is remarkable, though, how little effect the solutions had, however close to the mark the elucidations were. One can see an eventual general rise in GDP growth, driven partly by rising commodity prices, but huge leaps are absent. Indicative of this failure to launch are the evolving reform packages: when economic adjustment was insufficient, democracy was required; when the shrinking of the state did not provide the answer, the state was brought back in as a priority for reform; and when SAPs were not owned by governments, PRSPs were introduced. Of course, the liberal reforms in Africa have largely failed to have a significant impact just as socialist, Marxist and capitalist state-led packages mostly failed to do in their own time. Thoughts must then turn to political reasons beyond policy, and once again to state-society relations.

Sierra Leone was forced into austerity measures under Stevens and SAPs under his successor, Joseph Momoh. These measures were used politically by Stevens but by Momoh's time became another uncertainty for government. The most comprehensive attempts at liberal reform have, though, come in the post-conflict era and then redoubled in the post-Ebola era. In line with notions of liberal peace and the amalgamation of development and security concerns, Sierra Leone has been at the forefront of attempts to rebuild and reform 'failed' states, alongside other smaller countries like Liberia as well as much larger ones like the DRC, Iraq and Afghanistan. After fifteen years, as elsewhere, Sierra Leone's progress in this regard has not been absent but has been very slow. The state might be seen now as a patchwork of institutions that serve different purposes. The institutions themselves and many of their employees are caught in a net where they have multiple and simultaneous obligations: to their official functions, to their political bosses and to their kith and kin. This has always been the case, but is particularly acute now in the presence of far greater donor scrutiny and donor money riding on the results. Neo-patrimonialism has to some extent been once more refashioned. Whether liberal reform is best placed to address these continuing structural features of state-society relations is not at all clear.

Democratisation has also played its part. The argument for democratic consolidation in Sierra Leone is stronger than in many parts of Africa, partly because of the internal actors who have driven the changes, partly in recognition of the enthusiasm and knowledge of voters, but mostly because of the three momentous opposition victories at the ballot box, in particular the second and third in 2007 and 2018. It would be ranked slightly behind the African states judged as more democratically established—such as Ghana, Senegal, Botswana and Zambia—but probably on a par with others, including those with little likelihood of turnover such as Tanzania and Mozambique, and ahead of many more with greater accompanying violence, fraud and societal ruptures like Ethiopia, Nigeria and Rwanda. There are, however, still issues of stability in Sierra Leonean democracy, especially when considering the violence and attempted rigging, the fragility of institutions at election times and in between, and the ethno-regional division of the country which paradoxically paves the way for the turnovers. Again, the manner in which the electorate votes, which does vary somewhat over time, is still underpinned by local communal concerns and thus reflects the continuing imperative of parochial rather than national issues. Whether viewed from the top or from the bottom, patronage trumps policy in many circumstances. One might note that Sierra Leone does not have the education, development or class formation to underpin a consolidated liberal democracy, and so must be constructing its own rather more fragile type. Most, though, do not envisage a return of the soldiers or a one-party regime in the current international and indeed national climate, despite, or perhaps because of, the country's military and political history.

Beyond the conflict and post-conflict reforms, Sierra Leone also finds itself at the forefront of international discourse owing to its part in the current experimentations with transitional justice in the form of the SLSC and the TRC. The Rwandan and Yugoslav trials paved the way, but the SLSC was intended to provide a more compact and cheaper hybrid model. In contrast to the simultaneously emerging ICC, and partly driven by US concerns over the ICC, the SLSC was a stand-alone court, being part-UN and part-Sierra Leonean. It proved to be compact, trying only nine indictees, but not cheaper pro rata. More importantly, it managed to complete the trials with relatively minor repercussions in Sierra Leone. The SLSC was indeed fortunate that the SLA factions had disintegrated and the RUF was disintegrating, leaving only the Kamajors as the group likely to disturb the peace because of the trials. One might observe that, despite being overshadowed by the SLSC, the TRC had some rather indirect reconciliatory effects and helped form a national narrative of the war. It is unclear what effect, if any, the trial of eight second rung commanders plus the Liberian Charles Taylor has had in Sierra Leone, but assumptions of its transferability to other conflict arenas have already and rather hastily been made. It is the contention here that legal solutions do not provide lasting frameworks for the conclusion of what are in essence political and social struggles, even in this corner of West Africa.

Sierra Leone has been buffeted by international winds, changing in direction from colonialism to Cold War pragmatism and finally to post-Cold War economic, political and judicial liberalism. Each era has brought tough challenges and the general centre-periphery global system has always marginalised and indeed continues to marginalise the country, although there are clearly periods when global commodity prices are highly advantageous. There is now the hint of further change with the addition of China, India and various others onto the African international scene, although the iron ore debacle indicates that this is not simply an open treasure chest. Purported solutions to many problems in Sierra Leone, including to some extent the war and Ebola, have often come from the outside rather than being internally generated. However, despite the seemingly overwhelming strength of these forces, the suggestion that Sierra Leone is powerless in this relationship would be historically incorrect and would only serve to remove Sierra Leonean structures and agency from consideration. All regimes have used outside bodies, whether they are states, NGOs or business, to either bolster their political position or push for development. Indeed, on a smaller scale, some Sierra Leoneans now benefit from the creation of domestic NGOs that strive for Northern state and NGO funding, which is put to a similar wide range of purposes.

Indeed there are lessons here for those who would reform, democratise and liberalise Sierra Leone and other African states, whether they are indigenous or foreign. The history of Sierra Leone is littered with reform programmes which have faltered on contradictions; from the early colonial efforts to the more serious late colonists, through the conservative Margais and the political experiments of Stevens to the current liberal programmes. The fortunes of the latest batch of reforms similarly hang in the balance. It is not yet clear whether outsiders are propping up experiments in reform and concealing tensions within, or indeed if some sort of intersection or hybrid state-society relationship is emerging. It is also not clear which has to come first: reform or societal change. States and democracies from the unconstructed Congo, to the deconstructed Mali and Côte d'Ivoire, to the painstakingly and precariously reconstructed Ghana, Ethiopia and Rwanda, show a range of processes, none of which has yet consolidated.

Thus, it is within Sierra Leone that many of the most important processes are taking place. The themes of continuity and change running through the book, and whether change is of a structural or procedural variety, culminate here. There is continuity in the struggles to build a nation and a functioning state. The overriding popular concerns for local level survival and opportunities keep emphasis on the parochial, the familial and the ethnic and away from the nation and the state. The importance and legitimacy of 'traditional' authority and values, in an environment in which organs of the state largely fail to penetrate, is high in such crucial issues as spirituality, policing, justice, land, and indeed a public health crisis. This is a familiar scenario in many African countries but one with probably deeper foundations in Sierra Leone with its long history of politically conservative and pragmatic or even cynical elite politics. Postcolonial authorities, like their colonial predecessors, have used and manipulated but have been unable or unwilling to significantly challenge the power of the local. There have been, at the same time, other often violent challenges to the local and the national: from the Hut Tax War to the 1950s riots through to the civil war and the present day, there has been sporadic popular resistance.

This is not to suggest that the 'traditional' provides all the internal problems and the state all the answers. That would be to give the state too large a role that historically it has been unable to fulfil, and to ignore the fact that many see customary institutions as more legitimate even if particular incumbents are not. It is to suggest that there are fundamental *disconnections* between the ideas of the 'modern' state and the 'traditional' local. Indeed, the notions of modern and traditional have become decidedly blurred and it might be more useful to think of *connections* which alter the way the supposedly modern and the purportedly traditional work. One such connection is clearly networks of patron-clientelism which have for a long time filled some of the gaps between state and local, but there are others, some of old vintage and some much more recent. For instance, in July 2011, a typical story appeared in the Freetown media. It was a story of *juju*, of how one night club owner had allegedly employed a *juju* man to kill another, and whether the role of *juju* men was to kill or cure. Importantly, the events were all considered as the central part of a trial in Sierra Leone's state courts, emphasising the continued interweaving of the two spheres. In addition, some chiefs are now educated to a high level, sometimes abroad, and find themselves with a foot in each camp; 'traditional' practices and values are seen as both a source of contagion and an effective weapon within the response to the Ebola epidemic; politicians deny ethnic attachments while everyone knows who they stand for; government ministers fund FC/FGM rituals; women and youth have to some extent begun to circumscribe chiefly authority; and women have taken the issue of chieftaincy eligibility to the highest state courts.

It is also to suggest that local processes of change are where we may find the keys to the future. However, it will probably not be as expected or planned for at national and international level. It will be more likely as an amalgamation of international liberal concerns with, more importantly, semi-organic societal processes emerging from the war and Ebola and from other changes in the environment. More assertive youth organisations, changes in patron-client patterns, shifts in livelihoods and continuing enthusiasm for democracy, however we understand it, may offer very slowly shifting movements in what are still important and resilient ways of living in much of Sierra Leone. Clearly, there are strong structural conditions that militate against change, or at least rapid change, but there is also, as always, space for agency. The space is circumscribed in Sierra Leone, but the country's history teaches us that there are decisions to be made: Milton and Albert Margai, Stevens, Momoh, Strasser, Kabbah and Koroma all took different options in governing the country that resulted in diverging outcomes. Some options were dictated from outside, but most often the course of action was driven by an interaction of outside and personal beliefs and imperatives. Indeed, some options have left extremely disadvantageous national legacies, while others have been kinder in their impact even if they have not made significant long-term alterations to the body politic. The agency, then, of national and local leaders cannot be discounted in the face of resilient societal and structural conditions.

Current societal and state dynamics could indeed be seen as the latest phase in the ongoing creation of a Sierra Leonean modernity. Despite the presence of the overbearing liberal agenda, the historic reliance of Sierra Leonean elites on outside forces and ideas, and the conservative underpinnings of Sierra Leonean politics, the dynamics may also represent an internal development of ways of managing a phenomenally intricate and difficult pre-colonial, colonial and post-colonial legacy. As elsewhere in Africa, but particularly in Sierra Leone, the likelihood of an Arab-style Spring as in Egypt or Tunisia is very limited. These North African societies and their relation to the state are utterly different. The possibility of a return to war cannot, of course, be ruled out in a state as fragile as Sierra Leone. This is particularly true if not enough progress is made in certain sectors, if state resources are badly managed and if outside influence once again works against peace in Sierra Leone. Botswana, however, emerges again as a tentative comparison, not just in its reliance on diamonds, but in the equally conservative and yet much more stable nature, despite recent perturbations, of its state-society relations. The role of Sierra Leonean government, then, remains at best difficult. Its work in a best case scenario is to navigate a rocky path between staying in power, satisfying its societal obligations, convincing its funders, handling global economic fluctuations, reigning in its corrupt tendencies, and finally reforming and responding to the changes in society.

The Sierra Leonean state and nation was imposed from outside in a creation process utterly different from that experienced by the countries of the colonisers and with little consultation with those who became Sierra Leoneans. To believe that there is still no ownership of the state and nation by Sierra Leoneans would, however, be a grave mistake. Sierra Leone has now created its own distinct national narrative and myths, of which the Krios, the chiefs, Bai Bureh, the Margais, Stevens and of course the war and Ebola are very much a part. One outcome of the very national catastrophes that were the war and Ebola paradoxically could be their contribution to the making of the nation, if not yet the state. Everyone was involved in some way in both crises and none ever thought to secede during the war. There has long been a unifying Krio language and religious tolerance, but alongside the national story and more banal manifestations of nationhood—such as the anthem, the tricolour flag, the Cotton Tree, the fondness attached to the country's other name, *Salone*, popular musicians including S.E. Rogie, Abdul Tee-Jay and more recently Daddy Saj and Emmerson, and the football team and its one-time hero, Mohamed Kallon—there is now a much stronger notion of Sierra Leone. Of course, national identity continues to compete with local identities and is yet to get a firm grip on the state. Equally, it comes with quirks intrinsic and largely necessary in all national manifestations, such as the stereotyped view of the 'other', particularly in this case neighbouring Liberians, and historic and persistent allegiances, for example to Britain. However, over half a century after independence, it can now firmly be said that Sierra Leone exists as a separate unit of analysis. More importantly, notwithstanding its various appearances in the international spotlight, the pressure to conform from outside and the continued global economic imbalances, it is a country in charge, to a greater degree than is often believed, of its own future.

NOTES

2. THE RISE AND WANE OF KRIO DOMINANCE, 1787–1951

1. Fyfe, C., *A Short History of Sierra Leone* (London: Longman, 1979), p. 39.
2. Cohen, A., *The Politics of Elite Culture: Explorations in the Dramaturgy of Power in a Modern African Society* (Berkeley, CA: University of California Press, 1981), p. 226.
3. Harrell Bond, B. and D. Skinner, 'Misunderstandings Arising from the Use of the Term 'Creole' in the Literature on Sierra Leone', *Africa*, 47/3, 1977, pp. 305–20.
4. Porter, A., *Creoledom* (Oxford University Press, 1963).
5. Chabal, P. (ed.), *The Postcolonial Literature of Lusophone Africa* (Johannesburg: Witwatersrand University Press, 1996), pp. 17–19.
6. Caulker, P., *The Autochthonous Peoples, British Colonial Policies, and the Creoles in Sierra Leone: The Genesis of the Modern Sierra Leone Dilemma of National Integration* (Ann Arbor, MI: Temple University, 1976), p. 3.
7. Wyse, A., *H. C. Bankole-Bright and Politics in Colonial Sierra Leone 1919–1958* (Cambridge University Press, 1990), p. 28.
8. Messiant, C., 'Angola: the Challenge of Statehood' in Birmingham, D. and P. Martin (eds), *History of Central Africa: The Contemporary Years since 1960*, Vol. 3 (London: Longman, 1998), p. 157.
9. Fyfe, *A Short History of Sierra Leone*, p. 100.
10. Wyse, *H.C. Bankole-Bright*, p. 21.
11. Alie, J.A.D., *A New History of Sierra Leone* (London: Macmillan, 1990), p. 183.
12. Wyse, *H.C. Bankole-Bright*, p. 29.
13. Ibid., p. 26.
14. R. Corby and T.S. Alldridge, respectively, quoted in Kandeh, J., 'Politicization of Ethnic Identities in Sierra Leone', *African Studies Review*, 35/1, 1992, p. 86.
15. Wylie, K., *The Political Kingdoms of the Temne* (New York: Africana Publishing Co., 1977), p. 91.
16. Wyse, *H.C. Bankole-Bright*, pp. 16 and 18.
17. Wylie, *The Political Kingdoms*, p. 149.

18. Young, C., *The African Colonial State in Comparative Perspective* (New Haven: Yale University Press, 1994).

19. Berry, S., 'Hegemony on a Shoestring: Indirect Rule and Access to Agricultural Land', *Africa* 62/3, 1992, pp. 327–55.

20. Herbst, J., *States and Power in Africa: Comparative Lessons in Authority and Control* (Princeton: Princeton University Press, 2000), p. 78.

21. Ibid., p. 67.

22. Conklin, A., 'Colonialism and Human Rights, A Contradiction in Terms? The Case of France and West Africa', *American Historical Review*, 103(2), 1998, pp. 419–42.

23. Hobsbawm, E. and T. Ranger, *The Invention of Tradition* (Cambridge University Press, 1992); and Spear, T., 'Neo-traditionalism and the Limits of Invention in British Colonial Africa', *Journal of African History*, 44, 2003, pp. 3–27.

24. Fyfe, *A Short History of Sierra Leone*, p. 17.

25. Fyfe, C., *Sierra Leone Inheritance* (London: Oxford University Press, 1964), pp. 13–15.

26. Ibid., pp. 196 and 259.

27. Wylie, *The Political Kingdoms*, p. 181.

28. Fyfe, *Sierra Leone Inheritance*, pp. 263–7.

29. Abraham, A., *Topics in Sierra Leone History* (Freetown: Leone Publishers, 1976), pp. 62–7.

30. Magbaily Fyle, C., *The History of Sierra Leone* (London: Evans Brothers, 1981), pp. 105–7.

31. Fyfe, *Sierra Leone Inheritance*, p. 14.

32. Fanthorpe, R., 'Locating the Politics of a Sierra Leonean Chiefdom', *Africa*, 68/4, 1998, pp. 558–83; and Abraham, A., *Mende Government and Politics under Colonial Rule* (Oxford University Press, 1978), pp. 244–65.

33. Fyfe, *A Short History of Sierra Leone*, p. 124.

34. Fyfe, C., '1787–1887–1987: Reflections on a Sierra Leone Bicentenary' in Fyfe (ed.), *Sierra Leone 1787–1987: Two Centuries of Intellectual Life* (Manchester University Press, 1987), p. 417; and Wyse, *H.C. Bankole-Bright*, p. 29.

35. Editorial in *Sierra Leone Weekly News*, 27 March 1915, reprinted in Fyfe, *Sierra Leone Inheritance*, pp. 307–8.

36. Fyfe, *A Short History of Sierra Leone*, pp. 126–8.

37. Mamdani, M., *Citizen and Subject: Contemporary Africa and the Legacy of Late Colonialism* (Princeton, NJ: Princeton University Press, 1996).

38. See Lonsdale, J., "States and Social Processes in Africa: A Historiographical Survey," *African Studies Review*, 24/2–3, 1981, pp. 139–225.

39. Zack-Williams, A., *Tributors, Supporters and Merchant Capital: Mining and Underdevelopment in Sierra Leone* (Aldershot: Avebury, 1995), p. 38.

40. Ibid., pp. 47–53.

41. Reno, W., *Corruption and State Politics in Sierra Leone* (Cambridge University Press), p. 53.

42. Alie, *A New History of Sierra Leone*, p. 133.

43. Fyfe, *Sierra Leone Inheritance*, p. 190.

44. Bo School Prospectus, *Sierra Leone Gazette*, 29 September 1905, reprinted in Ibid., pp. 304–7.

45. Letters between Governor Major-General Charles Turner (1824–26) and Secretary of State Earl Bathurst, December 1825 and January 1826, reprinted in Ibid., pp. 186–8.

46. Wylie, *The Political Kingdoms*, p. 86.

47. Abraham, *Topics in Sierra Leone History*, pp. 31–9.

48. Koso-Thomas, O., *The Circumcision of Women: A Strategy for Eradication* (London: Zed Books, 1987); many still quote this figure of around 90 per cent, particularly in reference to the rural areas.

49. Kilson, M., *Political Change in a West African State: A Study of the Modernization Process in Sierra Leone* (Cambridge, MA: Harvard University Press, 1966), p. 40.

50. Thanks go to Tom Young for this formulation.

51. E.g. Kees van Donge, J., 'An Episode from the Independence Struggle in Zambia: a Case Study from Mwase Lundazi', *African Affairs*, 84/335, 1985, pp. 265–77.

52. Wyse, *H.C. Bankole-Bright*, p. 132.

53. Kilson, *Political Change*, p. 157.

54. Wyse, *H.C. Bankole-Bright*, pp. 160–63.

55. Biographical notes on the Margais, Stevens and other prominent 1950s politicians are included in Chapter 3.

56. Clapham, C., *Sierra Leone: the Political Economy of Internal Conflict*, CRU Working Paper 20 (The Hague: Clingendael Institute, 2003), p. 13.

57. Mamdani, *Citizen and Subject*.

58. Cohen, *The Politics of Elite Culture*, p. xix.

59. Wyse, A., *The Krio of Sierra Leone: An Interpretive History* (London: Hurst, 1989), p. 116.

60. Yoder, J.C., *Popular Political Culture, Civil Society, and State Crisis in Liberia* (New York: Mellen, 2003).

61. Bayart, J-F., *The State in Africa: The Politics of the Belly* (London: Longman, 1993); and Chabal, P. and Daloz, J.-P., *Africa Works: Disorder as Political Instrument* (Bloomington, IN: Indiana University Press, 1999).

3. KEY PLAYERS IN A DECEPTIVELY QUIET DECOLONISATION, 1951–1961

1. Reno, *Corruption and State Politics*, p. 60.

2. Fyfe, *A Short History of Sierra Leone*, p. 146.

3. Reno, *Corruption and State Politics*, pp. 62–5.

4. Zack-Williams, *Tributors, Supporters*, pp. 57–8.

5. Alie, *A New History of Sierra Leone*, pp. 201–5.

6. Wyse, *H.C. Bankole-Bright*, pp. 170–71.

7. Cohen, *The Politics of Elite Culture*, p. 115.

8. Ibid., p. 114, although this burgeoning and indeed any political purpose of Freemasonry at this time is questioned by Robert Hammond (University of Bradford PhD, forthcoming).

9. Denzer, L., 'Women in Freetown Politics, 1914–61: A Preliminary Study' in Fyfe, C, (ed.), *Sierra Leone 1787–1987: Two Centuries of Intellectual Life* (Manchester University Press, 1987), pp. 449–50.

10. Fanthorpe, R., 'Neither Citizen nor Subject? Lumpen Agency and the Legacy of Native Administration in Sierra Leone', *African Affairs*, 100/400, 2001, pp. 363–86.

11. Tangri, R., 'Conflict and Violence in Contemporary Sierra Leone Chiefdoms', *Journal of Modern African Studies*, 14/2, 1976, pp. 311–21.

12. Kilson, *Political Change*, p. 59.

13. Ibid., p. 237.

14. Cartwright, J., *Political Leadership in Sierra Leone* (Toronto: Toronto Press, 1978), p. 61.

15. Kilson, *Political Change*, p. 233.

16. Wyse, *H.C. Bankole-Bright*, p. 177.

17. Kilson, *Political Change*, pp. 257–8.

18. From 1959, he was entitled Sir Milton Margai. In this text, for the purposes of simplicity and to avoid confusion with his half-brother, they will be referred to as Milton and Albert.

19. Kilson, *Political Change*, p. 257.

20. Peter Dumbuya calls his style 'cautious conservatism' in *Reinventing the Colonial State: Constitutionalism, One-Party Rule, and Civil War in Sierra Leone* (Bloomington, IN: iUniverse, 2008), p. 22.

21. Cartwright, *Political Leadership*, p. 93.

22. Ibid., p. 95.

23. Alie, *A New History of Sierra Leone*, p. 226.

24. Kilson, *Political Change*, p. 255.

25. Ibid.

26. Ibid.

27. See e.g. Brennan, J., 'Youth, the TANU Youth League and Managed Vigilantism in Dar es Salaam, Tanzania 1925–73', *Africa*, 76/2, 2006, pp. 221–46; Kees van Donge, 'An Episode from the Independence Struggle'; and Chabal, P. and Vidal, N. (eds), *Angola: The Weight of History* (New York: Columbia University Press, 2008).

28. Tilly, C., *Coercion, Capital and European States, AD 900–1992* (Oxford: Blackwell, 1992).

29. Jackson, R., *Quasi-States: Sovereignty, International Relations and the Third World* (Cambridge University Press, 1993).

30. Herbst, *States and Power in Africa*.

31. One of Joel Migdal's case studies is Sierra Leone in *Strong States and Weak Societies* (Princeton, NJ: Princeton University Press, 1988).

32. Clapham, *Sierra Leone: the Political Economy of Internal Conflict*, p. 10.

4. IMMEDIATE AND SEVERE CHALLENGES: DEMOCRACY AND COUPS, 1961–1968.

1. Hayward, F. and Kandeh, J., 'Perspectives on Twenty-five Years of Elections in Sierra Leone' in Hayward, F. (ed.), *Elections in Independent Africa* (Boulder, CO: Westview, 1987), p. 25.
2. Ibid., p. 40; and Fisher, H., 'Elections and Coups in Sierra Leone, 1967', *Journal of Modern African Studies*, 7/4, 1969, p. 613.
3. Fisher, 'Elections and Coups', p. 612.
4. Cartwright, *Political Leadership*, p. 73.
5. Kilson, *Political Change*, p. 276.
6. Ibid., p. 277.
7. For an eloquent study of Nigeria, see Ekeh, P., 'Colonialism and the Two Publics: A Theoretical Statement', *Comparative Studies in Society and History*, 17/1, 1975, pp. 91–112.
8. Bangura, Y., 'Strategic Policy Failure and Governance in Sierra Leone', *Journal of Modern African Studies*, 38/4, 2000, pp. 566–8.
9. Kandeh, 'Politicization of Ethnic Identities', p. 91.
10. Cartwright, *Political Leadership*, p. 73.
11. Kandeh, 'Politicization of Ethnic Identities', p. 93.
12. For democracy following development, see Lipset, S., *Political Man* (New York: Anchor Books, 1960) and Moore, B., *Social Origins of Dictatorship and Democracy* (Harmondsworth: Penguin, 1966); and for the reverse, see World Bank, *Sub-Saharan Africa: From Crisis to Sustainable Growth* (Washington, DC: 1989).
13. Kilson, *Political Change*, pp. 279–80.
14. Cohen, *The Politics of Elite Culture*, p. 136.
15. Ibid., p. 43.
16. Ibid., pp. 129–36.
17. Kandeh, 'Politicization of Ethnic Identities', p. 93.
18. Cox, T., *Civil-military Relations in Sierra Leone: a Case Study of African Soldiers in Politics* (Cambridge, MA: Harvard University Press, 1976), p. 75.
19. Ibid., p. 52.
20. Alie, *A New History of Sierra Leone*, p. 228.
21. Quoted in Kandeh, 'Politicization of Ethnic Identities', p. 92.
22. Alie, *A New History of Sierra Leone*, p. 236.
23. Forrest, J., 'The Quest for State 'Hardness' in Africa', *Comparative Politics*, 20/4, 1988, pp. 423–42.
24. Alie, *A New History of Sierra Leone*, pp. 230–31.
25. Fisher, 'Elections and Coups', p. 618.
26. Cartwright, *Political Leadership*, pp. 81–2.
27. Hayward, F., 'Sierra Leone: State Consolidation, Fragmentation and Decay' in Cruise O'Brien, D., Dunn, J. and Rathbone, R. (eds), *Contemporary West African States* (Cambridge University Press, 1989), p. 167.

28. Quoted in Hayward and Kandeh, 'Perspectives on Twenty-five Years', p. 40.

29. Cartwright, *Political Leadership*, p. 82.

30. Fisher, 'Elections and Coups', p. 625.

31. Ibid., p. 627.

32. Ibid., pp. 629–30.

33. Cox, *Civil-military Relations*, pp. 117–19.

34. Fisher, 'Elections and Coups', pp. 634–5.

35. For a much lengthier discussion, see Decalo, S., *Coups and Army Rule in Africa: Motivations and Constraints* (New Haven, CT: Yale University Press, 1990).

5. THE CHOICES OF SIAKA STEVENS: VIOLENCE, PATRONAGE AND THE ONE-PARTY STATE, 1968–1991.

1. Cox, *Civil-military Relations*, p. 209.

2. Nelson-Williams, A., 'Restructuring the Republic of Sierra Leone Armed Forces (RSLAF)', *GFNSSR Working Paper Series*, No. 3, 2008, p. 3.

3. Krogstad, E.G., 'Security, Development and Force: Revisiting Police Reform in Sierra Leone', *African Affairs*, 111/443, 2012, p. 274.

4. Cox, *Civil-military Relations*, pp. 216–17.

5. Ibid, p. 211; and Hayward, 'Sierra Leone: State Consolidation', p. 169.

6. See Forna, A., *The Devil that Danced on Water: A Daughter's Memoir* (London: Flamingo, 2002).

7. Alie, *A New History of Sierra Leone*, p. 242.

8. Kandeh, 'Politicization of Ethnic Identities', p. 93.

9. Hayward and Kandeh, 'Perspectives', p. 47.

10. Ferme, M., 'The Violence of Numbers: Consensus, Competition, and the Negotiation of Disputes in Sierra Leone', *Cahiers d'Études Africaines*, 150/38-2–4, 1998, p. 567.

11. Hayward, 'Sierra Leone: State Consolidation', p. 169.

12. Ferme, 'The Violence of Numbers', p. 566.

13. Hayward and Kandeh, 'Perspectives', p. 34.

14. Fred Hayward's interview with Stevens, Freetown, 3 June 1986 (Ibid., p. 35); and Alie, *A New History of Sierra Leone*, p. 245.

15. Hayward and Kandeh, 'Perspectives', pp. 36–8.

16. Alie, *A New History of Sierra Leone*, p. 244; and Conteh-Morgan, E. and Dixon-Fyle, M., *Sierra Leone at the End of the Twentieth Century: History, Politics and Society* (New York: Peter Lang, 1999), p. 106.

17. Kandeh, J., 'Ransoming the State: Elite Origins of Subaltern Terror in Sierra Leone', *Review of African Political Economy*, 81/26, 1999, p. 361.

18. Abdullah, I., 'Bush Path to Destruction: the Origin and Character of the Revolutionary United Front (RUF/SL)', *Africa Development*, 22/3–4, 1997, pp. 45–76; and Abdullah, I. and Muana, P., 'The RUF of Sierra Leone: a Revolt of the Lumpenproletariat' in Clapham, C. (ed.), *African Guerrillas* (Oxford: James Currey, 1998).

19. Fanthorpe, 'Neither Citizen', p. 381; and Tangri, R., 'Central-local Politics in Contemporary Sierra Leone', *African Affairs*, 77/307, 1978, pp. 165–73.

20. Hayward's interview with Stevens, August 1970 (Hayward, 'Sierra Leone: State Consolidation', p. 168).

21. Tangri, 'Conflict and Violence', pp. 318–20.

22. Richards, P., 'Green Book Millenarians? The Sierra Leone War within the Perspective of an Anthropology of Religion' in Kastfelt, N. (ed.), *Religion and African Civil Wars* (London: Hurst, 2005), p. 123.

23. Chabal and Daloz, *Africa Works*.

24. Kourouma, A., *Waiting for the Wild Beasts to Vote* (London: Heinemann, 2003), p. 221.

25. Bayart, *The State in Africa*.

26. Smith, D., *A Culture of Corruption: Everyday Deception and Popular Discontent in Nigeria* (Princeton, NJ: Princeton University Press, 2007).

27. Bayart, *The State in Africa*.

28. Chabal and Daloz, *Africa Works*.

29. Erdmann, G. and Engel, U., 'Neopatrimonialism Reconsidered: Critical Review and Elaboration of an Elusive Concept', *Journal of Commonwealth & Comparative Politics*, 45/1, 2007, pp. 95–119.

30. For an interesting comparison to Sierra Leone, see Helle-Valle, J., 'Seen From Below: Conceptions of Politics in a Botswana Village', *Africa* 72/2, 2002, pp. 179–202.

31. Reno, *Corruption and State Politics*.

32. Hayward, 'Sierra Leone: State Consolidation', p. 167.

33. Schatzberg, M., *Political Legitimacy in Middle Africa: Father, Family, Food* (Bloomington, IN: Indiana University Press, 2001).

34. Reno, *Corruption and State Politics*, pp. 108–110.

35. Partnership Africa Canada, *The Heart of the Matter: Sierra Leone, Diamonds and Human Security* (Ottawa: PAC, 2000), p. 4.

36. Ross, M., 'The Political Economy of the Resource Curse', *World Politics*, 51, 1999, pp. 297–322.

37. Clapham, *Sierra Leone: the Political Economy of Internal Conflict*, pp. 11–12.

38. Keen, D., *Conflict and Collusion in Sierra Leone* (Oxford: James Currey, 2005), p. 24.

39. Reno, *Corruption and State Politics*, p. 110.

40. Keen, *Conflict and Collusion*, p. 27.

41. Reno, *Corruption and State Politics*, p. 134.

42. Clapham, *Sierra Leone: the Political Economy of Internal Conflict*, p. 22.

43. Reno, *Corruption and State Politics*, p. 134.

44. Clapham, *Sierra Leone: the Political Economy of Internal Conflict*, p. 22.

45. Keen, *Conflict and Collusion*, pp. 28–9.

46. Rodney, W., *How Europe Underdeveloped Africa* (London: Bogle-L'Ouverture Publications, 1973); and Bernstein, H., *Underdevelopment and Development* (Harmondsworth: Penguin, 1973).

47. Bayart, J-F., 'Africa in the World: a History of Extraversion', *African Affairs*, 99/395, 2000, pp. 217–67.

48. Alie, *A New History of Sierra Leone*, pp. 268–9.

49. Ibid., p. 247.

50. Reno, *Corruption and State Politics*, p. 176.

51. Conteh-Morgan and Dixon-Fyle, *Sierra Leone at the End of the Twentieth Century*, p. 126.

52. Chabal and Daloz, *Africa Works*, p. 122.

53. See Reno, *Corruption and State Politics*, pp. 141–6 for Sierra Leonean examples.

54. Keen, *Conflict and Collusion*, pp. 32–3; and Conteh-Morgan & Dixon-Fyle, *Sierra Leone at the End of the Twentieth Century*, p. 125.

55. Richards, P., *Fighting for the Rainforest: War, Youth and Resources in Sierra Leone* (Oxford: International African Institute, 1996), p. 22.

6. CIVIL WAR AND THE INCENDIARY DEBATES OVER ITS PROVENANCE, 1991–1996

1. Nelson-Williams, A., 'Restructuring the RSLAF', pp. 3–4.

2. Reyntjens, F., 'The Privatisation and Criminalisation of Public Space in the Geopolitics of the Great Lakes Region', *Journal of Modern African Studies*, 43/4, 2005, pp. 587–607.

3. Abdullah, 'Bush Path to Destruction', pp. 45–76.

4. Sawyer, A., 'Violent Conflicts and Governance Challenges in West Africa: the Case of the Mano River Basin Area', *Journal of Modern African Studies*, 42/3, 2004, p. 445.

5. Douglas Farah, quoted in Polgreen, L., 'A master plan drawn in blood', *New York Times*, 2 April 2006.

6. Quoted in Wax, E., 'In exile, Taylor still exerts control', *Washington Post*, 17 September 2003.

7. Harris, D., 'From 'Warlord' to 'Democratic' President: how Charles Taylor Won the 1997 Liberian Elections', *Journal of Modern African Studies*, 37/3, 1999, pp. 431–55.

8. Gberie, L., *A Dirty War in West Africa: the RUF and the Destruction of Sierra Leone* (London: Hurst, 2005), p. 60.

9. Ibid., p. 63.

10. Early 1992 is the time quoted in Richards, *Fighting for the Rainforest*, p. 8.

11. BBC, 'Taylor Sierra Leone war crimes trial verdict welcomed', 27 April 2012.

12. For the former, see Farah, D., 'Al Qaeda cash tied to diamond trade', *Washington Post*, 2 November 2001; and Global Witness, *The Usual Suspects: Liberia's Weapons and Mercenaries in Côte d'Ivoire and Sierra Leone* (London: March 2003), p. 51. For the latter, see Gberie, *A Dirty War in West Africa*, pp. 168–9.

13. See for example Bazenguissa-Ganga, R., 'The Spread of Political Violence in Congo-Brazzaville', *African Affairs*, 98/390, 1999, pp. 37–54.

14. See for Sierra Leone: Reno, *Corruption and State Politics*; and in general: Young, C., 'The End of the Post-Colonial State in Africa? Reflections on Changing African Political Dynamics', *African Affairs*, 103/410, 2004, pp. 23–49.

15. Jackson, R., 'Violent Internal Conflict and the African State: Toward a Framework of Analysis', *Journal of Contemporary African Studies*, 20/1, 2002, pp. 29–52.

16. Collier, P. and Hoeffler, A., *Justice-seeking and Loot-seeking in Civil War* (Washington, DC: World Bank, 1999).

17. Note that 'youth' is a not a strictly age-dependent term as in the West. In Africa, it is also imbued with notions of having not yet attained status, such as marriage and wealth, and can thus be applied to someone much older than the age of 16 or 18.

18. For an example of such debates, see Mkandawire, T., 'The Terrible Toll of Post-colonial 'Rebel Movements' in Africa: Toward an Explanation of the Violence against the Peasantry', *Journal of Modern African Studies*, 40/2, 2002, pp. 181–215; Ellis, S., 'Violence and History: a Response to Thandika Mkandawire', *Journal of Modern African Studies*, 41/3, 2003, pp. 457–75; and Mkandawire, T., 'Rejoinder to Stephen Ellis', *Journal of Modern African Studies*, 41/3, 2003, pp. 477–83.

19. There is an impressive range of Sierra Leonean child soldier novels, including *A Long Way Gone: Memoirs of a Boy Soldier* by the former child soldier Ishmael Beah (New York: Sarah Crichton Books, 2007). Beah strikingly noted that 'dehumanising children is a relatively easy task'. At the same time, notwithstanding the brutality, some have noted that the recent focus on child soldiers is more attributable to humanitarian discourse than an actual increase in numbers and that, in the same discourse, children are always presented as victims and thus any agency in recruitment is overlooked. Thanks go to Stacey Hind for these insights.

20. Truth and Reconciliation Commission, *Report* (Freetown, October 2004).

21. Abdullah, 'Bush Path to Destruction'.

22. Kandeh, J., 'Subaltern Terror in Sierra Leone' in Zack-Williams, T., Frost, D. and Thomson, A. (eds), *Africa in Crisis: New Challenges and Possibilities* (London: Pluto, 2002); and Muana, 'The RUF of Sierra Leone'.

23. Abdullah, 'Bush Path to Destruction'.

24. Ibid..

25. Gberie, *A Dirty War in West Africa*, pp. 66 and 76–7.

26. Collier, P., *Doing Well out of War* (Washington, DC: World Bank, 1999), p. 8.

27. Kaldor, M., *New and Old Wars: Organized Violence in a Global Era* (Cambridge: Polity, 1999).

28. Gberie, *A Dirty War in West Africa*, p. 7.

29. Partnership Africa Canada, *The Heart of the Matter*.

30. Zwick, E., *Blood Diamond* (Warner Bros, 2006); and Ibrahim Kamara, quoted on *Sierra Leone Web*, 5 July 2000. The phrase 'heart of the matter' is taken from Graham Greene's claustrophobic novel of the same name (New York: Viking Press, 1948) about World War II-era Freetown, where Greene had worked, but is not related to diamonds in this book.

31. Collier and Hoeffler, *Justice-seeking*.

32. Ballentine, K., 'Beyond Greed and Grievance: Reconsidering the Economic Dynamics of Armed Conflict', in Ballentine and Sherman, J. (eds), *The Political Economy of Armed Conflict: Beyond Greed and Grievance* (Boulder, CO: Lynne Rienner, 2003).

33. Ross, M., 'What do we Know about Natural Resources and Civil War?', *Journal of Peace Research*, 41/3, 2004, pp. 337–56.

34. Collier, P., Hoeffler, A. and Rohner, D., 'Beyond Greed and Grievance: Feasibility and Civil War', *Oxford Economic Papers*, 61, 2009, p. 2.

35. Ibid., p. 24.

36. Gberie, *A Dirty War in West Africa*, pp. 68–9.

37. Ibid., p. 75.

38. Ibid., p. 70.

39. Ibid., pp. 73–4.

40. Opala, J., '"Ecstatic Renovation": Street Art Celebrating Sierra Leone's 1992 Revolution', *African Affairs*, 93/371, 1994, pp. 195–218.

41. Abdullah and Muana, 'The RUF of Sierra Leone', p. 187; and *Focus on Sierra Leone*, 3/1 (1997).

42. Manning, C., 'Constructing Opposition in Mozambique: Renamo as a Political Party', *Journal of Southern African Studies*, 24/1, 1998, pp. 161–91.

43. Abdullah, 'Bush Path to Destruction'.

44. Söderberg Kovacs, M. & Bangura, I., 'Shape-shifters in the Struggle for Survival: Post-war Politics in Sierra Leone' in Themnér, A. (ed.), Warlord Democrats in Africa: Ex-Military Leaders and Electoral Politics (London: Zed Books, 2017), p. 189.

45. Richards, *Fighting for the Rainforest*, p. 33.

46. Kaplan, R., 'The Coming Anarchy: How Scarcity, Crime, Over-population and Diseases are Rapidly Destroying our Planet', *Atlantic Monthly*, February 1994, pp. 44–76.

47. Bangura, Y., 'Understanding the Political and Cultural Dynamics of the Sierra Leone War: A Critique of Paul Richards' Fighting for the Rain Forest', *Africa Development*, 22/3–4, 1997, pp. 117–47.

48. Richards, 'Green Book Millenarians?'.

49. Peters, K. and Richards, P., 'Understanding Post-Cold War Armed Conflicts in Africa', *Africa*, 77/3, 2007, pp. 183–210.

50. Richards, P., 'Converts to Human Rights? Popular Debate about War and Justice in Rural Central Sierra Leone', *Africa*, 72/3, 2002, p. 357.

51. Richards, 'Green Book Millenarians?', p. 120.

52. Keen, *Conflict and Collusion*, p. 56.

53. Richards, P., 'Youth, Food and Peace: a Reflection on Some African Security Issues at the Millennium' in Zack-Williams, T., Frost, D. and Thomson, A. (eds), *Africa in Crisis: New Challenges and Possibilities* (London: Pluto, 2002), p. 36.

54. Richards, 'Converts to Human Rights?', p. 345.

55. Peters, K., *Re-examining Voluntarism: Youth Combatants in Sierra Leone* (Pretoria: ISS, 2004).
56. Manning, C., 'Constructing opposition', p. 170.
57. Richards, P., 'To Fight or to Farm? Agrarian Dimensions of the Mano River Conflicts (Liberia and Sierra Leone)', *African Affairs*, 104/417, 2005, pp. 571–90.
58. Richards, 'Converts to Human Rights?', p. 351.
59. Ibid., p. 356.
60. Chauveau, J-P., and Richards, P., 'West African Insurgencies in Agrarian Perspective: Côte d'Ivoire and Sierra Leone Compared, *Journal of Agrarian Change*, 8/4, 2008, p. 515.
61 Fanthorpe, 'Neither Citizen', p. 385.
62. Richards, 'To Fight or to Farm?'.
63. Keen, *Conflict and Collusion*, p. 20.
64. Fanthorpe, R., 'On the Limits of Liberal Peace: Chiefs and Democratic Decentralization in Post-conflict Sierra Leone', *African Affairs*, 104/417, 2006, pp. 27–49. David Brown is highly sceptical of this methodology and entirely refutes the notion in Liberia (personal communication). However, the different histories of colonial and pseudo-colonial pacification in the two countries most likely left diverse chiefly legacies: in Liberia, with its greater number of stateless societies and with its Americo-Liberian oligarchy which had more to lose and more to gain, chiefs were more marginalised and had less authority.
65. Vincent, J., 'A Village-Up View of Sierra Leone's Civil War and Reconstruction: Multilayered and Networked Governance', *IDS Research Report* 75, 2012, pp. 18–21.
66. Mitton, K., 'Engaging Disengagement: The Political Reintegration of Sierra Leone's Revolutionary United Front', *Conflict, Security and Development*, 8/2, 2008, p. 193.
67. Peters, K., *War and the Crisis of Youth in Sierra Leone* (Cambridge University Press, 2011).
68. Gberie, *A Dirty War in West Africa*, p. 85.
69. Hoffman, D., 'The Kamajors of Sierra Leone' (Durham, NC: Duke University PhD, 2004), p. 105.
70. For a detailed analysis by a specialist on the Kamajors, see Hoffman, D., *The War Machines: Young Men and Violence in Sierra Leone and Liberia* (Durham, NC: Duke University Press, 2011), pp. 55–123; see also Muana, P., 'The Kamajoi Militia: Violence, Internal Displacement and the Politics of Counter-insurgency', *Africa Development*, 22/3–4, 1997, pp. 77–100.
71. For Liberia, Ellis, S., *The Mask of Anarchy: the Destruction of Liberia and the Religious Dimension of an African Civil War* (London: Hurst, 1999); and for Sierra Leone, Hoffman, *The War Machines*, pp. 79–83.
72. Wlodarczyk, N., *Magic and Warfare: Appearance and Reality in Contemporary African Conflict and Beyond* (Basingstoke: Palgrave Macmillan, 2009), pp. 5–6.
73. Ferme, M., *The Underneath of Things: Violence, History and the Everyday in Sierra Leone* (Berkeley, CA: University of California Press, 2001).

74. Richards, 'Green Book Millenarians?'.
75. Fithen, C., 'Rebellion, Resistance and Resources' (Oxford: 'State Conflict and Intervention in Sierra Leone' conference, May 2000).
76. Keen, *Conflict and Collusion*, p. 276.
77. Truth and Reconciliation Commission, *Report*.
78. Wlodarczyk, *Magic and Warfare*, p. 25; for a general discussion see Ellis, S. and ter Haar, G., *Worlds of Power: Religious Thought and Political Practice in Africa* (London: Hurst, 2003).
79. Kaldor, *New and Old Wars*.
80. Cramer, C., 'Homo Economicus Goes to War: Methodological Individualism, Rational Choice and the Political Economy of War', *World Development*, 30/11, 2002, p. 1854.
81. Herbst, *States and Power in Africa*.

7. THE ESCALATION AND ENDING OF THE CIVIL WAR, 1996–2002

1. See Harris, D., *Civil War and Democracy in West Africa: Conflict Resolution, Elections and Justice in Sierra Leone and Liberia* (London: I.B. Tauris, 2011), pp. 94–103; and Kandeh, J., 'Transition Without Rupture: Sierra Leone's Transfer Election of 1996', *African Studies Review*, 41/2, 1998, pp. 91–111.
2. Jimmy Kandeh notes an increase in religion-based campaigning in 1996 (Kandeh, 'Transition without Rupture'), but this must not be over-emphasised as electoral gains would be highly uncertain in a historically tolerant society where religion cross-cuts ethnicity, particularly by comparison with other campaign methods like patronage and ethno-regionalism.
3. Kabbah, A.T., *Coming Back From the Brink in Sierra Leone* (Accra: EPP, 2012); one commentator has viewed this assertion as plausible (Gberie, L., 'Tejan Kabbah: This is my Life', *New African*, 1 February 2012).
4. Author's interviews with former INEC Commissioner for the Western Area (later INEC Chairman) Ahmed Fadlu-Deen (Freetown, 16 April 2002); and INEC Commissioner for the Northern Province, Almami Cyllah (Zwedru, Liberia, 10 October 2005). Fadlu-Deen considered that the end result was fair, whereas Cyllah was convinced of its partiality.
5. For details of letters from Sankoh to Libyan contacts, see Gberie, *A Dirty War in West Africa*, p. 63; and for the guarantors' lack of interest, see the comments of US Ambassador, John Hirsch, in Hirsch, J., *Sierra Leone: Diamonds and the Struggle for Democracy* (Boulder, CO: Lynne Rienner, 2001), p. 97.
6. A former adviser to the RUF remains convinced that, despite its inadequacies, the group could have been transformed into a political organisation in 1996, particularly given the presence of the more educated and politically-inclined (rather than militarily-inclined) members (author's interview, London, 1 July 2004).
7. Garcia, E. (ed.), *A Time of Hope and Transformation: Sierra Leone Peace Process, Reports and Reflections* (London: International Alert, 1997).

8. For a version of the Executive Outcomes story and the influence it exercised in Sierra Leone from the company's founder, see Barlow, E., Executive Outcomes: Against All Odds (Johannesburg: Galago Publishing, 2007)

9. Hoffman, *The Kamajors of Sierra Leone*, p. 106.

10. Keen, *Conflict and Collusion*, pp. 200–1.

11. Riley, S., 'Sierra Leone: the Militariat Strikes Again', *Review of African Political Economy*, 24/72, 1997, pp. 287–92.

12. Gberie, L., 'The May 25 Coup d'état in Sierra Leone: a Militariat Revolt?', *Africa Development*, 22/3–4, 1997, pp. 149–70.

13. Gberie, *A Dirty War in West Africa*, pp. 107–10.

14. Keen, *Conflict and Collusion*, p. 211.

15. Gberie, L., 'An Interview with Peter Penfold', *African Affairs*, 104/414, 2005, p. 122.

16. See Kargbo, M.S. British foreign policy and the conflict in Sierra Leone, 1991–2001, Oxford: Peter Lang, 2006.

17. Gberie, *A Dirty War in West Africa*, p. 115.

18. For his side of the story, see Penfold, P., *Atrocities, Diamonds and Diplomacy* (Barnsley: Pen & Sword, 2012).

19. Gallagher, J., *Britain and Africa under Blair: In Pursuit of the Good State* (Manchester University Press, 2011).

20. Gberie, *A Dirty War in West Africa*, pp. 122–3.

21. Keen, *Conflict and Collusion*, pp. 221–3.

22. See Sorious Samura's extraordinary footage in his documentary *Cry Freetown* (CNN, 1999).

23. The TRC Report (2004) held the AFRC 'primarily responsible.' No RUF leaders tried by the SLSC were found guilty for the invasion.

24. Gberie, *A Dirty War in West Africa*, p. 130.

25. Samura, *Cry Freetown*.

26. For shame, see Keen, *Conflict and Collusion*, p. 56.

27. Mitton, K., *Understanding Atrocity in the Sierra Leonean Civil War* (London: Hurst, 2015).

28. Keen, *Conflict and Collusion*, pp. 230 and 233.

29. Mitton, K., 'Irrational Actors and the Process of Brutalisation: Understanding Atrocity in the Sierra Leonean Conflict (1991–2002)', *Civil Wars*, 14/1, 2012, pp. 104–22—although the concern here is also for child soldiers who knew only the RUF world.

30. For the unfolding of this relationship, see Mahony, C., 'Prioritising International Sex Crimes before the Special Court for Sierra Leone: One more Instrument of Political Manipulation?' in Bergsmo, M. (ed.), *Thematic Prosecution of International Sex Crimes* (Beijing: Torkel Opsahl Academic EPublisher, 2012).

31. Gberie, *A Dirty War in West Africa*, p. 159.

32. Clapham, *Sierra Leone: the Political Economy of Internal Conflict*, p. 32.

33. Mahony, 'Prioritising International Sex Crimes', pp. 66–7.

34. Gberie, *A Dirty War in West Africa*, pp. 168–9.
35. Mahony, 'Prioritising International Sex Crimes', pp. 68–9.
36. Gberie, *A Dirty War in West Africa*, pp. 172–3.
37. International Crisis Group, *Sierra Leone after Elections: Politics as Usual?* (Freetown and Brussels: ICG, July 2002), p. 9.
38. Clapham, *Sierra Leone: the Political Economy of Internal Conflict*, p. 27.
39. See again Bayart, 'Africa in the World'.
40. Tilly, *Coercion, Capital and European States*.
41. Chabal, P., 'Violence, Power and Rationality: a Political Analysis of Conflict in Contemporary Africa' in Chabal, Engel, U. and Gentili, A-M., *Is Violence Inevitable in Africa? Theories of Conflict and Approaches to Conflict Prevention* (Leiden: Brill, 2005), p. 1.
42. Cramer, C., *Civil War is not a Stupid Thing: Accounting for Violence in Developing Countries* (London: Hurst, 2006).

8. THE POST-CONFLICT DISPENSATION: *PLUS ÇA CHANGE?* 2002–2007

1. Campaign for Good Governance, *Report on the Electoral Process in Sierra Leone, March 2001–May 2002* (Freetown: August 2002), pp. 10–20.
2. For fuller stories, see Harris, *Civil War and Democracy in West Africa*; and Kandeh, J., 'Sierra Leone's Post-conflict Elections of 2002', *Journal of Modern African Studies*, 41/2, 2003, pp. 189–216.
3. *For di People*, Freetown, 21 May 2002.
4. Author's interview with Dr Dennis Bright, Freetown, 3 May 2002; and European Union, *Presidential and Parliamentary Elections in Sierra Leone: Preliminary Statement* (Freetown: 15 May 2002).
5. Embassy of the United States to Sierra Leone, press release (Freetown, 12 March 2002).
6. Author's interview with Francis Hindowa, Bo, 1 May 2002; he was later tried and convicted for corruption.
7. Author's interview with National Election Watch (NEW) chairman Rev. Llewellyn Rogers-Wright, Freetown, 8 May 2002.
8. Author's interview with Ricken Patel, Adviser to MOP, Freetown, 27 April 2002.
9. Söderberg Kovacs & Bangura, 'Shape-shifters in the Struggle for Survival, p. 189.
10. Author's interview with BBC correspondent Lansana Fofana, Freetown, 26 April 2002.
11. Author's interview with Alimamy Pallo Bangura, Freetown, 21 May 2002.
12. Author's interviews with ex-combatant RUFP candidates, e.g. Mohammed Sowa and Patrick Kamara who were numbers three and six on the RUFP Pujehun list, but both more interested in carpentry 'projects', Bo, 1 May 2002.
13. Quotes and some details in this paragraph taken from author's interview with Alimamy Pallo Bangura, Freetown, 21 May 2002.
14. Author's interview with PLP Secretary General (and presidential candidate in 2007) Dr Kandeh Baba Conteh, Freetown, 10 May 2002.

15. Author's interview with Alimamy Pallo Bangura, Freetown, 21 May 2002.

16. Author's interview with Osman Yansaneh, Freetown, 29 April 2002.

17. UN Official Communiqué of the Security Council, 21 June 2000.

18. Commonwealth Observer Group, *The Presidential and Parliamentary Elections* (London: 2002), p. 18.

19. Quoted in *Awoko*, Freetown, 27 January 2003.

20. Lindberg, S.I., "'It's our Time to Chop": Do Elections in Africa Feed Neo-patrimonialism rather than Counteract it?' *Democratization*, 10/2, 2003, pp. 121–40.

21. Quoted in Jackson, M., *In Sierra Leone* (Durham, NC: Duke University Press, 2004), pp. 164–5.

22. Author's interviews with IMATT and British Army officers, London, 15 June 2004 and 26 April 2006, and Freetown, 7 July 2010. See also Nelson-Williams, A., 'Restructuring the RSLAF'; and Le Grys, B., 'British Military Involvement in Sierra Leone, 2001–2006' in Jackson, P. and Albrecht, P. (eds), *Security Sector Reform in Sierra Leone 1997–2007: Views from the Front Line* (Geneva: LIT, 2010).

23. Charley, J.C. and M'Cormack, F.I., 'A 'Force for Good'? Police Reform in Post-conflict Sierra Leone', *IDS Research Report* 70, 2011.

24. Krogstad, 'Security, Development and Force', pp. 274–8.

25. Charley and M'Cormack, 'A "Force for Good"?', p. 39.

26. Vincent, 'A Village-Up View', pp. 25–7.

27. Mitton, 'Engaging Disengagement'; Menzel, A., 'Between Ex-Combatization and Opportunities for Peace: The Double-Edged Qualities of Motorcycle-Taxi Driving in Urban Postwar Sierra Leone', *Africa Today*, 58/2, 2011, pp. 97–127; and Utas, M. and Christensen, M., 'Mercenaries of Democracy: The 'Politrix' of Remobilized Combatants in the Sierra Leone 2007 General Elections', *African Affairs*, 107/429, 2008, pp. 515–39; Enria, L., 'Love and Betrayal: The Political Economy of Youth Violence in Post-War Sierra Leone', *Journal of Modern African Studies*, 53/4, 2015, pp. 637–60.

28. Thomson, B., *Sierra Leone: Reform or Relapse? Conflict and Governance Reform* (London: Chatham House, 2007), p. 15.

29. See Cubitt, C., *Local and Global Dynamics of Peacebuilding: Post-Conflict Reconstruction in Sierra Leone* (London: Routledge, 2012).

30. Robinson, J., *Governance and Political Economy Constraints to World Bank CAS Priorities in Sierra Leone* (Washington, DC: World Bank, 2008), p. 23.

31. Thomson, *Sierra Leone: Reform or Relapse?*, p. 22.

32. Vincent, 'A Village-Up View', pp. 18–21. Paramount Chiefs, who must come from chiefly lineages, are elected for life by chiefdom councillors who have in turn been elected by taxpayers.

33. Ibid, pp. 22–3.

34. Fanthorpe, 'On the Limits of Liberal Peace', p. 27.

35. Fanthorpe, R., *Humanitarian Aid in Post-War Sierra Leone: The Politics of Moral*

Economy (London: Overseas Development Institute, 2003); Sawyer, E., 'Remove or Reform? A Case for (Restructuring) Chiefdom Governance in Post-Conflict Sierra Leone', *African Affairs*, 107/428, 2008, pp. 387–403; and Hanlon, J., 'Is the International Community Helping to Recreate the Preconditions for War in Sierra Leone', *The Round Table*, 94, 2005, pp. 459–72.

36. See the 2009 Chieftaincy Act, which codified existing rules on Paramount Chief elections, and the guidelines in the 2012 Chiefdom and Tribal Administration Policy.

37. Author's interview with a senior adviser working for a major Western donor, Freetown, 8 July 2010; Paul Richards' work also leans somewhat in this direction, for instance in his references to 'community failure' and warnings about 'community-driven reconstruction' (Chauveau and Richards, 'West African Insurgencies', p. 546).

38. The numbers are almost identical to before, with the addition of just one District Council in rural Western Area.

39. International Crisis Group, *Liberia and Sierra Leone: Rebuilding Failed States* (Dakar and Brussels: December 2004), p. 18.

40. Thomson, *Sierra Leone: Reform or Relapse?*, p. 23; and Jackson, P., 'Reshuffling an Old Deck of Cards? The Politics of Local Government Reform in Sierra Leone', *African Affairs*, 106/422, 2007, pp. 102–9.

41. Manning, R., *The Landscape of Local Authority in Sierra Leone: How 'Traditional' and 'Modern' Justice Systems Interact* (Washington, DC: World Bank, 2009), pp. 7–8; and Jackson, Ibid., p. 100.

42. See Fanthorpe, 'On the Limits of Liberal Peace'; and Vincent, 'A Village-Up View', pp. 22–3.

43. Manning, *The Landscape of Local Authority*, p. 16. In the 2011 Decentralisation Policy, it was amended so that councils became 'the highest development and service delivery authorities' and chiefs 'the traditional component of local government administration'.

44. Conteh, FM., 'Politics, development and the instrumentalisation of (de)centralisation in Sierra Leone', Review of African Political Economy, 44/151, 2017, pp. 30–46.

45. Balogun, P. and Gberie, L., *Assessing the Performance of the Long-Term Partnership Agreement between the Governments of Sierra Leone and the UK* (London: DFID, 2005); and World Bank, *Sierra Leone Programmatic Governance and Reform Grant* (Washington, DC: 2006).

46. See Cargill, T., *Sierra Leone a Year after Elections: Still in the Balance*, Chatham House, September 2008, p. 3. Also, author's interview with former SLPP Minister of Information Julius Spencer, who was otherwise very much in favour of the DFID and an even tougher approach, Freetown, 15 July 2010; and author's interview with donor staff, Freetown, 17 July 2010.

47. For details and critique, see Ainley, K. et al (eds.), Evaluating Transitional Justice: Accountability and Peacebuilding in Post-Conflict Sierra Leone (London: Palgrave, 2015).

48. Special Court for Sierra Leone, *Agreement between the United Nations and the Government of Sierra Leone on the Establishment of the Special Court for Sierra Leone* (Freetown, 16 January 2002).

49. For differing viewpoints, see Clark, P., *The Gacaca Courts, Post-Genocide Justice, and Reconciliation in Rwanda: Justice without Lawyers* (Cambridge University Press, 2010) and Waldorf, L., *Transitional Justice and DDR: The Case of Rwanda* (New York: International Center for Transitional Justice, 2009).

50. UN Security Council, *The Rule of Law and Transitional Justice in Conflict and Post-conflict Societies* (New York: 23 August 2004), p. 14.

51. Robertson, G., *Crimes Against Humanity: The Struggle for Global Justice* (New York: New Press, 2000); and Branch, A., 'International Justice, Local Injustice', *Dissent*, Summer 2004, pp. 22–6, respectively. See also Brett, P., 'A Critical Introduction to the "Legalisation of World Politics"', *e-International Relations*, March 2012.

52. Mahony, 'Prioritising International Sex Crimes', p. 81.

53. Harris, D. and Lappin, R., 'Taylor is Guilty, is that all there is? The Collision of Justice and Politics in the Domestic Arena' in Ainley et al, *Evaluating Transitional Justice*.

54. Davies, L., and Gabbatt, A., 'Mia Farrow contradicts Naomi Campbell in Charles Taylor trial', *The Guardian*, 9 August 2010.

55. *Sierra Leone Web*, 5 June 2003.

56. Mahony, 'Prioritising International Sex Crimes', p. 75.

57. Robertson, *Crimes Against Humanity*.

58. Mahony, 'Prioritising International Sex Crimes', p. 75.

59. Gowan, *The Global Gamble: Washington's Faustian Bid for World Dominance* (London: Verso, 1999), p. 146.

60. Tutu, D., *No Future without Forgiveness* (New York: Doubleday, 1999); and for criticism, Wilson, R., *The Politics of Truth and Reconciliation in South Africa: Legitimizing the Post-Apartheid State* (Cambridge University Press, 2001).

61. Bishop Joseph Humper, Chairman of the Sierra Leonean TRC, interviewed in *The Analyst*, 12 May 2006; and author's interview with UN Human Rights Officer Boubacar Dieng, Freetown, 14 April 2002. This scenario shows many signs of being repeated in Kenya.

62. Harris, D. and Lappin, R., 'The Liberian Truth and Reconciliation Commission: reconciling or Re-dividing Liberia?', *Alternatives*, 9/1, 2010, pp. 181–91.

63. Kelsall, T., 'Truth, Lies, Ritual: Preliminary Reflections on the Truth and Reconciliation Commission in Sierra Leone', *Human Rights Quarterly*, 27, 2005, pp. 361–91.

64. Shaw, R., *Rethinking Truth and Reconciliation Commissions: Lessons from Sierra Leone* (Washington, DC: United States Institute of Peace, 2005), p. 8.

65. Yoder, *Popular Political Culture*, p. 237.

66. Stovel, L., '"There's no Bad Bush to Throw Away a Bad Child": "Tradition"-inspired Reintegration in Post-war Sierra Leone', *Journal of Modern African Studies*, 46/2, 2008, pp. 305–24.

67. Baines, E., 'The Haunting of Alice: Local Approaches to Justice and Reconcili-ation in Northern Uganda', *International Journal of Transitional Justice*, 1/1, 2007, pp. 91–114; and Allan, T., 'Ritual (Ab)use? Problems with Traditional Justice in Northern Uganda' in Waddell, N. and Clark, P., *Courting Conflict? Justice, Peace and the ICC in Africa* (London: Royal African Society, 2008).

68. Kelsall, T., *Culture under Cross-Examination: International Justice and the Special Court for Sierra Leone* (Cambridge University Press, 2009), p. 17.

69. Douma, P. and De Zeeuw, J., *From Transitional to Sustainable Justice* (The Hague: Clingendael Conflict Research Unit, 2004), p. 2.

70. According to information collated from various reports, the Yugoslav and Rwan-dan trials cost seven and six times that of the SLSC, but the SLSC costs per completed case (US$21.7 million, including all cases of deceased defendants but not including Taylor who was on appeal at the time) and costs per conviction (US$32.5 million, not including Taylor) were actually greater than for the Yugoslav trials and just below those for the Rwandan version (both the ex-Yugoslavia and Rwanda tribunals still having ongoing cases). See also Jalloh, C., 'Special Court for Sierra Leone: Achieving Justice?' *Michigan Journal of Interna-tional Law*, 32/395, 2010, pp. 395–460.

71. The first SLSC Registrar, Robin Vincent, quoted in Dougherty, B., 'Right-sizing International Criminal Justice: the Hybrid Experiment at the Special Court for Sierra Leone', *International Affairs*, 80/2 (2004), p. 326.

9. POLITICAL SHIFTS IN SIERRA LEONE: ELECTIONS, LIBERAL REFORM, SOCIETY AND THE NEW MULTIPOLAR WORLD, 2007–12

1. For fuller stories see Kandeh, J., 'Rogue Incumbents, Donor Assistance and Sierra Leone's Second Post-Conflict Election of 2007', *Journal of Modern African Stud-ies*, 46/4, 2008; and Harris, *Civil War and Democracy in West Africa*.

2. Zambia is a pertinent case study of a predominant party system which then experienced a turnover (Burnell, P., 'The Party System and Party Politics in Zam-bia: Continuities Past, Present and Future', *African Affairs* 100/399, 2001, pp. 239–63).

3. Nic Cheeseman notes that half of all presidential transfers of power from one party to another between 1990 and 2009 were in open-seat polls ('African Elec-tions as Vehicles for Change', *Journal of Democracy*, 21/4, 2010, pp. 139–53).

4. See European Union, *Presidential and Parliamentary Elections in Sierra Leone: Preliminary Statement* (Freetown: 10 September 2007); and National Democratic Institute, *Presidential and Parliamentary Elections in Sierra Leone: Preliminary Statement* (Freetown: 10 September 2007); the latter two instances were also related to the author by NDI and EU observers respectively, September 2007.

5. See Utas and Christensen, 'Mercenaries of Democracy; and the documentary film, *Jew-Man Business* (Christensen, M., 2011).

6. Taken from the author's observations and interviews in rural Kenema District and from observations made by other NDI and EU observers, September 2007.

7. Berewa, S., A New Perspective on Governance, Leadership, Conflict and Nation Building in Sierra Leone (Milton Keynes: AuthorHouseUK, 2011)

8. Kandeh, 'Rogue Incumbents', p. 625.

9. International Crisis Group, Sierra Leone: The Election Opportunity (Dakar and Brussels: July 2007).

10. See Kandeh, 'Rogue Incumbents', p. 615.

11. Wyrod, C., 'Sierra Leone: A Vote for Better Governance', Journal of Democracy, 19/1, 2008, pp. 70–83.

12. See again Schatzberg, Political Legitimacy.

13. Huntington, S., The Third Wave: Democratization in the Late Twentieth Century (Norman, OK: University of Oklahoma Press, 1991).

14. Chabal, P., 'A Few Considerations on Democracy in Africa', International Affairs 74/2, 1998, pp. 289–303.

15. See again Lipset, Political Man; Moore, Social Origins; and World Bank, Sub-Saharan Africa.

16. Thanks go to the late Donal Cruise O'Brien for this notion of ritual.

17. See Ake, C., The Feasibility of Democracy in Africa (Dakar, CODESRIA, 2000).

18. Karlstrom, M., 'Imagining Democracy: Political Culture and Democratisation in Buganda', Africa 66/4, 1996, pp. 485–505.

19. Author's interview with an adviser working for the government, Freetown, 20 July 2011.

20. Bhandari, M., 'Health check for Sierra Leone', The Guardian, 24 June 2011; and Nossiter, A., 'Sierra Leone's health care system becomes a cautionary tale for donors', New York Times, 13 April 2013. Further muddying the anti-corruption waters, Daoh was seen by many of the author's interviewees as one of the more professional civil servants (Freetown 2010 and 2011).

21. Author's interview with a senior consultant working for the government, Freetown, 19 July 2010; and with the same consultant a year later, Freetown, 18 July 2011.

22. Author's interview with donor staff, Freetown, 19 July 2011.

23. Author's interview with donor staff, Freetown, 26 July 2011.

24. Author's interview with donor staff, 8 July 2010, and different staff from the same agency a year later, Freetown, 22 July 2011.

25. For a detailed study, see Fanthorpe, R., Lavali, A. and Sesay. M.G., Decentralization in Sierra Leone: Impact, Constraints and Prospects (Purley: Fanthorpe Consultancy Ltd, 2011).

26. Author's interview with donor staff, Freetown, 25 July 2011; see also Vincent, 'A Village-Up View', pp. 22–3.

27. Robinson, Governance and Political Economy, pp. 34–7.

28. Commonwealth Expert Team, Sierra Leone Local Elections 2008 (London: July 2008).

29. Africa Research Institute, 'Old Tricks, Young Guns: Elections and Violence in Sierra Leone', Briefing Note 1102, April 2011, pp. 3–4.

30. United Nations Environment Programme (UNEP), *Sierra Leone: Environment, Conflict and Peacebuilding Assessment* (Geneva: 2010).

31. Patriotic Vanguard, 'Public Inquiry on Bumbuna Events', 6 June 2012.

32. Le Billon, P. and Levin, E., 'Building Peace with Conflict Diamonds? Merging Security and Development in Sierra Leone', *Development and Change*, 40/4, 2009, pp. 693–715.

33. Little, A., 'Can Britain Lift Sierra Leone out of Poverty?', *BBC Newsnight*, 23 June 2010.

34. Africa Governance Initiative, http://www.africagovernance.org, accessed 10 July 2012.

35. For a study in Zambia, see von Soest, C., 'How Does Neopatrimonialism Affect the African State? The Case of Tax Collection in Zambia', *Journal of Modern African Studies*, 45(4), 2007, pp. 621–45; the quote is from Richmond, O., 'Resistance and the Post-liberal Peace', *Millennium*, 38/3, 2010, p. 667.

36. DFID, *Drivers of Change* (London: 2003).

37. Author's interview with donor staff, Freetown, 16 July 2010.

38. Author's interview (Freetown, 12 July 2010) and continued personal communication with an adviser working for the government.

39. Author's interview with donor staff, Freetown, 16 July 2010.

40. Richmond, O., *The Transformation of Peace* (London: Palgrave, 2008); and Richmond, O., 'Welfare and the Civil Peace: Poverty with Rights?' in Pugh, M. Cooper, N. and Turner, M. (eds), *Whose Peace? Critical Perspectives on the Political Economy of Peacebuilding* (London: Palgrave, 2008); see Cubitt, *Local and Global Dynamics*, for Sierra Leone.

41. E.g. Mistry, P.S., 'Reasons for Sub-Saharan Africa's Development Deficit that the Commission for Africa did not Consider', *African Affairs*, 104/417, 2005, pp. 665–78; and Moyo, D., *Dead Aid: Why Aid is Not Working and How There is a Better Way for Africa* (New York: Farrar Straus & Giroux, 2009).

42. E.g. Smith, D., *Towards a Strategic Framework for Peacebuilding: Getting Their Act Together* (Oslo: Royal Norwegian Ministry of Foreign Affairs, 2004).

43. Richmond, O., 'A Post-liberal Peace: Eirenism and the Everyday', *Review of International Studies*, 35/3, 2009, pp. 557–80.

44. For the penultimate idea, seen from different angles, Duffield, M., *Global Governance and the New Wars: The Merging of Development and Security* (London: Zed Books, 2001); and IDS Bulletin, 'Transforming Security and Development in an Unequal World', 40/2, 2009; and for Sierra Leone, see Denney, S., 'Reducing Poverty with Teargas and Batons: the Security-Development Nexus in Sierra Leone', *African Affairs*, 110/439, 2011, pp. 1–20. For the latter idea, see Leftwich, A., *From Drivers of Change to the Politics of Development* (London: DFID, 2006); and DFID, *Building Peaceful States and Societies* (London: 2010).

45. Kelsall, T., 'Going with the Grain in African Development?', *Development Policy*

Review, 26/6, 2008, pp. 627–55; and author's interviews with donor staff, Freetown, 2010–2011.

46. DFID, 'The Politics of Poverty: Elites, Citizens and States', paper based on a stakeholder event, June 2010, p. 5.

47. See again Ekeh, 'Colonialism and the Two Publics'; and Chabal and Daloz, *Africa Works*.

48. Taylor, I., 'Earth Calling the Liberals: Locating the Political Culture of Sierra Leone as the Terrain for 'Reform', in Newman, E., Paris, R. and Richmond, O. (eds), *New Thinking on Liberal Peacebuilding*, (Tokyo: UN University Press, 2009).

49. For Zambia, see von Soest, 'How does Neopatrimonialism'.

50. See Young, T., '"A Project to be Realised": Global Liberalism and Contemporary Africa', *Millennium*, 24/3, 1995, pp. 527–46; and Duffield, *Global Governance*.

51. Cramer, 'Homo Economicus goes to War'; and Spagnoli, F., *Homo-Democraticus: On the Universal Desirability and the not so Universal Possibility of Democracy and Human Rights* (Cambridge Scholars Press, 2003).

52. Kate Meagher stridently warns us against static conceptions of African society in 'Cultural Primordialism and the Post-structuralist Imaginaire: Plus ça Change…', *Africa*, 76(4), 2006, pp. 590–97.

53. See again Cramer, *Civil War is not a Stupid Thing*.

54. E.g. Chauveau and Richards, 'West African Insurgencies'.

55. Kahler, M., 'Aid and State Building', paper delivered at the *Annual Meeting of the American Political Science Association*, 2007, p. 40.

56. DFID, 'The Politics of Poverty', p. 6.

57. See Paris, R., 'International Peacebuilding and the "*Mission Civilisatrice*"', *Review of International Studies*, 28, 2002, pp. 637–56.

58. See again Bayart, 'Africa in the World'.

59. Author's interview with a Paramount Chief, Freetown, 21 July 2010.

60. James Vincent ('A Village-Up View', p. 21) also notes that during and after the war 'chiefs made a major change to include youth and women in their governance practices'.

61. Richmond, 'Resistance and the Post-liberal Peace', pp. 672 and 688.

62. Diouf, M., 'Urban Youth and Senegalese Politics: Dakar 1988–1994', *Public Culture*, 8/2, 1996, pp. 225–50.

63. Boersch-Supan, J., 'The Generational Contract in Flux: Intergenerational Tensions in Post-Conflict Sierra Leone', *Journal of Modern African Studies*, 50/1, 2012, pp. 25–51.

64. Fanthorpe, R. and Maconachie, R., 'Beyond the 'Crisis of Youth'? Mining, Farming, and Civil Society in Post-War Sierra Leone', *African Affairs*, 109/435, 2010, pp. 270–72.

65. For the former observation, see Manning, *The Landscape of Local Authority*, p. 7. The latter was, for instance, expressed to the author by a bank employee shortly after the end of the war, Freetown, 2 May 2002; judging by the subsequent

occurrence of stories of *juju* in society and the press and even at the SLSC, this was somewhat optimistic.

66. Fanthorpe and Maconachie, 'Beyond the 'Crisis of Youth'?', pp. 260–68.
67. See Orvis, S., 'Civil Society in Africa or African Civil Society?' *Journal of Asian and African Studies* 36/1, 2001, pp. 17–38.
68. Maconachie, R., 'Re-Agrarianising Livelihoods in Post-Conflict Sierra Leone? Mineral Wealth and Rural Change in Artisanal and Small-Scale Mining Communities', *Journal of International Development*, 23/8, 2011, pp. 1054–67; and Maconachie, R. and Hilson, G., 'Artisanal Gold Mining: A New Frontier in Post-Conflict Sierra Leone?' *Journal of Development Studies*, 47/4, 2011, pp. 595–616.
69. Tripp, A.M., 'Women in Movement: Transformations in African Political Landscapes' in Cornwall, A., *Readings in Gender in Africa* (Oxford: James Currey, 2005).
70. Reticker, G., *Pray the Devil Back to Hell* (Fork Films, 2008); note that women have long held some 'traditional' and societal positions of power in Sierra Leone.
71. Castilejo, C., 'Women's Political Participation and Influence in Sierra Leone', *Fride Working Paper*, 83, 2009, pp. 14–16.
72. Samba, A., 'In Sierra Leone, Bernadette Lahai Defends Judiciary as Chief Justice Reconciles with Madam Torto', *Awareness Times*, 9 June 2010.
73. Manning, *The Landscape of Local Authority*, p. 7.
74. Parker, M., 'Rethinking Female Circumcision', *Africa*, 65/4, 1995, pp. 506–23; and Pedersen, S., 'National Bodies, Unspeakable Acts: The Sexual Politics of Colonial Policy Making', *Journal of Modern History* 63/4, 1991, pp. 647–80. Note that the choice of name is loaded with significance.
75. Parker, Ibid.; and Boddy, J., 'Gender Crusades: The Female Circumcision Controversy in Cultural Perspective' in Hernlund, Y. and Shell-Duncan, B. (eds), *Transcultural Bodies: Female Genital Cutting in Global Context* (Rutgers University Press, 2007).
76. In 2005, UNICEF reported that 94 per cent of women in Sierra Leone had undergone FC/FGM. Five years later, the rate had reportedly dropped to 84 per cent (IRIN, Sierra Leone: the Political Battle on FGM/C, 17 December 2012).
77. Inter Press Service, 'In Sierra Leone they just cut you, and there's not much problem with that', 8 August 2007.
78. International Federation of Journalists, 'IFJ Condemns Strip Humiliation of Women Journalists in Sierra Leone', 12 February 2009.
79. Paris, R., 'Saving Liberal Peacebuilding', *Review of International Studies* 36/2, 2010, pp. 337–65; and Cooper, N., 'Review Article: On the Crisis of the Liberal Peace', *Conflict, Security and Development*, 7/4, 2007, p. 606.
80. Respectively, Lee, M.C., 'The 21st Century Scramble for Africa', *Journal of Contemporary African Studies*, 24/3, 2006, pp. 303–30; and Clapham, C., 'Fitting China In', *Brenthurst Discussion Paper*, 2006.
81. Harris, D. and Vittorini, S., 'New Topographies of Power? Africa Negotiating

an Emerging Multipolar World' in Dietz T. et al (eds), *African Engagements: Africa Negotiating an Emerging Multipolar World* (Leiden: Brill, 2011).

82. Datzberger, S., 'China's silent storm in Sierra Leone' SAAII Policy Briefing 71, 2013.

83. Oakland Institute, *Understanding Land Investment Deals in Africa Country Report: Sierra Leone* (Oakland, CA: 2011).

84. Wade, A., 'Time for the West to practice what it preaches', *Financial Times*, 24 January 2008.

10. MULTIPLE CRISES AND RESPONSES: EBOLA, IRON ORE AND HARD TIMES, 2012–2018

1. For a fuller story, see Conteh, FM and Harris, D., 'Swings and Roundabouts: the Vagaries of Democratic Consolidation and "Electoral Rituals" in Sierra Leone', *Critical African Studies*, 6/1, 2014, pp. 57–70.

2. Blyden, S., 'Will our Vice-President Speak Publicly?: Sam-Sumana in a Fresh "Corruption" Scandal from USA', *Awareness Times*, 23 July 2012.

3. Sama, Poindexter, 'SLPP & PMDC say "Christiana Thorpe Wants to Turn Salone into a One Party State"', *Awoko*, 2 August 2012.

4. Author's observations of campaign material, Freetown and Kenema, November 2012.

5. Author's observations of campaign material, Freetown and Kenema, November 2012.

6. Conteh and Harris, 'Swings and Roundabouts', p. 63.

7. Author's observations, Kenema, November 2012.

8. *This is Sierra Leone* (no date), http://www.thisissierraleone.com/sierra-leone-new-years-day-broadcast-by-president-koroma/, accessed 18 February 2020.

9. Rashid Thomas, A., 'Will Sierra Leone's economy grow by 50% in 2012?' *The Sierra Leone Telegraph*: Freetown, n.d.; and *International Monetary Fund*, Country Report No. 11/361', 2011, http://www.imf.org/external/pubs/ft/scr/2011/cr11361.pdf, accessed 18 February 2020.

10. Conteh, FM. And Harris, D., 'Government-Donor Relations in Sierra Leone: Who's in the Driving Seat?', Journal of Modern African Studies, 58/1, 2020.

11. Ibid.

12. Datzberger, 'China's silent storm', p. 1.

13. Author's interviews with Western donor officials, Freetown, July 2011 and July 2016.

14. Author's interview with a government official, Freetown, 25 July 2016.

15. Mihalyi, D., 'The miracle that became a debacle: Iron ore in Sierra Leone', *Natural Resource Governance Institute*, 2015, http://www.resourcegovernance.org/blog/miracle-became-debacle-iron-ore-sierra-leone, accessed 18 February 2020.

16. Author's interviews with donor and government officials, Freetown, July 2016.

17. Davis, P., *Ebola in Sierra Leone: Economic Impact and Recovery* (London: Adam

Smith International, 2015), https://pdfs.semanticscholar.org/3807/bb4f3428b-45657feb49bfb883efa53893efb.pdf, accessed 18 February 2020.

18. For a fascinating overview from ground-level, see Walsh, S. and Johnson, O., *Getting to Zero: A Doctor and a Diplomat on the Ebola Frontline* (London, Zed Books, 2018).

19. Ross, E., Honwana Welch, G. and Angelides, P., 'Sierra Leone's response to the Ebola outbreak: Management strategies and key responder experiences', *Royal Institute of International Affairs*, 2017, p. 2.

20. *Médecins Sans Frontières*, 'Ebola in West Africa: Epidemic requires massive deployment of resources', 21 June 2014, http://www.msf.org/en/article/ebola-west-africa-epidemic-requires-massive-deployment-resources, accessed 18 February 2020.

21. *Médecins Sans Frontières*, 'We need help to fight against Ebola', 26 August 2014, http://msf-seasia.org/news/15830, accessed 18 February 2020.

22. *BBC*, 'Ebola outbreak: Sierra Leone workers dump bodies in Kenema', 25 November 2014, http://www.bbc.co.uk/news/world-africa-30191938, accessed 18 February 2020.

23. Ross et al, *'Sierra Leone's response'*, pp. 7–10.

24. Author's interviews with donor officials, Freetown, 11 and 17 July 2016.

25. Ross et al, *'Sierra Leone's response'*, pp. 29–30.

26. *World Health Organisation*, 'Factors that contributed to undetected spread of the Ebola virus and impeded rapid containment,' January 2015, http://www.who.int/csr/disease/ebola/one-year-report/factors/en/, accessed 18 February 2020.

27. Fofana, U, 'Ebola center in Sierra Leona under guard after protest march', *Reuters*, 26 July 2014, http://www.reuters.com/article/us-health-ebola-africa-idUSKBN-0FV0NL20140726, accessed 18 February 2020; and *Sierra Express Media*, 'APC Invents Ebola As 100th Tactic' 28 June 2014, http://sierraexpressmedia.com/?p=68583, accessed 18 February 2020.

28. Author's correspondence with Dr Luisa Enria, April 2015.

29. Wilkinson, A. and Fairhead, J., 'Comparison of social resistance to Ebola response in Sierra Leone and Guinea suggests explanations lie in political configurations not culture', *Critical Public Health* 27/1, 2017, pp. 14–27.

30. Ibid.

31. Richards, P., *Ebola: How a People's Science Helped End an Epidemic* (London: Zed Books, 2016); and Walsh and Johnson, *Getting to Zero*.

32. Richards, *Ebola*, p. 114.

33. Enria, L. and Harris, D, 'Book Review: Ebola: How a People's Science Helped End an Epidemic, by Paul Richards, Zed Books, 2016', *African Affairs*, 116/463, 2017, pp. 356–7.

34. Author's interview with donor officials, Freetown, 22 July and 24 November 2016.

35. Author's interview with donor and government officials, Freetown, July and November 2016.

36. Author's interview with donor and government officials, Freetown, 15 and 19 July 2016.
37. Author's interview with donor and government officials, Freetown, July 2016.
38. Author's interview with NGO official, Freetown, 16 July 2016.
39. Yumkella, K., 'Press Statement', *Global Times*, 3 July 2017, http://globaltimes-sl. com/full-statement-of-dr-kandeh-kolleh-yumkella-on-the-suspension-of-his-campaign-for-the-slpp-flagbearer-nomination/, accessed 18 February 2020.
40. Rashid Thomas, A., 'Supreme Court adjourns Samura Kamara's case', *The Sierra Leone Telegraph*, 1 March 2018, http://www.thesierraleonetelegraph.com/ supreme-court-adjourns-samura-kamaras-case/, accessed 18 February 2020.
41. Rashid Thomas, A., 'APC witch-hunt against Yumkella now goes to the Supreme Court', *The Sierra Leone Telegraph*, 6 February 2018, http://www.thesierraleone-telegraph.com/apc-witch-hunt-against-yumkella-now-goes-to-the-supreme-court/, accessed 18 February 2020.
42. *Citifmonline*, 'ECOWAS court declares 2015 removal of Sierra Leone Veep illegal', 27 November 2017, http://citifmonline.com/2017/11/27/ecowas-court-declares-2015-removal-of-sierra-leone-veep-illegal/, accessed 18 February 2020.
43. Hitchen, J., 'The WhatsApp rumours that infused Sierra Leone's tight election', *African Arguments*, 10 April 2018, http://africanarguments.org/2018/04/10/ the-whatsapp-rumours-infused-sierra-leone-tight-election-social-media/, accessed 18 February 2020.
44. Inveen, C., and Maclean, R, 'Sierra Leone: Violence fears as tense election reaches runoff', *The Guardian*, 21 Mar 2018, https://www.theguardian.com/world/2018/ mar/21/sierra-leone-political-violence-tribal-rhetoric-rival-parties-face-runoff, accessed 18 February 2020; and *Sierra Express Media*, 'Political Violence Erupts Across The Country', 22 April 2018, http://sierraexpressmedia.com/?p=83929, accessed 18 February 2020.
45. *Aljazeera*, 'Emmerson: The pop star challenging Sierra Leone's presidents', 27 March 2018, https://www.aljazeera.com/news/2018/03/emmerson-pop-star-challenging-sierra-leone-presidents-180327103105289.html, accessed 18 February 2020.
46. All results and electoral data are taken from the Sierra Leone National Elections Commission website, http://necsl.org, accessed 18 February 2020.
47. *Premium Times*, 'Sierra Leone High Court vacates interim injunction on Tuesday's presidential run-off', 26 March 2018, https://www.premiumtimesng.com/for-eign/west-africa-foreign/263138-sierra-leone-high-court-vacates-interim-injunction-on-tuesdays-presidential-run-off.html, accessed 18 February 2020.
48. Rashid Thomas, A., 'I am putting Sierra Leone first—Yumkella's agenda for change lives on', *The Sierra Leone Telegraph*, 22 March 2018, http://www.thesier-raleonetelegraph.com/i-am-putting-sierra-leone-first-yumkellas-agenda-for-change/, accessed 18 February 2020; and *Cocorioko*, 'Chief Sam Sumana declares for APC', 29 March 2018, https://cocorioko.net/breaking-news-chief-sam-sumana-declares-for-apc/, accessed 18 February 2020.

49. Rashid Thomas, A., 'Sierra Leone government Hajj scholarships sold to foreigners and the rich', *The Sierra Leone Telegraph*, 21 August 2017, http://www.thesierraleonetelegraph.com/sierra-leone-government-hajj-scholarships-sold-to-foreigners-and-the-rich/, accessed 18 February 2020.

50. Available at Sierra Leone Presidential Debate, https://www.youtube.com/watch?v=6Whe5fbzmLg

51. For a discussion, see Bangura, Y., 'Why the APC has more MPs than the SLPP even though the SLPP won the Presidency', *The Sierra Leone Telegraph*, 26 April 2018, http://www.thesierraleonetelegraph.com/why-apc-has-more-mps-than-slpp-despite-slpp-winning-the-presidency/, accessed 18 February 2020.

52. Ibid.

53. James, L., 'Sierra Leone: Are brawls in parliament a sign of things to come?', *African Arguments*, 26 April 2018, http://africanarguments.org/2018/04/26/sierra-leone-are-brawls-in-parliament-a-sign-of-things-to-come/, accessed 18 February 2020.

54. Mumbere, D., 'Sierra Leone president names cabinet, as opposition files petition challenging his victory', *africanews*, 12 April 2018, http://www.africanews.com/2018/04/12/sierra-leone-president-names-cabinet-as-opposition-files-petition-challenging/, accessed 18 February 2020.

55. Kamara, M., 'Over-Voting Uncovered in 400 Polling Stations', *Cocorioko*, 23 March 2018, http://cocorioko.net/over-voting-uncovered-in-400-polling-stations/, accessed 18 February 2020.

56. Bangura, Y., 'A Resilient Duopoly?: Understanding the March 7, 2018 Election', *Premium Times*, 18 March 2018, https://opinion.premiumtimesng.com/2018/03/18/a-resilient-duopoly-understanding-the-march-7-2018-elections-by-yusuf-bangura/, accessed 18 February 2020.

57. *The Commonwealth*, 'Sierra Leone: Presidential run-off was 'credible and transparent', 2 April 2018, http://thecommonwealth.org/media/news/presidential-run-was-credible-and-transparent, accessed 18 February 2020; and *European Union Election Observation Mission Sierra Leone*, 'Presidential, Parliamentary and Local Council Elections 2018 Preliminary Statement', 9 March 2018, https://eeas.europa.eu/sites/eeas/files/eu_eom_sierra_leone_preliminary_statement090318_1.pdf, accessed 18 February 2020.

58. *GhanaWeb*, 'I didn't rig elections—Mahama cries in Sierra Leone', 5 April 2018, https://www.ghanaweb.com/GhanaHomePage/NewsArchive/I-didn-t-rig-elections-Mahama-cries-in-Sierra-Leone-640481, accessed 18 February 2020.

59. Rashid Thomas, A., Controversy over appointment of chief minister of Sierra Leone', *The Sierra Leone Telegraph*, 2 May 2018, http://www.thesierraleonetelegraph.com/controversy-over-appointment-of-chief-minister-of-sierra-leone/, accessed 18 February 2020.

BIBLIOGRAPHY

Books, articles and reports directly related to Sierra Leone

Abdullah, I., 'Bush Path to Destruction: the Origin and Character of the Revolutionary United Front (RUF/SL)', *Africa Development*, 22/3–4, 1997, pp. 45–76.

Abdullah, I. and Muana, P., 'The RUF of Sierra Leone: a Revolt of the Lumpenproletariat' in Clapham, C. (ed.), *African Guerrillas* (Oxford: James Currey, 1998).

Abdullah, I. (ed.), *Between Democracy and Terror: The Sierra Leone Civil War* (Dakar: CODESRIA, 2004).

Abraham, A., *Topics in Sierra Leone History* (Freetown: Leone Publishers, 1976).

——— *Mende Government and Politics under Colonial Rule* (Oxford University Press, 1978).

Africa Research Institute, 'Old Tricks, Young Guns: Elections and Violence in Sierra Leone', Briefing Note 1102, April 2011.

Ainley, K. et al (eds), *Evaluating Transitional Justice: Accountability and Peacebuilding in Post-Conflict Sierra Leone* (London: Palgrave, 2015).

Alie, J.A.D., *A New History of Sierra Leone* (London: Macmillan, 1990).

Audit Service Sierra Leone, *Report on the Audit of the Management of the Ebola Funds: May to October 2014* (Freetown: February 2015).

Balogun, P. and Gberie, L., *Assessing the Performance of the Long-Term Partnership Agreement between the Governments of Sierra Leone and the UK* (London: DFID, 2005).

Bangura, Y., 'Understanding the Political and Cultural Dynamics of the Sierra Leone War: A Critique of Paul Richards' "Fighting for the Rain Forest"', *Africa Development*, 22/3–4, 1997, pp. 117–47.

——— 'Strategic Policy Failure and Governance in Sierra Leone', *Journal of Modern African Studies*, 38/4, 2000, pp. 551–77.

Barlow, E., *Executive Outcomes: Against All Odds* (Johannesburg: Galago Publishing, 2007).

Beah, I., *A Long Way Gone: Memoirs of a Boy Soldier* (New York: Sarah Crichton Books, 2007).

Berewa, S., *A New Perspective on Governance, Leadership, Conflict and Nation Building in Sierra Leone* (Milton Keynes: AuthorHouseUK, 2011).

Boersch-Supan, J., 'The Generational Contract in Flux: Intergenerational Tensions in Post-Conflict Sierra Leone', *Journal of Modern African Studies*, 50/1, 2012, pp. 25–51.

Campaign for Good Governance, *Report on the Electoral Process in Sierra Leone, March 2001–May 2002* (Freetown: August 2002).

Cargill, T., *Sierra Leone a Year after Elections: Still in the Balance* (London: Chatham House, September 2008).

Cartwright, J., *Political Leadership in Sierra Leone* (Toronto: Toronto Press, 1978).

Castilejo, C., 'Women's Political Participation and Influence in Sierra Leone', *Fride Working Paper*, 83, 2009.

Caulker, P., *The Autochthonous Peoples, British Colonial Policies, and the Creoles in Sierra Leone: The Genesis of the Modern Sierra Leone Dilemma of National Integration* (Ann Arbor, MI: Temple University, 1976).

Charley, J.C. and M'Cormack, F.I., 'A "Force for Good"? Police Reform in Post-conflict Sierra Leone', *IDS Research Report* 70, 2011.

Chauveau, J-P. and Richards, P., 'West African Insurgencies in Agrarian Perspective: Côte d'Ivoire and Sierra Leone Compared', *Journal of Agrarian Change*, 8/4, 2008, pp. 515–52.

Clapham, C., *Sierra Leone: the Political Economy of Internal Conflict*, CRU Working Paper 20 (The Hague: Clingendael Institute, 2003).

Cohen, A., *The Politics of Elite Culture: Explorations in the Dramaturgy of Power in a Modern African Society* (Berkeley, CA: University of California Press, 1981).

Commonwealth Expert Team, *Sierra Leone Local Elections 2008* (London: July 2008).

Commonwealth Observer Group, *The Presidential and Parliamentary Elections* [report on Sierra Leone elections] (London: 2002).

Conteh, F.M., 'Politics, development and the instrumentalisation of (de)centralisation in Sierra Leone', *Review of African Political Economy*, 44/51, 2017, pp. 30–46.

Conteh, F.M. and Harris, D., 'Swings and Roundabouts: the Vagaries of Democratic Consolidation and 'Electoral Rituals' in Sierra Leone', *Critical African Studies*, 6/1, 2014, pp. 57–70

——— 'Government-Donor Relations in Sierra Leone: Who's in the Driving Seat?', *Journal of Modern African Studies*, 58/1, 2020, pp. 45–65.

Conteh-Morgan, E. and Dixon-Fyle, M., *Sierra Leone at the End of the Twentieth Century: History, Politics and Society* (New York: Peter Lang, 1999).

Cox, T., *Civil-military Relations in Sierra Leone: a Case Study of African Soldiers in Politics* (Cambridge, MA: Harvard University Press, 1976).

Cubitt, C., *Local and Global Dynamics of Peacebuilding: Post-Conflict Reconstruction in Sierra Leone* (London: Routledge, 2012).

Datzberger, S., 'China's silent storm in Sierra Leone' *SAAII Policy Briefing* 71, 2013.

Davis, P., *Ebola in Sierra Leone: Economic Impact and Recovery* (London: Adam Smith International, 2015)

Denney, S., 'Reducing Poverty with Teargas and Batons: the Security-Development Nexus in Sierra Leone', *African Affairs*, 110/439, 2011, pp. 1–20.

Denzer, L., 'Women in Freetown Politics, 1914–61: A Preliminary Study' in Fyfe, C. (ed.), *Sierra Leone 1787–1987: Two Centuries of Intellectual Life* (Manchester University Press, 1987).

Dougherty, B., 'Right-sizing International Criminal Justice: the Hybrid Experiment at the Special Court for Sierra Leone', *International Affairs*, 80/2 (2004).

Dumbuya, P., *Reinventing the Colonial State: Constitutionalism, One-Party Rule, and Civil War in Sierra Leone* (Bloomington, IN: iUniverse, 2008).

Embassy of the United States to Sierra Leone, press release (Freetown, 12 March 2002).

Enria, L., 'Love and Betrayal: The Political Economy of Youth Violence in Post-War Sierra Leone', *Journal of Modern African Studies*, 53/4, 2015, pp. 637–60.

Enria, L. and Harris, D., 'Book Review: Ebola: How a People's Science Helped End an Epidemic, by Paul Richards, Zed Books, 2016', *African Affairs*, 116/463, 2017, pp. 356–7.

European Union, *Presidential and Parliamentary Elections in Sierra Leone: Preliminary Statement* (Freetown, 15 May 2002).

——— *Presidential and Parliamentary Elections in Sierra Leone: Preliminary Statement* (Freetown, 10 September 2007).

Fanthorpe, R., 'Locating the Politics of a Sierra Leonean Chiefdom', *Africa*, 68/4, 1998, pp. 558–83.

——— 'Neither Citizen nor Subject? Lumpen Agency and the Legacy of Native Administration in Sierra Leone', *African Affairs*, 100/400, 2001, pp. 363–86.

——— *Humanitarian Aid in Post-War Sierra Leone: The Politics of Moral Economy* (London: Overseas Development Institute, 2003).

——— 'On the Limits of Liberal Peace: Chiefs and Democratic Decentralization in Post-conflict Sierra Leone', *African Affairs*, 104/417, 2006, pp. 27–49.

Fanthorpe, R. and Maconachie, R., 'Beyond the 'Crisis of Youth'? Mining, Farming, and Civil Society in Post-War Sierra Leone', *African Affairs*, 109/435, 2010.

Fanthorpe, R., Lavali, A. and Sesay, M.G., *Decentralization in Sierra Leone: Impact, Constraints and Prospects* (Purley: Fanthorpe Consultancy Ltd, 2011).

Ferme, M., 'The Violence of Numbers: Consensus, Competition, and the Negotiation of Disputes in Sierra Leone', *Cahiers d'Études Africaines*, 150/38–2–4, 1998, pp. 555–80.

——— *The Underneath of Things: Violence, History and the Everyday in Sierra Leone* (Berkeley, CA: University of California Press, 2001).

BIBLIOGRAPHY

Fisher, H., 'Elections and Coups in Sierra Leone, 1967', *Journal of Modern African Studies*, 7/4, 1969, pp. 611–36.

Fithen, C., 'Rebellion, Resistance and Resources' (Oxford: 'State Conflict and Intervention in Sierra Leone' conference, May 2000).

Forna, A., *The Devil that Danced on Water: A Daughter's Memoir* (London: Flamingo, 2002).

Fyfe, C., *Sierra Leone Inheritance* (London: Oxford University Press, 1964).

——— *A Short History of Sierra Leone* (London: Longman, 1979).

——— '1787–1887–1987: Reflections on a Sierra Leone Bicentenary' in Fyfe, C. (ed.), *Sierra Leone 1787–1987: Two Centuries of Intellectual Life* (Manchester University Press, 1987).

Gallagher, J., *Britain and Africa under Blair: In Pursuit of the Good State* (Manchester University Press, 2011).

Garcia, E. (ed.), *A Time of Hope and Transformation: Sierra Leone Peace Process, Reports and Reflections* (London: International Alert, 1997).

Gberie, L., 'The May 25 Coup d'état in Sierra Leone: a Militariat Revolt?', *Africa Development*, 22/3–4, 1997, pp. 149–70.

——— 'An Interview with Peter Penfold', *African Affairs*, 104/414, 2005, pp. 117–25.

——— *A Dirty War in West Africa: the RUF and the Destruction of Sierra Leone* (London: Hurst, 2005).

Global Witness, *The Usual Suspects: Liberia's Weapons and Mercenaries in Côte d'Ivoire and Sierra Leone* (London: March 2003).

Greene, G., *The Heart of the Matter* (New York: Viking Press, 1948).

Hanlon, J., 'Is the International Community Helping to Recreate the Preconditions for War in Sierra Leone', *The Round Table*, 94, 2005, pp. 459–72.

Harrell Bond, B. and Skinner, D., 'Misunderstandings Arising from the Use of the Term 'Creole' in the Literature on Sierra Leone', *Africa*, 47/3, 1977, pp. 305–20.

Harris, D., *Civil War and Democracy in West Africa: Conflict Resolution, Elections and Justice in Sierra Leone and Liberia* (London: I.B. Tauris, 2011).

Harris, D. and Lappin, R., 'Taylor is Guilty, is that all there is? The Collision of Justice and Politics in the Domestic Arena' in Ainley, K. et al (eds.), *Evaluating Transitional Justice: Accountability and Peacebuilding in Post-Conflict Sierra Leone* (London: Palgrave, 2015).

Hayward, F., 'Sierra Leone: State Consolidation, Fragmentation and Decay' in Cruise O'Brien, D., Dunn, J. and Rathbone, R. (eds), *Contemporary West African States* (Cambridge University Press, 1989).

Hayward, F. and Kandeh, J., 'Perspectives on Twenty-five Years of Elections in Sierra Leone' in Hayward, F. (ed.), *Elections in Independent Africa* (Boulder, CO: Westview, 1987).

Hirsch, J., *Sierra Leone: Diamonds and the Struggle for Democracy* (Boulder, CO: Lynne Rienner, 2001).

Hoffman, D., 'The Kamajors of Sierra Leone' (Durham, NC: Duke University PhD, 2004).

────── *The War Machines: Young Men and Violence in Sierra Leone and Liberia* (Durham, NC: Duke University Press, 2011).

International Crisis Group, *Sierra Leone after Elections: Politics as Usual?* (Freetown and Brussels: ICG, July 2002).

────── *Liberia and Sierra Leone: Rebuilding Failed States* (Dakar and Brussels: December 2004).

────── *Sierra Leone: The Election Opportunity* (Dakar and Brussels: July 2007).

International Monetary Fund, *Country Report No. 11/361*, 2011.

Jackson, M., *In Sierra Leone* (Durham, NC: Duke University Press, 2004).

Jackson, P., 'Reshuffling an Old Deck of Cards? The Politics of Local Government Reform in Sierra Leone', *African Affairs*, 106/422, 2007, pp. 95–111.

Jalloh, C., 'Special Court for Sierra Leone: Achieving Justice?' *Michigan Journal of International Law*, 32/395, 2010, pp. 395–460.

Kabbah, A.T., *Coming Back From the Brink in Sierra Leone* (Accra: EPP, 2012).

Kandeh, J., 'Politicization of Ethnic Identities in Sierra Leone', *African Studies Review*, 35/1, 1992, pp. 81–99.

────── 'Transition Without Rupture: Sierra Leone's Transfer Election of 1996', *African Studies Review*, 41/2, 1998, pp. 91–111.

────── 'Ransoming the State: Elite Origins of Subaltern Terror in Sierra Leone', *Review of African Political Economy*, 81/26, 1999, pp. 349–66.

────── 'Subaltern Terror in Sierra Leone' in Zack-Williams, T., Frost, D. and Thomson, A. (eds), *Africa in Crisis: New Challenges and Possibilities* (London: Pluto, 2002).

────── 'Sierra Leone's Post-conflict Elections of 2002', *Journal of Modern African Studies*, 41/2, 2003, pp. 189–216.

────── 'Rogue Incumbents, Donor Assistance and Sierra Leone's Second Post-Conflict Election of 2007', *Journal of Modern African Studies*, 46/4, 2008, pp. 603–35.

Kargbo, M.S. *British Foreign Policy and the Conflict in Sierra Leone, 1991–2001* (Oxford: Peter Lang, 2006).

Keen, D., *Conflict and Collusion in Sierra Leone* (Oxford: James Currey, 2005).

Kelsall, T., 'Truth, Lies, Ritual: Preliminary Reflections on the Truth and Reconciliation Commission in Sierra Leone', *Human Rights Quarterly*, 27, 2005, pp. 361–91.

────── *Culture under Cross-Examination: International Justice and the Special Court for Sierra Leone* (Cambridge University Press, 2009).

Kilson, M., *Political Change in a West African State: A Study of the Modernization Process in Sierra Leone* (Cambridge, MA: Harvard University Press, 1966).

Krogstad, E.G., 'Security, Development and Force: Revisiting Police Reform in Sierra Leone', *African Affairs*, 111/443, 2012, pp. 261–80.

Le Billon, P. and Levin, E., 'Building Peace with Conflict Diamonds? Merging

Security and Development in Sierra Leone', *Development and Change*, 40/4, 2009, pp. 693–715.

Le Grys, B., 'British Military Involvement in Sierra Leone, 2001–2006' in Jackson, P. and Albrecht, P. (eds), *Security Sector Reform in Sierra Leone 1997–2007: Views from the Front Line* (Geneva: LIT, 2010).

Maconachie, R., 'Re-Agrarianising Livelihoods in Post-Conflict Sierra Leone? Mineral Wealth and Rural Change in Artisanal and Small-Scale Mining Communities', *Journal of International Development*, 23/8, 2011, pp. 1054–67.

Maconachie, R. and Hilson, G., 'Artisanal Gold Mining: A New Frontier in Post-Conflict Sierra Leone?' *Journal of Development Studies*, 47/4, 2011, pp. 595–616.

Magbaily Fyle, C., *The History of Sierra Leone* (London: Evans Brothers, 1981).

Mahony, C., 'Prioritising International Sex Crimes before the Special Court for Sierra Leone: One More Instrument of Political Manipulation?' in Bergsmo, M. (ed.), *Thematic Prosecution of International Sex Crimes* (Beijing: Torkel Opsahl Academic EPublisher, 2012).

Manning, R., *The Landscape of Local Authority in Sierra Leone: How 'Traditional' and 'Modern' Justice Systems Interact* (Washington, DC: World Bank, 2009).

Menzel, A., 'Between Ex-Combatization and Opportunities for Peace: The Double-Edged Qualities of Motorcycle-Taxi Driving in Urban Postwar Sierra Leone', *Africa Today*, 58/2, 2011, pp. 97–127.

Migdal, J., *Strong States and Weak Societies* (Princeton, NJ: Princeton University Press, 1988).

Mitton, K., 'Engaging Disengagement: The Political Reintegration of Sierra Leone's Revolutionary United Front', *Conflict, Security and Development*, 8/2, 2008, pp. 193–222.

———— 'Irrational Actors and the Process of Brutalisation: Understanding Atrocity in the Sierra Leonean Conflict (1991–2002)', *Civil Wars*, 14/1, 2012, pp. 104–22.

———— *Rebels in a Rotten State: Understanding Atrocity in the Sierra Leonean Civil War* (London: Hurst, 2015).

Muana, P., 'The Kamajoi Militia: Violence, Internal Displacement and the Politics of Counter-insurgency', *Africa Development*, 22/3–4, 1997, pp. 77–100.

National Democratic Institute, *Presidential and Parliamentary Elections in Sierra Leone: Preliminary Statement* (Freetown, 10 September 2007).

Nelson-Williams, A., 'Restructuring the Republic of Sierra Leone Armed Forces (RSLAF)' *GFNSSR Working paper Series*, No. 3, 2008.

Oakland Institute, *Understanding Land Investment Deals in Africa Country Report: Sierra Leone* (Oakland, CA: 2011).

Opala, J., '"Ecstatic Renovation": Street Art Celebrating Sierra Leone's 1992 Revolution', *African Affairs*, 93/371, 1994, pp. 195–218.

Partnership Africa Canada, *The Heart of the Matter: Sierra Leone, Diamonds and Human Security* (Ottawa: PAC, 2000).

Penfold, P., *Atrocities, Diamonds and Diplomacy* (Barnsley: Pen & Sword, 2012).

Peters, K., *Re-examining Voluntarism: Youth Combatants in Sierra Leone* (Pretoria: ISS, 2004).

—— War and the Crisis of Youth in Sierra Leone (Cambridge University Press, 2011).

Peters, K. and Richards, P., 'Understanding Post-Cold War Armed Conflicts in Africa', *Africa*, 77/3, 2007, pp. 183–210.

Porter, A., *Creoledom* (Oxford University Press, 1963).

Reno, W., *Corruption and State Politics in Sierra Leone* (Cambridge University Press).

Richards, P., *Fighting for the Rainforest: War, Youth and Resources in Sierra Leone* (Oxford: International African Institute, 1996).

—— 'Converts to Human Rights? Popular Debate about War and Justice in Rural Central Sierra Leone', *Africa*, 72/3, 2002, pp. 339–67.

—— 'Youth, Food and Peace: a Reflection on Some African Security Issues at the Millennium' in Zack-Williams, T., Frost, D. and Thomson, A. (eds), *Africa in Crisis: New Challenges and Possibilities* (London: Pluto, 2002).

—— 'Green Book Millenarians? The Sierra Leone War within the Perspective of an Anthropology of Religion' in Kastfelt, N. (ed.), *Religion and African Civil Wars* (London: Hurst, 2005).

—— 'To Fight or to Farm? Agrarian Dimensions of the Mano River Conflicts (Liberia and Sierra Leone)', *African Affairs*, 104/417, 2005, pp. 571–90.

—— *Ebola: How a People's Science Helped End an Epidemic* (London: Zed Books, 2016).

Riley, S., 'Sierra Leone: the Militariat Strikes Again', *Review of African Political Economy*, 24/72, 1997, pp. 287–92.

Robinson, J., *Governance and Political Economy Constraints to World Bank CAS Priorities in Sierra Leone* (Washington, DC: World Bank, 2008).

Ross, E., Honwana Welch, G. and Angelides, P., 'Sierra Leone's response to the Ebola outbreak: Management strategies and key responder experiences', *Royal Institute of International Affairs*, 2017.

Sawyer, A., 'Violent Conflicts and Governance Challenges in West Africa: the Case of the Mano River Basin Area', *Journal of Modern African Studies*, 42/3, 2004.

Sawyer, E., 'Remove or Reform? A Case for (Restructuring) Chiefdom Governance in Post-Conflict Sierra Leone', *African Affairs*, 107/428, 2008, pp. 387–403.

Shaw, R., *Rethinking Truth and Reconciliation Commissions: Lessons from Sierra Leone*, (Washington, DC: United States Institute of Peace, 2005).

Söderberg Kovacs, M. and Bangura, I., 'Shape-shifters in the Struggle for Survival: Post-war Politics in Sierra Leone' in Themnér, A. (ed.), *Warlord*

Democrats in Africa: Ex-Military Leaders and Electoral Politics (London: Zed Books, 2017).

Special Court for Sierra Leone, *Agreement between the United Nations and the Government of Sierra Leone on the Establishment of the Special Court for Sierra Leone* (Freetown, 16 January 2002).

Stovel, L., "'There's no Bad Bush to Throw Away a Bad Child": "Tradition"-inspired Reintegration in Post-war Sierra Leone', *Journal of Modern African Studies*, 46/2, 2008, pp. 305–24.

Tangri, R., 'Conflict and Violence in Contemporary Sierra Leone Chiefdoms', *Journal of Modern African Studies*, 14/2, 1976, pp. 311–21.

——— 'Central-local Politics in Contemporary Sierra Leone', *African Affairs*, 77/307, 1978, pp. 165–73.

Taylor, I., 'Earth Calling the Liberals: Locating the Political Culture of Sierra Leone as the Terrain for 'Reform', in Newman, E., Paris, R. and Richmond, O. (eds), *New Thinking on Liberal Peacebuilding* (Tokyo: UN University Press, 2009).

Thomson, B., *Sierra Leone: Reform or Relapse? Conflict and Governance Reform* (London: Chatham House, 2007).

Truth and Reconciliation Commission, *Report* (Freetown, October 2004).

Vincent, J., 'A Village-Up View of Sierra Leone's Civil War and Reconstruction: Multilayered and Networked Governance', *IDS Research Report* 75, 2012.

United Nations Environment Programme (UNEP), *Sierra Leone: Environment, Conflict and Peacebuilding Assessment* (Geneva: 2010).

United Nations Official Communiqué of the Security Council, 21 June 2000.

Utas, M. and Christensen, M., 'Mercenaries of Democracy: The 'Politrix' of Remobilized Combatants in the Sierra Leone 2007 General Elections', *African Affairs*, 107/429, 2008, pp. 515–539.

Walsh, S. and Johnson, O., *Getting to Zero: A Doctor and a Diplomat on the Ebola Frontline* (London: Zed Books, 2018).

Wilkinson, A. and Fairhead, J., 'Comparison of social resistance to Ebola response in Sierra Leone and Guinea suggests explanations lie in political configurations not culture', *Critical Public Health* 27/1, 2017, pp. 14–27.

Wlodarczyk, N., *Magic and Warfare: Appearance and Reality in Contemporary African Conflict and Beyond* (Basingstoke: Palgrave Macmillan, 2009).

World Bank, *Sierra Leone Programmatic Governance and Reform Grant* (Washington, DC: 2006).

Wylie, K., *The Political Kingdoms of the Temne* (New York, Africana Publishing Co., 1977).

Wyrod, C., 'Sierra Leone: A Vote for Better Governance', *Journal of Democracy*, 19/1, 2008, pp. 70–83.

Wyse, A., *The Krio of Sierra Leone: An Interpretive History* (London: Hurst, 1989).

——— *H.C. Bankole-Bright and Politics in Colonial Sierra Leone 1919–1958* (Cambridge University Press, 1990).

Zack-Williams, A., *Tributors, Supporters and Merchant Capital: Mining and Underdevelopment in Sierra Leone* (Aldershot: Avebury, 1995).

Books, articles and reports related to the wider context

Ake, C., *The Feasibility of Democracy in Africa* (Dakar, CODESRIA, 2000).

Allan, T., 'Ritual (Ab)use? Problems with Traditional Justice in Northern Uganda' in Waddell, N. and Clark, P., *Courting Conflict? Justice, Peace and the ICC in Africa* (London: Royal African Society, 2008).

Baines, E., 'The Haunting of Alice: Local Approaches to Justice and Reconciliation in Northern Uganda', *International Journal of Transitional Justice*, 1/1, 2007, pp. 91–114.

Ballentine, K., 'Beyond Greed and Grievance: Reconsidering the Economic Dynamics of Armed Conflict', in Ballentine and Sherman, J. (eds), *The Political Economy of Armed Conflict: Beyond Greed and Grievance* (Boulder, CO: Lynne Rienner, 2003).

Bayart, J-F., *The State in Africa: The Politics of the Belly* (London: Longman, 1993).

———— 'Africa in the World: a History of Extraversion', *African Affairs*, 99/395, 2000, pp. 217–67.

Bazenguissa-Ganga, R., 'The Spread of Political Violence in Congo-Brazzaville', *African Affairs*, 98/390, 1999, pp. 37–54.

Bernstein, H., *Underdevelopment and Development* (Harmondsworth: Penguin, 1973).

Berry, S., 'Hegemony on a Shoestring: Indirect Rule and Access to Agricultural Land', *Africa*, 62/3, 1992, pp. 327–55.

Boddy, J., 'Gender Crusades: The Female Circumcision Controversy in Cultural Perspective' in Hernlund, Y. and Shell-Duncan, B. (eds), *Transcultural Bodies: Female Genital Cutting in Global Context* (Rutgers University Press, 2007).

Branch, A., 'International Justice, Local Injustice', *Dissent*, Summer 2004, pp. 22–6.

Brennan, J., 'Youth, the TANU Youth League and Managed Vigilantism in Dar es Salaam, Tanzania 1925–73', *Africa*, 76/2, 2006, pp. 221–46.

Brett, P., 'A Critical Introduction to the "Legalisation of World Politics"', *e–International Relations*, March 2012.

Burnell, P., 'The Party System and Party Politics in Zambia: Continuities Past, Present and Future', *African Affairs* 399, 2001, pp. 239–63.

Chabal, P., 'A Few Considerations on Democracy in Africa', *International Affairs* 74/2, 1998, pp. 289–303.

———— 'Violence, Power and Rationality: a Political Analysis of Conflict in Contemporary Africa' in Chabal, P., Engel, U. and Gentili, A-M., *Is Violence Inevitable in Africa? Theories of Conflict and Approaches to Conflict Prevention* (Leiden: Brill, 2005).

Chabal, P. and Daloz, J.-P., *Africa Works: Disorder as Political Instrument* (Bloomington, IN: Indiana University Press, 1999).

237

Chabal, P. and Vidal, N. (eds), *Angola: The Weight of History* (New York: Columbia University Press, 2008).

Chabal, P. (ed.), *The Postcolonial Literature of Lusophone Africa* (Johannesburg: Witwatersrand University Press, 1996).

Cheeseman, N., 'African Elections as Vehicles for Change', *Journal of Democracy*, 21/4, 2010, pp. 139–53.

Clapham, C., 'Fitting China In', *Brenthurst Discussion Paper*, 2006, pp. 1–6.

Clark, P., *The Gacaca Courts, Post-Genocide Justice, and Reconciliation in Rwanda: Justice without Lawyers* (Cambridge University Press, 2010).

Collier, P., *Doing Well out of War* (Washington, DC: World Bank, 1999).

Collier, P. and Hoeffler, A., *Justice-seeking and Loot-seeking in Civil War* (Washington, DC: World Bank, 1999).

Collier, P., Hoeffler, A. and Rohner, D., 'Beyond Greed and Grievance: Feasibility and Civil War', *Oxford Economic Papers*, 61, 2009, pp. 1–27.

Cooper, N., 'Review Article: On the Crisis of the Liberal Peace', *Conflict, Security and Development*, 7/4, 2007, pp. 605–16.

Cramer, C., 'Homo Economicus Goes to War: Methodological Individualism, Rational Choice and the Political Economy of War', *World Development*, 30/11, 2002, pp. 1845–64.

——— *Civil War Is Not a Stupid thing: Accounting for Violence in Developing Countries* (London: Hurst, 2006).

Decalo, S., *Coups and Army Rule in Africa: Motivations and Constraints* (New Haven, CT: Yale University Press, 1990).

Department for International Development (DFID), *Drivers of Change* (London, 2003).

——— *Building Peaceful States and Societies* (London, 2010).

——— 'The Politics of Poverty: Elites, Citizens and States', paper based on a stakeholder event, June 2010.

Diouf, M., 'Urban Youth and Senegalese Politics: Dakar 1988–1994', *Public Culture*, 8/2, 1996, pp. 225–50.

Douma, P. and De Zeeuw, J., *From Transitional to Sustainable Justice* (The Hague: Clingendael Conflict Research Unit, 2004).

Duffield, M., *Global Governance and the New Wars: The Merging of Development and Security* (London: Zed Books, 2001).

Ekeh, P., 'Colonialism and the Two Publics: A Theoretical Statement', *Comparative Studies in Society and History*, 17/1, 1975, pp. 91–112.

Ellis, S., *The Mask of Anarchy: the Destruction of Liberia and the Religious Dimension of an African Civil War* (London: Hurst, 1999).

——— 'Violence and History: a Response to Thandika Mkandawire', *Journal of Modern African Studies*, 41/3, 2003, pp. 457–75.

Ellis, S. and ter Haar, G., *Worlds of Power: Religious Thought and Political Practice in Africa* (London: Hurst, 2003).

Erdmann, G. and Engel, U., 'Neopatrimonialism Reconsidered: Critical Review and Elaboration of an Elusive Concept', *Journal of Commonwealth & Comparative Politics*, 45/1, 2007, pp. 95–119.

Forrest, J., 'The Quest for State 'Hardness' in Africa', *Comparative Politics*, 20/4, 1988, pp. 423–42.

Gowan, P., *The Global Gamble: Washington's Faustian Bid for World Dominance* (London: Verso, 1999).

Harris, D., 'From 'Warlord' to 'Democratic' President: how Charles Taylor Won the 1997 Liberian Elections', *Journal of Modern African Studies*, 37/3, 1999, pp. 431–55.

Harris, D. and Lappin, R., 'The Liberian Truth and Reconciliation Commission: Reconciling or Re-dividing Liberia?', *Alternatives*, 9/1, 2010, pp. 181–91.

Harris, D. and Vittorini, S., 'New Topographies of Power? Africa Negotiating an Emerging Multipolar World' in Dietz T. et al (eds), *African Engagements: Africa Negotiating an Emerging Multipolar World* (Leiden: Brill, 2011).

Helle-Valle, J., 'Seen From Below: Conceptions of Politics in a Botswana Village', *Africa*, 72/2, 2002, pp. 179–202.

Herbst, J., *States and Power in Africa: Comparative Lessons in Authority and Control* (Princeton, NJ: Princeton University Press, 2000).

Hobsbawm, E. and Ranger, T., *The Invention of Tradition* (Cambridge University Press, 1992).

Huntington, S., *The Third Wave: Democratization in the Late Twentieth Century* (Norman, OK: University of Oklahoma Press, 1991).

IDS Bulletin, 'Transforming Security and Development in an Unequal World', 40/2, 2009.

Jackson, R., *Quasi-States: Sovereignty, International Relations and the Third World* (Cambridge University Press, 1993).

——— 'Violent Internal Conflict and the African State: Toward a Framework of Analysis', *Journal of Contemporary African Studies*, 20/1, 2002, pp. 29–52.

Kahler, M., 'Aid and State Building', paper delivered at the Annual Meeting of the American Political Science Association, 2007.

Kaldor, M., *New and Old Wars: Organized Violence in a Global Era* (Cambridge: Polity, 1999).

Kaplan, R., 'The Coming Anarchy: How Scarcity, Crime, Over-population and Diseases are Rapidly Destroying our Planet', *Atlantic Monthly*, February 1994, pp. 44–76.

Karlstrom, M., 'Imagining Democracy: Political Culture and Democratisation in Buganda'. *Africa*, 66/4, 1996, pp. 485–505.

Kees van Donge, J., 'An Episode from the Independence Struggle in Zambia: a Case Study from Mwase Lundazi', *African Affairs*, 84/335, 1985, pp. 265–77.

Kelsall, T., 'Going with the Grain in African Development?', *Development Policy Review*, 26/6, 2008, pp. 627–55.

Koso-Thomas, O., *The Circumcision of Women: A Strategy for Eradication* (London: Zed Books, 1987).

Kourouma, A., *Waiting for the Wild Beasts to Vote* (London: Heinemann, 2003).

Lee, M.C., 'The 21st Century Scramble for Africa', *Journal of Contemporary African Studies*, 24/3, 2006, pp. 303–30.

Leftwich, A., *From Drivers of Change to the Politics of Development* (London: DFID, 2006).

Lindberg, S.I., '"It's our Time to Chop": Do Elections in Africa Feed Neo-patrimonialism rather than Counteract it?' *Democratization*, 10/2, 2003, pp. 121–40.

Lipset, S., *Political Man* (New York: Anchor Books, 1960).

Mamdani, M., *Citizen and Subject: Contemporary Africa and the Legacy of Late Colonialism* (Princeton, NJ: Princeton University Press, 1996).

Manning, C., 'Constructing Opposition in Mozambique: Renamo as a Political Party', *Journal of Southern African Studies*, 24/1, 1998, pp. 161–91.

Meagher, K., 'Cultural Primordialism and the Post-structuralist Imaginaire: Plus ça Change…', *Africa*, 76(4), 2006, pp. 590–97.

Messiant, C., 'Angola: the Challenge of Statehood' in Birmingham, D. and Martin, P. (eds), *History of Central Africa: The Contemporary Years since 1960*, Vol. 3 (London: Longman, 1998).

Mistry, P.S., 'Reasons for Sub-Saharan Africa's Development Deficit that the Commission for Africa did not Consider', *African Affairs*, 104/417, 2005, pp. 665–78.

Mkandawire, T., 'The Terrible Toll of Post-colonial 'Rebel Movements' in Africa: Toward an Explanation of the Violence against the Peasantry', *Journal of Modern African Studies*, 40/2, 2002, pp. 181–215.

―――― 'Rejoinder to Stephen Ellis', *Journal of Modern African Studies*, 41/3, 2003, pp. 477–83.

Moore, B., *Social Origins of Dictatorship and Democracy* (Harmondsworth: Penguin, 1966).

Moyo, D., *Dead Aid: Why Aid is Not Working and How There is a Better Way for Africa* (New York: Farrar Straus & Giroux, 2009).

Orvis, S., 'Civil Society in Africa or African Civil Society?' *Journal of Asian and African Studies*, 36/1, 2001, pp. 17–38.

Paris, R., 'International Peacebuilding and the "*Mission Civilisatrice*"', *Review of International Studies*, 28, 2002, pp. 637–56.

―――― 'Saving Liberal Peacebuilding', *Review of International Studies*, 36/2, 2010, pp. 337–65.

Parker, M., 'Rethinking Female Circumcision', *Africa*, 65/4, 1995, pp. 506–23.

Pedersen, S., 'National Bodies, Unspeakable Acts: The Sexual Politics of Colonial Policy Making', *Journal of Modern History*, 63/4, 1991, pp. 647–80.

Reyntjens, F., 'The Privatisation and Criminalisation of Public Space in the Geopolitics of the Great Lakes Region', *Journal of Modern African Studies*, 43/4, 2005, pp. 587–607.

BIBLIOGRAPHY

Richmond, O., *The Transformation of Peace* (London: Palgrave, 2008).

———— 'Welfare and the Civil Peace: Poverty with Rights?' in Pugh, M., Cooper, N. and Turner, M. (eds), *Whose Peace? Critical Perspectives on the Political Economy of Peacebuilding* (London: Palgrave, 2008).

———— 'A Post-liberal Peace: Eirenism and the Everyday', *Review of International Studies*, 35/3, 2009, pp. 557–80.

———— 'Resistance and the Post-liberal Peace', *Millennium*, 38/3, 2010, pp. 665–92.

Robertson, G., *Crimes Against Humanity: The Struggle for Global Justice* (New York: New Press, 2000).

Rodney, W., *How Europe Underdeveloped Africa* (London: Bogle-L'Ouverture Publications, 1973).

Ross, M., 'The Political Economy of the Resource Curse', *World Politics*, 51, 1999, pp. 297–322.

———— 'What do we Know about Natural Resources and Civil War?', *Journal of Peace Research*, 41/3, 2004, pp. 337–56.

Schatzberg, M., *Political Legitimacy in Middle Africa: Father, Family, Food* (Bloomington, IN: Indiana University Press, 2001).

Smith, D., *Towards a Strategic Framework for Peacebuilding: Getting Their Act Together*, (Oslo: Royal Norwegian Ministry of Foreign Affairs, 2004).

———— *A Culture of Corruption: Everyday Deception and Popular Discontent in Nigeria* (Princeton, NJ: Princeton University Press, 2007).

Spagnoli, F., *Homo-Democraticus: On the Universal Desirability and the not so Universal Possibility of Democracy and Human Rights* (Cambridge Scholars Press, 2003).

Spear, T., 'Neo-traditionalism and the Limits of Invention in British Colonial Africa', *Journal of African History*, 44, 2003, pp. 3–27.

Tilly, C., *Coercion, Capital and European States, AD 900–1992* (Oxford: Blackwell, 1992).

Tripp, A.M., 'Women in Movement: Transformations in African Political Landscapes' in Cornwall, A., *Readings in Gender in Africa* (Oxford: James Currey, 2005).

Tutu, D., *No Future without Forgiveness* (New York: Doubleday, 1999).

United Nations Security Council, *The Rule of Law and Transitional Justice in Conflict and Post-conflict Societies* (New York, 23 August 2004).

von Soest, C., 'How Does Neopatrimonialism Affect the African State? The Case of Tax Collection in Zambia', *Journal of Modern African Studies*, 45(4), 2007, pp. 621–45.

Waldorf, L., *Transitional Justice and DDR: The Case of Rwanda* (New York: International Center for Transitional Justice, 2009).

Wilson, R., *The Politics of Truth and Reconciliation in South Africa: Legitimizing the Post-Apartheid State* (Cambridge University Press, 2001).

World Bank, *Sub-Saharan Africa: From Crisis to Sustainable Growth* (Washington, DC, 1989).

Yoder, J. C., *Popular Political Culture, Civil Society, and State Crisis in Liberia* (New York: Mellen, 2003).

Young, C., *The African Colonial State in Comparative Perspective* (New Haven, CT: Yale University Press, 1994).

—— 'The End of the Post-Colonial State in Africa? Reflections on Changing African Political Dynamics', *African Affairs*, 103/410, 2004, pp. 23–49.

Young, T., '"A project to be Realised": Global Liberalism and Contemporary Africa', *Millennium*, 24/3, 1995, pp. 527–46.

Newspapers, websites and films

Africa Governance Initiative, http://www.africagovernance.org.

Al Jazeera, 'Emmerson: The pop star challenging Sierra Leone's presidents', 27 March 2018.

Awoko, Freetown, 27 January 2003.

Bangura, Y., 'A Resilient Duopoly?: Understanding the March 7, 2018 Election', *Premium Times*, 18 March 2018.

—— 'Why the APC has more MPs than the SLPP even though the SLPP won the Presidency', *The Sierra Leone Telegraph*, 26 April 2018.

BBC, 'Taylor Sierra Leone war crimes trial verdict welcomed', 27 April 2012.

—— 'Ebola outbreak: Sierra Leone workers dump bodies in Kenema', 25 November 2014.

Bhandari, M., 'Health check for Sierra Leone', *The Guardian*, 24 June 2011.

Blyden, S., 'Will our Vice-President Speak Publicly?: Sam-Sumana in a Fresh 'Corruption' Scandal from USA', *Awareness Times*, 23 July 2012.

Carter Center, 'Expert Mission Report on Sierra Leone's March 7 Elections', 23 March 2018.

Christensen, M., *Jew-Man Business* (2011).

Citifmonline, 'ECOWAS court declares 2015 removal of Sierra Leone Veep illegal', 27 November 2017.

Cocorioko, 'Chief Sam Sumana declares for APC', 29 March 2018.

Davies, L. and Gabbatt, A., 'Mia Farrow contradicts Naomi Campbell in Charles Taylor trial', *The Guardian*, 9 August 2010.

European Union Election Observation Mission Sierra Leone, 'Presidential, Parliamentary and Local Council

Elections 2018 Preliminary Statement', 9 March 2018.

Farah, D., 'Al Qaeda cash tied to diamond trade', *Washington Post*, 2 November 2001.

Focus on Sierra Leone, 3/1 (1997).

Fofana, U., 'Ebola center in Sierra Leona under guard after protest march', *Reuters*, 26 July 2014.

For di People, Freetown, 21 May 2002.

Gberie, L., 'Tejan Kabbah: This Is My Life', *New African*, 1 February 2012.

Hitchen, J., 'The WhatsApp rumours that infused Sierra Leone's tight election', *African Arguments*, 10 April 2018.

Inter Press Service, 'In Sierra Leone they just cut you, and there's not much problem with that', 8 August 2007.

International Federation of Journalists, 'IFJ Condemns Strip Humiliation of Women Journalists in Sierra Leone', 12 February 2009.

Inveen, C., and Maclean, R., 'Sierra Leone: Violence fears as tense election reaches runoff', *The Guardian*, 21 March 2018.

IRIN, 'Sierra Leone: the political battle on FGM/C', 17 December 2012.

James, L., 'Sierra Leone: Are brawls in parliament a sign of things to come?', *African Arguments*, 26 April 2018.

Kamara, M., 'Over-Voting Uncovered in 400 Polling Stations', *Cocorioko*, 23 March 2018.

Little, A., 'Can Britain lift Sierra Leone out of poverty?', *BBC Newsnight*, 23 June 2010.

Médecins Sans Frontières, 'Ebola in West Africa: Epidemic requires massive deployment of resources', 21 June 2014.

———— 'We need help to fight against Ebola', 26 August 2014.

Mihalyi, D., 'The miracle that became a debacle: Iron ore in Sierra Leone', *Natural Resource Governance Institute*, 2015.

Mumbere, D., 'Sierra Leone president names cabinet, as opposition files petition challenging his victory', *africanews*, 12 April 2018.

Nossiter, A., 'Sierra Leone's health care system becomes a cautionary tale for donors, *New York Times*, 13 April 2013.

Patriotic Vanguard, 'Public Inquiry on Bumbuna Events', 6 June 2012.

Polgreen, L., 'A master plan drawn in blood', *New York Times*, 2 April 2006.

Premium Times, 'Sierra Leone High Court vacates interim injunction on Tuesday's presidential run-off', 26 March 2018.

Rashid Thomas, A., 'Will Sierra Leone's economy grow by 50% in 2012?' *The Sierra Leone Telegraph*: Freetown, n.d.; and International Monetary Fund, Country Report No. 11/361', 2011.

———— 'Sierra Leone government Hajj scholarships sold to foreigners and the rich', *The Sierra Leone Telegraph*, 21 August 2017.

———— 'APC witch-hunt against Yumkella now goes to the Supreme Court', *The Sierra Leone Telegraph*, 6 February 2018.

———— 'Supreme Court adjourns Samura Kamara's case', *The Sierra Leone Telegraph*, 1 March 2018.

———— 'I am putting Sierra Leone first—Yumkella's agenda for change lives on', *The Sierra Leone Telegraph*, 22 March 2018.

———— 'Controversy over appointment of chief minister of Sierra Leone', *The Sierra Leone Telegraph*, 2 May 2018.

Reticker, G., *Pray the Devil Back to Hell* (Fork Films, 2008).

Sama, Poindexter, 'SLPP & PMDC say "Christiana Thorpe Wants to Turn Salone into a One Party State"', *Awoko*, 2 August 2012.

Samba, A., 'In Sierra Leone, Bernadette Lahai defends judiciary as Chief Justice reconciles with Madam Torto', *Awareness Times*, 9 June 2010.

Samora, S., *Cry Freetown* (CNN, 1999).

Sierra Express Media, 'APC Invents Ebola As 100th Tactic', 28 June 2014.

———— 'Political Violence Erupts Across The Country', 22 April 2018.

Sierra Leone 2018 Presidential Election Debate, available at https://www.youtube.com/watch?v=5f_XBAZ-j4E

Sierra Leone National Electoral Commission website, http://necsl.org

Sierra Leone Web, 5 June 2003.

Wade, A., 'Time for the West to practice what it preaches', *Financial Times*, 24 January 2008.

Wax, E., 'In exile, Taylor still exerts control', *Washington Post*, 17 September 2003.

Zwick, E., *Blood Diamond* (Warner Bros, 2006).

INDEX

Note: Page numbers followed by "*n*" refer to notes.